# CAMRA'S
# LONDON
# PUB WALKS

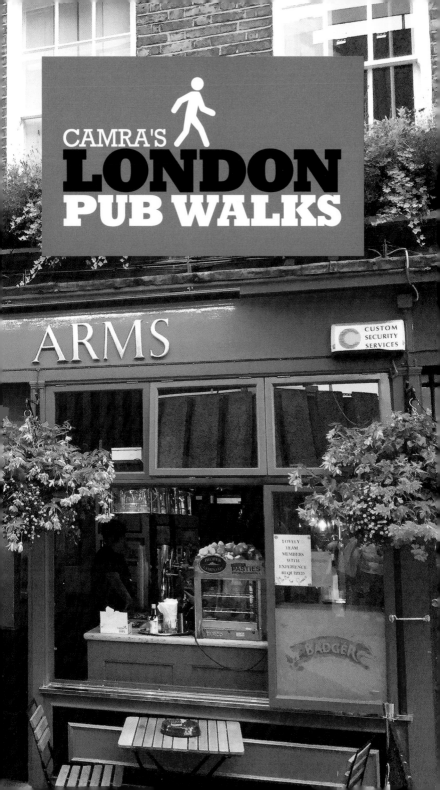

**Published by the Campaign for Real Ale Ltd.**
230 Hatfield Road
St Albans
Hertfordshire AL1 4LW
www.camra.org.uk/books

Design and layout © Campaign for Real Ale Ltd. 2016
Text © Bob Steel

First published 2006, reprinted with corrections 2006
Revised edition 2009, reprinted with corrections 2011
Second edition 2013

ISBN 978-1-85249-336-3

A CIP catalogue record for this book is available from
the British Library

Printed and bound in Malta by Latitude Press Ltd

Head of Publishing: **Simon Hall**
Project Editor: **Katie Button**
Editorial Assistance: **Emma Haines, Susannah Lord**
Design/Cartography: **Stephen Bere**
Cover design: **Stephen Bere**
Sales & Marketing: **David Birkett**

**Photography:** Bob Steel
**Additional photography:** Adam Bruderer/flickr p88; Alex Segre /
Shutterstock.com: p4 (b), 116-117; Bernt Rostad/flickr p86 (tl), p108 (tr);
Cath Harries: p9 (b), p19, p20 (l), p21, p25, p26, p28 (r), p31 (b), p47, p62
(b), p71, 73 (tl), 76, p78 (tr), p80 (br, tl), p97 (tr), p101, p102 (t), p103 (cr,
tl), p104 (b), p105 (br), p106, p108 (bl), p109 (bl), p110 (tl), p140 (tr), p143,
p165, p201 (bl), p202 (c); cohodas208c/flickr p122 (bl); Dan Atrill/flickr p99
(t); DncnH/flickr p107, p182; Ewan Munro p42 (tl), p73 (br), p78 (tl), p84 (tl);
FollowYourNose/flickr p111 (t); Fuller's p16, p39 (t), Garry Knight/flickr p36
(t), p77, p111 (br); Graham C99/flickr p167 (br), p169; Herry Lawford/flickr
p24, p63 (t), p109 (tr); jelm6/flickr p92 (bl), p93 (br); Jim Linwood/flickr p43
(tl), p185, p187, p199 (l); Luck Fisher/flickr p127; Matt Brown/flickr p60 (t),
p114; Maxwell Hamilton/flickr p177, p183, p184 (t), p195, p198 (t), p199 (r);
mira66/flickr p163 (bl); oatsy40/flickr p83; Paul Hudson/flickr p123 (tr); Paul
Wilkinson/flickr p146 (br); Pete McGill p171; Pter Trimming/flickr p166; Rob
Gale p89, p91 (t); Scott Wylie/flickr p121; Shaun O'Connor p176; Stephen
Bere: p2-3, p14 (bl), p15 (br), p27, p28 (bl), p29 (tl, tr), p31 (t), p32 (b,t), p33
(tl), p34, p35, p38 (b,t), p39 (b), p40, p41, p44 (tl, tr), p46, p59, p60 (b), p63
(c), p65, p66 (t), p75 (br , t), p78 (c), p79 (bl), p80 (tr), p124 (t), p125 (tl, tr),
p126 (bl, t), p201 (c, br), p204 (bl, br); Stephen May p45; Uri Baruchin/flickr
p96 (b); Visit Greenwich/flickr p147 (b)

(b) bottom; (bl) bottom left; (br) bottom right; (c) centre; (cr) centre right;
(l) left; (r) right; (t) top; (tr) top right; (tl) top left

**Cover photography:** Monica Wells / Alamy Stock Photo
(front cover, main); Roger Hutchings / Alamy Stock Photo
(front cover, inset); Jansos / Alamy Stock Photo (back cover, b)

**Acknowledgements**
As usual I would like to gratefully acknowledge the help provided by
CAMRA London branches in compiling this book; and to Geoff Strawbridge,
the CAMRA London Regional Director, for his co-ordinating assistance. Also,
and in particular, for help on specific routes, Roy Tunstall, John Pardoe and
James Watson for their detailed advice. Lastly, to Katie Button and the team
at CAMRA Head Office for putting everything together.

# contents

# Walk locator map

Numbers represent the approximate centre of each walk

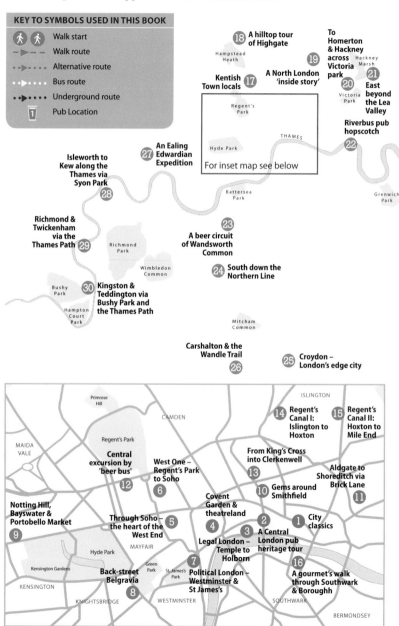

**KEY TO SYMBOLS USED IN THIS BOOK**

- Walk start
- Walk route
- Alternative route
- Bus route
- Underground route
- Pub Location

**18** A hilltop tour of Highgate

Hampstead Heath

**To Homerton & Hackney across Victoria park**

Hackney Marsh

Kentish Town locals **17**

A North London 'inside story'

**19**

**20**
Victoria Park

**21**
East beyond the Lea Valley

Regent's Park

Riverbus pub hopscotch
**22**

An Ealing Edwardian Expedition **27**

THAMES

Hyde Park

For inset map see below

Isleworth to Kew along the Thames via Syon Park

**28**

Battersea Park

Grenwich Park

Richmond & Twickenham via the Thames Path **29**

Richmond Park

A beer circuit of Wandsworth Common
**23**

Wimbledon Common

South down the Northern Line
**24**

Bushy Park

**30** Kingston & Teddington via Bushy Park and the Thames Path

Hampton Court Park

Mitcham Common

Carshalton & the Wandle Trail
**26**

Croydon – London's edge city
**25**

ISLINGTON

Primrose Hill

CAMDEN

**14** Regent's Canal I: Islington to Hoxton

**15** Regent's Canal II: Hoxton to Mile End

MAIDA VALE

Regent's Park

Central excursion by 'beer bus'
**12**

West One – Regent's Park to Soho
**6**

From King's Cross into Clerkenwell
**13**

Gems around Smithfield
**10**

Aldgate to Shoreditch via Brick Lane
**11**

Covent Garden & theatreland
**4**

Notting Hill, Bayswater & Portobello Market
**9**

Through Soho – the heart of the West End
**5**

**2**

**1** City classics

**3** A Central London pub heritage tour

Hyde Park

Kensington Gardens

Legal London – Temple to Holborn

MAYFAIR

Green Park

St James's Park

**7** Political London – Westminster & St James's

A gourmet's walk through Southwark & Boroughh
**16**

Back-street Belgravia
**8**

KENSINGTON

KNIGHTSBRIDGE

WESTMINSTER

SOUTHWARK

BERMONDSEY

# Introduction

It's ten years since the first edition of CAMRA's *London Pub Walks* was published, and three since the completely rewritten 2nd edition appeared. As Des de Moor makes clear in his survey of the London brewing scene (see p10) the capital continues to enjoy a vibrant growth and diversity as far as beer is concerned, and London is once again one of the world's great brewing cities, something that certainly could not be said in 2006. New microbreweries are undoubtedly continuing to lead the way in this, with younger brewers experimenting with all sorts of interesting recipes and providing a feast for the palate, alongside the more traditional British milds, bitters and stouts.

## The London beer scene

There has also been something of a revolution in the way we're drinking our beer, towards smaller measures of stronger beers in the continental tradition. In this sense, the term 'craft beer' which is being used to encapsulate this trend is appropriate, although the term has also now, confusingly, become synonymous with those new beers served in keg form, often filtered and/or pasteurised, chilled, and under some gas pressure. I am not going to venture too far in the controversy this has created both within and outside of CAMRA save to say that these new kegged beers are a galaxy apart from the appalling, gassy and tasteless liquids that caused CAMRA's birth in the early 1970s. What is undeniable is that interest in beer is at record levels in modern times and there has been renaissance in beer and pub culture as a result. And what better which to enjoy all this than London?

## The changing face of London's pubs

So the beer picture is a very encouraging one, but what of the pubs? Nationally they continue to succumb to closures and a range of threats, from predatory developers, retailers keen to expand their reach, to changing cultural patterns in some areas. And whilst many new bars are opening in High Streets, and real ale is now more widely available across the capital than at any time in living memory, suburban pubs in particular continue to face an uncertain future. However,

**Crate, based in Hackney, opened in 2012 in a former canalside print factory, and is one of a new breed of breweries springing up around he capital**

**The Hope in Carshalton is now owned by local shareholders**

there are signs that the tide may be turning: the designation of many public houses as Assets of Community Value (ACVs) following a long and continuing campaign by CAMRA has offered a way of protecting pubs from predators. Some councils in London are interested in following Wandsworth, in formally protecting pubs through planning guidance which acknowledges their architectural, community and heritage value and gives planners strong grounds to refuse applications for change of use or demolition.

The case of the Carlton Tavern in Maida Vale also attracted national attention. Summarily demolished by developers, it will now have to be rebuilt brick by brick after Westminster Council's tough stance was upheld by planning inspectors at appeal. Let's hope this marks a new chapter in the unhappy story of lost pubs where developers have been able to get away with derisory fines for flouting planning procedures.

As to whether people are deserting pubs for other sources of entertainment, perhaps the jury is still out: I suggested in the last edition that poorly-run and unattractive

pubs, and continuing price hikes by pubcos and family brewers were in part responsible for the demise of many pubs: however I pointed to the success of more traditional pubs run by enthusiastic management, free of tie if they're lucky, who have turned round pubs which the big boys claimed were not viable. The success of the campaign to save the Chesham Arms in Homerton (p137) and the way it has once again taken its place as a thriving community local, is one the latest examples, but there are others: the Ivy House in Nunhead was another pub whose days looked numbered, but a determined group of locals managed to save the pub and turn it into a profitable and vibrant enterprise as London's first community owned local. The Hope in Carshalton (p176), twice a winner of CAMRA's Greater London Pub of the Year award, and now also fully owned by its shareholders, was for many years a failing local; and the little Trafalgar in Merton (p164), the epitome of the plain backstreet boozer, is the current local CAMRA Pub of Year. Maybe if we could get more pubs out of the portfolio of big pubcos and brewers whose main aim often

**The Trafalgar, Merton**

appears to be asset stripping, and into the hands of community enthusiasts we would get even more people into the pubs and stem the tide of closures! After all, CAMRA's main aim has always been to safeguard traditional British beer, but we also need convivial pubs in which to drink.

## The routes

There have been a number of casualties since the second edition of this guide was published in 2013; so there are a small number of new routes here and rather more numerous smaller alterations to the routes documented in the last edition, rather than a comprehensive rewrite.

Most of these trails take you to five or six pubs, and many link to adjacent trails if you have the stamina! Wherever possible, trails start and end at an Underground station, or failing that a National Rail station. Visitors to London will find the public transport system pretty good, despite what its detractors say. It's probably worth buying a Travelcard at the start of the day – if you are making more than a couple of journeys by public transport it will be cost effective. There are several routes specifically designed around public transport – enabling you to navigate your way to the best London pubs by Tube, bus and Riverbus.

The first edition of London Pub Walks was, in part, a celebration of the work done by CAMRA to publicise the Real Heritage pubs of the capital, and to increase awareness of the fine range of architectural features – some grand, some more humble but increasingly rare – which survived as evidence of the pub as part of our social history. Many of London's finest surviving pub interiors, but of course, by no means all, can be visited on the routes set out in this current edition, and at least two routes are themed to focus on pubs with outstanding interiors. To get the full picture, I recommend the latest copy of CAMRA's publication Britain's best Real Heritage Pubs by Geoff Brandwood.

**The Adam & Eve, Homerton (p137)**

## Food

Food of course is now widely available in pubs; and the great majority of pubs in this book offer at least snacks and sandwiches. I have not religiously included food information for each pub. If you want to eat whilst on one of these trails, you should have no trouble, unless you decide to go at a very busy time or late in the evening.

## Opening times, and when to go

It's important to bear in mind that there are some weekend closures and restricted opening hours in parts of the capital. Broadly speaking, pubs in the City, towards the east of the central area, are more likely not to be open at weekends – most of those in the West End will be. Check the times on each entry, which were correct when going to press, but are subject to alteration.

**The Harp, Charing Cross (p40)**

Another thing to remember is that London pubs can get very busy – in the City at lunchtimes and after work; in the West End of an evening. Not everyone is able to go at quieter times, but I think a great time to enjoy pubs is in the morning, soon after they open – particularly if you want to appreciate the architecture!

*RWS*

# London's brewing

*Des de Moor*

A bottle shop in East Dulwich now has a section dedicated to beer from southeast London. At the beginning of the decade, a mere two bottling brewers would have qualified for these shelves. Now, there are more than 20 potential suppliers, a sure sign of the recent breathtaking expansion of London brewing.

**London was once the world beer capital** but the industry suffered relentless decline through the 20th century, culminating in a new low in 2006 when the closure of Young's brewery left only nine breweries. But then a trickle of promising start-ups appeared, and by 2010 the London Brewers Alliance had emerged specifically to promote London beer. By the end of 2011 there were 22 breweries, and a year later 36. There are now over 75, surely the highest figure since at least Victorian times, and London beers now appear on London bars with a frequency not seen since the 1970s.

These breweries are rather different beasts to the industrial giants of the past. The last remnant of old school big brewing disappeared at the end of 2015, when Watney's former Stag brewery at Mortlake mashed its last. Fuller's at Chiswick, London's last remaining old-established independent, is now its biggest and oldest brewery. Veteran London brewer Derek Prentice calculates that, compared with when CAMRA was founded in the early 1970s, seven times the number of breweries produce about a seventh of the quantity of beer.

Even so, there's enough of a buzz to attract the attentions of today's brewing giants. In 2015, Meantime in Greenwich, established in 2000 and now London's second oldest and second biggest brewery, was sold to multinational SABMiller, which in turn was bought out by the world's biggest brewing group, Anheuser-Busch InBev. Further controversy followed when AB InBev bought micro Camden Town, founded in a Hampstead pub cellar in 2006. Subsequently it announced it was selling Meantime, which will likely become part of Japan's Asahi.

**Brewing at the Kernal**

**The Kernel**

Most London breweries, though, remain small, artisanal operations. Perhaps the most famous and renowned, besides Fuller's, is the Kernel. Opened in 2010 in a Bermondsey railway arch, it inspired a new cluster of breweries that now form the so-called 'Bermondsey mile'. Between them, they turn a stretch of historic rail viaduct into an unlikely zythophile promenade every Saturday (although the Kernel itself no longer has a drink-in bar). One of the most interesting is Ubrew, opened in 2015 as a communal brewhouse which now provides a base not only for keen homebrewers but for around 10 small commercial beer firms.

Beer styles have also changed. While several newcomers make excellent cask beer, not to mention some superb revivals of historic London stouts and porters, much of the growth has been elsewhere, in 'craft keg', bottles, cans and US-inspired craft beer styles. Pretty much every London brewer now produces a pale ale liberally dosed with New World hops, but a good few see no reason to offer a best bitter. Then again, India Pale Ale was also a London invention, so in a sense it's come home at last.

*Des de Moor is the author of* The CAMRA Guide to London's Best Beer, Pubs and Bars

# Central London

→

# City classics

This compact walk traces a route right across the heart of London's financial district, close to many famous financial institutions like the Stock Market in Threadneedle Street, and the futuristic Lloyd's building. The Royal Exchange, which greets you at the start of the walk, is these days a swanky shopping centre but still well worth seeing. Another highlight is Leadenhall Market, which is relatively unspoilt in comparison with other London markets. The pubs themselves are a mixed bunch from the grand conversions to little tucked away side-street taverns; but expect them all to get very busy when the city workers spill out for lunch or at the end of the day.

**WALK 1**

- **Start:** ⊖⊖ Bank
- **Finish:** ⊖ Aldgate, or ⇌ Fenchurch Street
- **Distance:** 1.3 miles (2 km)
- **Key attractions:** The Royal Exchange; Bank of England; Leadenhall Market; Museum of London
- ▶ **THE PUBS:** Counting House; Crosse Keys; Lamb Tavern; Ship (Talbot Court); Ship (Hart Street); East India Arms. Try also: Cock & Woolpack; Peacock
- ▶ **Timing tips:** Almost all the pubs are shut at the weekend as is the norm in the City of London, so a weekday it must be. If you can start early (the Counting House opens at 11, the Crosse Keys as early as 9), or during the afternoon, you'll have more space to enjoy the pubs.

The splendid Lamb Tavern occupies a key corner site in Leadenhall Market

Emerging from your train at Bank, you're greeted immediately by the grand Royal Exchange building, rebuilt in the 1840s, and which, as noted above, is now used as an upmarket indoor shopping mall; but a flying visit is recommended if only for the architecture. Either way, proceed east along Cornhill. Depending upon the time (as it only opens at noon) and if you're keen to try an extra pub, you could look into the hidden little **7** **Cock & Woolpack** on narrow Finch Lane, a turning on the left (north side)

of Cornhill. It's a Shepherd Neame house, so expect a range from their portfolio.

Otherwise continue a little further to reach the **1** **Counting House**. This sumptuous late Victorian building was built as a bank, and has only been a pub

PAINTING AT THE ENTRANCE TO THE LAMB TAVERN

**KEY**

🚶 Walk start

– ▶ – Walk route

•••••• Detour

THREADNEEDLE STREET

FINCH LANE

**7**

**Bank**

CORNHILL

**1**

LEADENHALL STREET

BIRCHIN LANE

**Bank**

**2**

**3**

Leadenhall Market

KING WILLIAM STREET

GRACECHURCH STREET

LIME STREET

FENCHURCH STREET

FENCHU

CANNON STREET

THE TUCKED-AWAY SHIP

**4**

PHILPOT LANE

ROOD LANE

MINCING LANE

EASTCHEAP

**Monument**

GREAT TOWER STREET

THE SHIP

PUDDING LANE

ST MARY AT HILL

LOWER THAMES STREET

LONDON BRIDGE

THAMES

since 1997. An excellent refurbishment and conversion by Fuller's was rewarded by a City Heritage Award, the first time that this accolade has been won by a public house. There are plenty of interesting fixtures and fittings to admire, among which the enormous glass-domed skylight is an outstanding

**The circular bar of the Crosse Keys**

feature. The place offers a full range of Fuller's regular and seasonal beers, such as London Pride, Chiswick Bitter and ESB. It's worth a climb to the gallery to admire the splendour of the building from a height. Food is available throughout the day.

Leave the Counting House via the rear door leading to St Peter's Alley, one of numerous little alleyways that have survived in the City. Head past the tiny garden and this alley will disgorge you into Gracechurch Street, right opposite the striking entrance to Leadenhall Market. This will be the quarry after the next pub, which is a few yards down the street to the right.

You won't miss the **2** **Crosse Keys** on account of its sheer size: another former bank, built in 1912 for the Hong Kong & Shanghai Bank, this impressive Wetherspoon conversion opened in 1999 and occupies some 8,000 square feet – massive even by JDW's standards. It's named after the former Crosse Keys Inn, which was destroyed by the Great Fire of London in 1666. The building has a very high ceiling with glass-domed skylights, substantial marble pillars and a

ART DECO ELEGANCE AT THE PEACOCK

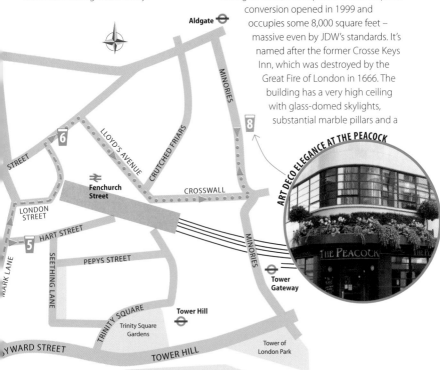

**The gallery of the Counting House provides a good view**

striking circular central bar in marble. One of the best parts of this Grade II-listed building is the elegant wood-panelled room at the rear. You'll be unlucky not to find a beer or two to suit you in here, for, although the numbers on at any time are variable, the choice of guests is usually one of the largest in Wetherspoon's London estate.

Cross the street and double back to the entrance to Leadenhall Market. On a site with a long history as a market, the current building – the work of the City's architect Sir Horace Jones, who was also the architect of Billingsgate and Smithfield Markets – dates to 1881. For most of its life it was a meat, game and poultry market and, although the latter survived into the 20th century, it's a cleaner and more sanitised place, though still highly impressive, today. Walk down the covered arcade past the New Moon

to the junction of malls, which is dominated by the **3 Lamb Tavern**. This magnificent building on three floors dates back to the reconstruction of the market. The interior still has some venerable old fittings: look out for the fine tiled panel depicting Christopher Wren explaining his plans for rebuilding London; and some decent etched glasswork to doors and windows. After being a free house until 1985 the Lamb is now owned by Young's, so expect beers from their stable; but in the past few years the atmospheric little downstairs cellar room, Old Tom's Bar, has branched out with its own more eclectic range of beers. Local guests, most frequently Sambrook's Wandle Ale, are supported by three on keg from the Meantime brewery, and a few interesting bottled offerings. Tempting-looking 'grazing plates' of cheese and meats are available too. On a more esoteric note, the Lamb has been a film location for both *Brannigan* starring John Wayne and *Winds of War* starring Robert Mitchum; and younger drinkers may know that more recently the market outside the pub was cast as Diagon Alley in the *Harry Potter* films.

Head out of the market by taking the mall opposite the Lamb (so, turn right, as if you hadn't entered the pub) which will bring you out onto Lime Street. Bear right, and cross Fenchurch Street into Philpot Lane. At the end of this street, turn right into Eastcheap, and now just a few steps along, by the sandwich bar and bus stop, right again into the little covered alley, Talbot Court, leading to the **4 Ship**. Not so far from the Monument, the pub's 'new' name dates back to the rebuilding after the fire, when it apparently became patronised by salty types from the river. These days of course it's city workers who are the patrons, but tucked away as it is, it's often possible to find a spot, especially in the little upstairs room, when other local places are brimming. Don't expect a 17th-century survivor – but it's a handsome building with a traditional interior, and has one of the larger ranges

**The traditional East India Arms**

of beers in the Nicholson's chain, so you'll be able to pick up something interesting on the beer front from a wide array of handpulls. This pub is the last serious call for food, which is available all day.

When it's time to 'jump ship' (groan!), return to Eastcheap and, turning left, continue down to the end and bear left

**The second Ship on our route has an elaborate frontage**

again into Mark Street. Head up to the first turning on the right, and just around the corner you'll see the sign for the tiny **5** **Ship**, jammed between two dismal modern office blocks. The exterior, narrow but elaborate, features two arched doorways flanking a central window. Ornate grape motifs decorate the elevation below the first-floor bay window.

Inside, there's a small bar (but there's a dining room upstairs too), which has had a recent makeover resulting in the removal of the huge bad taste tie collection. On the bar, up to four cask ales: the house beer is rebadged Caledonian 80/-, whilst Deuchars IPA is pretty regular.

The next pub isn't called the Ship, but it does retain the nautical connection. To get there, look for the lane (New London Street) a few yards up on the left beyond the Ship and head up the steps at the end of this, bringing you outside Fenchurch Street station. Walk around the handsome brick façade of the station and up to Fenchurch Street itself at the junction. Look right, and the distinctive red brick elevation of the **6 East India Arms** is right in front of you. There has been a pub on this site for almost 400 years. The current Grade II-listed building dates from the 1820s and is now the only London pub celebrating the East India Company, although the name is not the original. The little drinking booths have been lost and the opened-out interior is minimally furnished today, though not unattractive. The bar counter, around which the floorboarded drinking area wraps, is topped with an unusual glass gantry bearing the name of the pub's present owners, Shepherd Neame, whose beers you'll find on the four handpumps.

**East India Arms**

This is the final full entry on this walk. If Fenchurch Street station is of no use to you, continuing east along Fenchurch Street will lead to Aldgate Underground station in five minutes; alternatively, a similar walk in the opposite direction will bring you to Monument/Bank. If you're game for another pub, take the next turning right (Lloyd's Avenue), and at the railway bridge bear 45 degrees left onto Crosswall. At the second junction turn left again onto Minories, and a few yards up on the opposite side is the **8 Peacock**. Fans of the Streamline Moderne style of Art Deco will drool over the remarkable exterior of Ibex House, which hosts the pub in one corner. It's in the same style as the more well-known Daily Express building on Fleet Street. Expect to find at least a couple of beers on, of which the reliable Butcombe Bitter should be one, and if you're lucky up to two guests.

From here, Aldgate station is directly north along Minories, and Tower Gateway is a few minutes south.

## PUB INFORMATION

**1 COUNTING HOUSE**
50 Cornhill, EC3V 3PD
020 7283 7123 • www.the-counting-house.com
**Opening hours:** 11–11; closed Sat & Sun

**2 CROSSE KEYS**
7-12 Gracechurch Street, EC3V 0DR
020 7623 4824
**Opening hours:** 8am-11 (midnight Fri); 9am-10 Sat; 9am-8 Sun

**3 LAMB TAVERN**
10-12 Leadenhall Market, Gracechurch Street, EC3V 1LR
020 7626 2454 • www.lambtavernleadenhall.com
**Opening hours:** 11–11; closed Sat & Sun

**4 SHIP**
11 Talbot Court, Gracechurch Street, EC3V 0BP
020 7929 3903 • www.nicholsonspubs.co.uk/ theshiptalbotcourtlondon
**Opening hours:** 11-11 (6 Sat); closed Sun

**5 SHIP**
3 Hart Street, Lower Thames Street, EC3R 7NB
020 7702 4422 • www.shipec3.co.uk
**Opening hours:** 11.30-11.30; closed Sat & Sun

**6 EAST INDIA ARMS**
67 Fenchurch Street, EC3M 4BR
020 7265 5121
**Opening hours:** 11.30-11; closed Sat & Sun

**Try also:**

**7 COCK & WOOLPACK**
6 Finch Lane, Gracechurch Street, EC3V 3NA
020 7626 4799
**Opening hours:** 12-11; closed Sat & Sun

**8 PEACOCK**
41 Minories, EC3N 1DT
020 7488 3630
**Opening hours:** 12-midnight; closed Sat & Sun

# A Central London pub heritage tour

One of the key objectives of the first edition of CAMRA's *London Pub Walks*, published 10 years ago, was to promote London's rich heritage of pub interiors which had until that time, received very little attention or documentation. A good many of the pubs recommended in this new edition have features of architectural and/or historic interest, but this route, along with Walk 19, offers a concentrated dose of riches as far as heritage is concerned, and all the entries appear on CAMRA's inventory of 'Real Heritage Pubs'. Devotees of this subject should acquire a copy of *London Heritage Pubs – An Inside Story* by Geoff Brandwood & Jane Jephcote (CAMRA, 2008), where there is more detail on what to look for.

▶ **Start:** ⇌ ⊖ Blackfriars

▶ **Finish:** ⊖ Holborn

▶ **Distance:** 1.25 miles (2 km)

▶ **Key attractions:** Rich internal pub fittings and architecture; Sir John Soane's museum (www.soane. org); Lincoln's Inn Fields; Dr Johnson's house (www. drjohnsonshouse.org)

▶ **THE PUBS:** Black Friar; Olde Cheshire Cheese; Cittie of Yorke; Princess Louise Try also: Punch Tavern; Tipperary

▶ **Timing tip:** Some of the entries, including the optional additions, are closed at weekends, especially Sunday, so if you can, aim for a weekday, although Saturday sees most of the key entries open.

**The Princess Louise boasts fine tile and mirror work**

As well as the 'core' entries for this walk, there are links to other quality pubs that appear on other routes; and two or three additional pubs with some features of interest. Several of the pubs on this walk are in the estate of Yorkshire brewer Samuel Smith where the only real ale available is the unexciting Old Brewery Bitter; but the excellence of the fittings and fixtures makes a visit worthwhile, and, if it's your first time, frankly unmissable.

Start at the nicely revamped Blackfriars station with its excellent access via both Underground and Thameslink rail services (if arriving via the latter onto Blackfriars Bridge, exit on the north bank of the Thames). If you want to stretch your legs before starting the walk, why not take a stroll along the South Bank from, say, Waterloo, and cross via Blackfriars Bridge? The station exit at the north end of Blackfriars Bridge lies directly across the road from the first pub stop of the walk, and with its highly distinctive shape the **Black Friar** is hard to miss. In fact the view from across the street here shows the exterior at its best, with a huge black monk

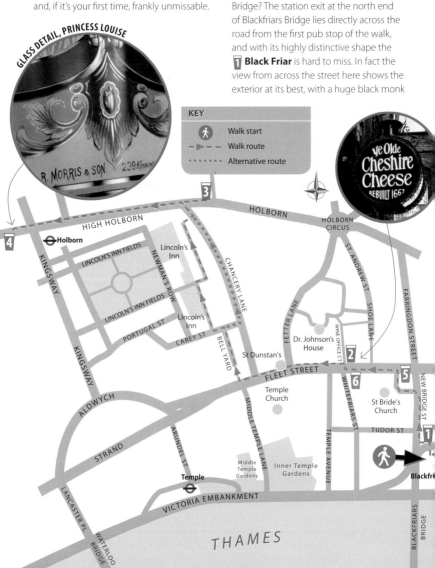

GLASS DETAIL, PRINCESS LOUISE

R. MORRIS & SON. 239 KENNIN

**KEY**

| | |
|---|---|
| 🚶 | Walk start |
| – ▶ – | Walk route |
| ••••• | Alternative route |

ye Olde Cheshire Cheese REBUILT 1667

HOLBORN

HIGH HOLBORN

🚇 Holborn

KINGSWAY

LINCOLN'S INN FIELDS

Lincoln's Inn

NEWMAN'S ROW

LINCOLN'S INN FIELDS

Lincoln's Inn

PORTUGAL ST

CAREY ST

CHANCERY LANE

BELL YARD

St Dunstan's

FLEET STREET

HOLBORN CIRCUS

ST ANDREW ST

SHOE LANE

FARRINGDON STREET

FETTER LANE

WINE OFFICE CT

Dr. Johnson's House

2

5

NEW BRIDGE ST

6

WHITEFRIARS ST

St Bride's Church

1

Temple Church

ALDWYCH

STRAND

ARUNDEL ST

MIDDLE TEMPLE LANE

Middle Temple Gardens

Inner Temple Gardens

TEMPLE AVENUE

TUDOR ST

🚇 Temple

KINGSWAY

LANCASTER PL

WATERLOO BRIDGE

VICTORIA EMBANKMENT

Blackfri

BLACKFRIARS BRIDGE

**THAMES**

**The interior at the Black Friar is not to be missed**

surveying the traffic carnage from the apex of the building. This Grade II*-listed pub was originally built circa 1875 on the site of a 13th-century Dominican Priory; this religious heritage gave the area its name and was the inspiration for the pub's design.

Once safely across the road, the exterior is worth closer examination. A plaque outside reminds us that some 50 years ago the Black Friar nearly followed thousands of other fine pubs into oblivion, but was saved following a spirited campaign led by the redoubtable John Betjeman. Look also for the copper signs directing customers to the former saloon bar at the left-hand extremity. The numerous doorways remind us that once there were several separate spaces – and even today, with these all interconnected, it's still easy to see, once inside, that the further one moves around to the left, the more sumptuous

**Stained glass window at the Black Friar**

the décor, culminating in the astonishing chapel-like snug in the far interior. And it is the interior, dating from an Art Nouveau refit from 1905 onwards, that makes this pub so remarkable: at that time, when austerity was replacing the glamour and confidence of the late-Victorian period, exuberant design of this kind was very rare. Royal Academy sculptor Henry Poole used high-quality materials such as marble and alabaster, while adorning the pub with the imaginary antics of the local Dominican friars. Look for the witty captions like 'Don't advertise, tell a gossip!' The crypt-like snug, dating from 1917, is especially notable, but the management has recently seen fit to allocate this area to diners, the only thing I can really find to criticise here. The main bar would originally have been partitioned with screens, but these have now gone.

It's not only the architecture that is worth sampling here: the beer list is better than ever, with London Pride joined by a changing range of interesting guests from Nicholson's list on the other seven taps. This is a great pub, best enjoyed outside the busy lunchtime and early evening periods.

One of London's most famous buried rivers, the Fleet, still dribbles into the Thames under Blackfriars Bridge; and as you walk up New Bridge Street, directly away from the river upon leaving the Black Friar, you're following the old river valley up towards Holborn Viaduct, where the valley was spanned nearly 150 years ago by what was effectively the first flyover in London. Just before reaching the traffic lights at Ludgate Circus, use the controlled pedestrian crossing to switch to the west side of the road by Bridewell Place. Walk north and take the next turning left, Bride Lane, a narrow road that takes you onto Fleet Street via an atmospheric little short cut. As you bear right and walk up the slope (once the old terrace of the River Thames), there's interest all around: on the right, the Crown & Sugarloaf is a good-quality renewal by Samuel Smith of what was once the western half of the Punch Tavern, just around the corner. It features some fine glass and woodwork.

The **5 Punch Tavern** itself, accessed by turning right onto Fleet Street, is of historical interest as it was on these premises in 1841 that *Punch* magazine was supposedly conceived. Staff of this satirical magazine met here for 150 years until it folded in 1992. If you have time, it's worth dropping in as it retains some fine early features, particularly the splendid tiled entrance corridor with mosaic floor, presided over by paintings of Mr and Mrs Punch. Inside, there are two fine skylights and a nicely proportioned bar-back boasting some rich etched glass. Geologists in particular will appreciate the

**Mr Punch, of course, in the lobby of the Punch Tavern Fleet street**

bar top in pink marble and the attractive fireplace. The pub is now aimed at affluent city workers, with prices to match; beers are less exciting than the architecture, from national brewers such as Sharp's and Marstons.

Back on Bride Lane, take the steps opposite the Crown & Sugarloaf leading up to an alley between the back of the Old Bell and the imposing St Bride's church, which traditionally had close connections with journalists and printers. The church has the highest Wren steeple in London and was apparently the inspiration for the traditional tiered wedding cake. The spire was built in 1701–3 and withstood the Second World War Blitz, although the rest of the church was destroyed in December 1940 and later rebuilt. The Old Bell was reputedly constructed to refresh the builders at work on the church. Despite alterations, it still has an atmospheric interior with plenty of wood and glass, and there is a striking floor mosaic in the entrance to the back door.

**The quaint little Tipperary**

The alley brings you onto Fleet Street, where turn left. Look out on the opposite side of the road for two of the finest monuments to the long-gone days of Fleet Street's newspaper culture. No. 135, the old Daily Telegraph building, was a very bold building for such a conservative newspaper, but was architecturally outflanked shortly afterwards by the glass curtain wall of the old Daily Express HQ just to the east, nicknamed the 'Black Lubyanka' by *Private Eye*.

Another little pub with some features of heritage interest worth a visit (particularly if you haven't been before) is a little further along on the left, and so overshadowed by modern office blocks that the narrow frontage is easy to miss. The **6** **Tipperary** claims to be the earliest Irish pub in London, a boast backed by the words on its exterior board: that it was acquired and refitted by J.G. Mooney & Co. of Dublin in 1895. The well-worn remains of the Mooney name appear on a slate at the entrance, and shamrocks are found in the mosaic flooring. Starting life as the Boar's Head, the pub was renamed the Tipperary in 1918 to commemorate the Great War song. The ground-floor bar is a long narrow room with wood panelling, inset mirrors and an imposing bar-back. Independent once again, it offers Marstons Pedigree and three rotating guests.

Fleet Street used to run more or less along the Thames' shore, and the area retains many of the alleys and courtyards typical of medieval cities. It is in one of these that the next pub is found, with the hanging lantern sign visible across the street to the right, on looking across from the Tipperary. To reach the **7** **Olde Cheshire Cheese** in one piece, use the crossing and head right for a few yards to an alley with the distinctive name of Wine Office Court. Here stands the atmospheric entrance to an important survivor in the social history of the urban tavern, with its exterior pendant lantern giving the date of 1667, the year after the Great Fire. Inside, the original pub retains a domestic-style layout that is very rare in London pubs. Two rooms lead off the

**St Paul's Cathedral and the Olde Cheshire Cheese**

entrance corridor, conjuring up a sense of homeliness with their large fireplaces, and the vintage panelling is possibly the oldest of any London pub. It's easy to imagine the right-hand room without its Victorian bar counter, a remainder of a time when bar counters did not exist and drinks were brought to customers at their table in jugs or pitchers from the cellar.

The Cheese stems from the tavern rather than the alehouse tradition, as it sold mainly wine and food and thereby catered for the upper and middle classes. The rear left-hand room continues in that tradition, with a long history of use as a dining room, going back at least to the days of Dr Johnson, who was reputedly a patron here. In the dining room hangs a Reynolds portrait of the sturdy lexicographer with the following inscription beneath:

'The Favourite Seat of Dr. Johnson … born 18th Septr, 1709. Died 13th Decr, 1784. In him a noble understanding and a

**The grounds of Lincoln's Inn**

masterly intellect were united with grand independence of character and unfailing goodness of heart, which won him the admiration of his own age, and remain as recommendations to the reverence of posterity. 'No, Sir! There is nothing which has yet been contrived by man by which so much happiness has been produced as by a good tavern.'

Perhaps the best of the many poems penned in praise of this venerable house is that 'Ballade' written by John Davidson (1857–1909) the Scottish poet, one stanza of which reads:

> 'I know a house of antique ease
> Within the smoky city's pale,
> A spot wherein the spirit sees
> Old London through a thinner veil.
> The modern world so stiff and stale,
> You leave behind you when you please,
> For long clay pipes and great old ale
> And beefsteaks in the Cheshire Cheese.'

The Cheese also has cellar rooms and an upstairs eatery, but the two ground-floor rooms are the kernel of the old tavern. Other curios are the old fly screens with 'OCC' inscribed on them, and above the doorway to the bar room there is an old warning: 'Gentlemen only served in this bar.'

Beyond the staircase, a 1991 extension has significantly increased the area of the pub; which is a good thing, for it gets very busy, with tourists popping in to gaze in awe. Despite this, the main bar room is frequently quiet enough to enable one to appreciate the wonderful panelling and glazing unimpeded. The Cheese is owned by Sam Smith of Tadcaster, so expect Old Brewery Bitter on handpump.

If it's a weekday, you might wish to take in another classic London pub, the Olde Mitre, the full description for which appears in Walk 10. To get there, follow Wine Office Court, and take the first right onto Shoe Lane, following it north until it becomes St Andrew Street, which brings you to Holborn Circus; then regain the main route at the Cittie of Yorke by walking west along High Holborn. Another cultural diversion is a visit to Dr Johnson's house at 17 Gough Square – turn right out of the Olde Cheshire Cheese, then first left. Otherwise return to Fleet Street and turn right past the lavishly refurbished Old Bank of England, and up Bell Yard to Carey Street. The Seven Stars, 100 yards to the left, is another premier division heritage pub, which would take its place alongside the entries described here. Originally built at the end of Elizabeth I's reign in 1602, the current timbered ground-floor frontage probably dates from the mid- to late-Victorian period. For a full description see Walk 3.

During weekdays, until 7pm, whether or not taking in the Seven Stars, turn left along Carey Street and then right through the gate by No. 57 (where the late David Bowie once worked) into Lincoln's Inn New Square, walking right through the Inn into Old Buildings at the north-eastern end, where a gateway exits into Chancery Lane. This was named after the Inns of Chancery, which were attached to and, for a while, were training institutions for the Inns of Court. If the New Square gate to Lincoln's Inn is closed, turn right on Carey Street, passing the Knights Templar, and then left into Chancery Lane.

At the top of Chancery Lane, turn right on High Holborn, crossing to the north side, and walk along a few yards until you reach the striking clock protruding from the

**The Cittie of Yorke's timber hall is unique in English pub design**

**3** **Cittie of Yorke**. Named after a pub that occupied a site across the road until the 1970s, this is the finest survivor of a pub style popular during the interwar years, which tried to evoke a return to an Olde England of medieval banqueting halls. Despite the apparent antiquity of the place, the ground-floor pub dates back only as far as 1923, when it was rebuilt as a Henekey's wine bar. Enter via a corridor, and to the left is a panelled mock-Tudor room. A cellar bar, a remnant of a much older building, is sometimes open and also worth a look. However, it is the rear room, built in the style of a great timber hall with a high-pitched roof, that is the jewel here. There is little like it in any English pub, with its arcade under clerestory windows, an array of small railway carriage-style booths and, above the servery, a walkway to serve the huge casks, which at one time contained wine. Don't miss the fine old early 19th-century triangular stove in the centre of the room, another unique fixture with an unusual flue that exits downwards. The pub is owned by Samuel Smith's of Tadcaster, so the only real ale on sale here is Old Brewery Bitter. Good food is available most of the day from a modern server at the near end of the room, but this is a pub to enjoy first and foremost for its architecture.

Upon leaving, a few yards' detour to the left will enable you to view, across the road, Staple Inn – the rickety-looking half-timbered buildings – which is the only surviving Inn of Chancery. The onward route continues west along High Holborn, first to the junction with Kingsway by Holborn Underground station, and straight across here to the final pub on this walk just 100 yards further on the left. And the **4** **Princess Louise** is a fitting finale to this route for, since the fine restoration

**The striking Cittie of Yorke**

**The wonderful stillion at the Princess Louise**

carried out by Samuel Smith in 2007, this late Victorian building has arguably the finest surviving authentic Victorian pub interior in the capital. Named after one of Queen Victoria's daughters, the pub, rather plain on the outside, has some of the best mirror and tile work in any pub, a testimony to the skills of the celebrated firms of R. Morris and W.B. Simpson respectively. The rich mirrors represent a technique known as French embossing, which was applied with tremendous results here by Morris. The wonderful stillion with its pendant lights, probably the work of W.H. Lascelles, must surely be one of the finest survivors of this kind and it can still be enjoyed without the intrusion of a glasses gantry on the counter to obstruct the view. The rich lincrusta ceiling, attractive bar counter and appropriate seating are all pleasing. In contrast to most modern restoration work, the quality of wood and glass in the replaced screens that faithfully divide the interior into separate booths, just as in the original pub, is superb. The same goes for the new floor mosaic work in the newly recreated corridors running down each side of the interior. Yet again, Samuel Smiths deserve praise for returning this now treasured building (which once was in a rather sorry condition) to its former glory, even if it offers only its own single real ale, as usual in its London estate.

From here it is but a minute's walk back along High Holborn to Holborn Underground station, on the Piccadilly and Central lines; or, if you prefer, buses to virtually all parts.

## PUB INFORMATION

**1 BLACK FRIAR**
174 Queen Victoria Street, EC4V 4EG
020 7236 5474 • www.nicholsonspubs.co.uk/
theblackfriarblackfriarslondon
**Opening hours:** 9am-11; 12-10.30 Sun

**2 OLDE CHESHIRE CHEESE**
145 Fleet Street, EC4A 2BU
020 7353 6170
**Opening hours:** 11.30-11; closed Sun

**3 CITTIE OF YORKE**
22 High Holborn, WC1V 6BN
020 7242 7670
**Opening hours:** 11.30-11; closed Sun

**4 PRINCESS LOUISE**
208 High Holborn, WC1V 7BW
020 7405 8816 • princesslouisepub.co.uk
**Opening hours:** 11.30-11; 12-10.30 Sun

**Try also:**

**5 PUNCH TAVERN**
99 Fleet Street, EC4Y 1DE
020 7353 6658 • www.punchtavern.com
**Opening hours:** 7.30am-11 (midnight Thu-Fri);
11-11 Sat; 11-10 Sun

**6 TIPPERARY**
66 Fleet Street, EC4Y 1HT
020 7583 6470
**Opening hours:** 11-11; 12-6 Sat; 12-5 Sun

# Legal London – Temple to Holborn

A south-to-north meander through three of the four Inns of Court takes us through an attractive area of the capital largely untouched by noisy traffic and modernisation, except at the end. There are tranquil gardens, lawns and squares, with classy pubs never too far away to break up the tour. The 'Inns' themselves though have nothing directly to do with drink! It is the collective name for the four ancient 'honourable societies' that have the exclusive right of admission to the Bar, that is, the right to practise law. If you're doing the culture as well as the pubs, a visit to the stunning 16th-century Middle Temple Hall with its wonderful hammerbeam roof is highly recommended, but access is limited and it's as well to check ahead. The pubs are a mixture of the classy (even the recent conversions) and venerable, with a brash new youngster to shake you up at the end. They are close together, so feel free to miss one or two out unless you're ticking them off.

▶ **Start:** ⊖ Temple

▶ **Finish:** ⊖ Holborn

▶ **Distance:** 1.1 miles (1.8 km)

▶ **Key attractions:** Inns of Court; Prince Henry's Room (tel: 020 7936 4004); Royal Courts of Justice; Churches of St Dunstan's and St Clement Danes; Lincoln's Inn Fields; Soane Museum

▶ **THE PUBS:** Edgar Wallace; Devereux; Old Bank of England; Knights Templar; Seven Stars; Ship Tavern; Holborn Whippet. Try also: Temple Brew House

▶ **Timing tip:** This is a walk best done in the week since some of the Inns of Court, as well as many of the pubs, are closed at weekends.

Squares and gardens outside Middle Temple

Start at Temple Underground station on the Embankment and exit into Temple Gardens adjacent to the station (if the gates are shut, bear left then right into Temple Place and rejoin the route at Milford Lane). On the way you will pass

several statues, notably those of philosopher John Stuart Mill, and of Lady Somerset, a 19th-century champion of temperance who would no doubt frown upon us if only she knew. Exit and cross the road to the old red phone box opposite and walk up Milford Lane to the steps ahead, taking us up into Essex Street. The street is named after the Earl of Essex, Robert Devereux, and

**THE SHIP TAVERN**

**KEY**

| | |
|---|---|
| 🚶 | Walk start |
| ▷ – – – | Walk route |
| • • • • • | Alternative route |

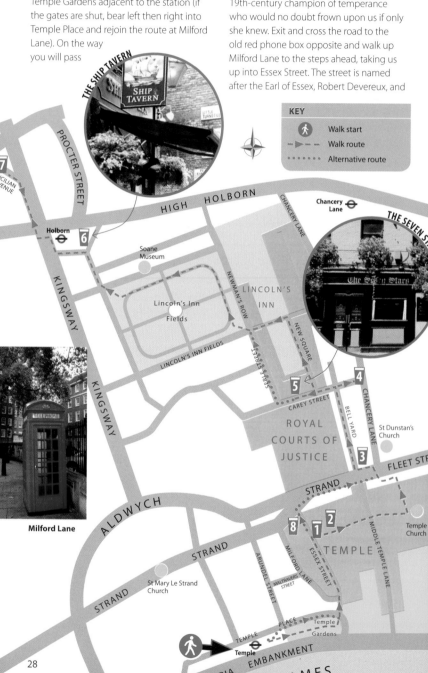

**Milford Lane**

THAMES

**The Edgar Wallace has fine floral displays**

**The spectacular Old Bank of England**

two of the best surviving pubs in this little area used both to carry his name. The first call was formerly known as the Essex Head, but now it's called the ⬛ **Edgar Wallace** after the celebrated journalist, novelist and playwright. Revitalised over the past few years it's now a fine pub for the discerning ale drinker, offering eight interesting ales, which you can expect to be in very good condition. The 'retro' ads on the wall, notably for seventies hip tipple Babycham, are worth a look. Food is available, but it does get busy at lunchtimes (there's more seating upstairs).

Leaving the pub, you might like to detour north a few yards on Essex Street to visit the ⬛ **Temple Brew House** at No. 46. This modern bar set in a handsome older building boasts an on-site brewery visible from the bar, which is a single-room design with minimal decor and some tables set aside for eating. 'Essex Street Brewery' ales include regular and one-off brews alongside a couple of guest and several keg 'craft' beers.

The main route continues on the narrow lane, Devereux Court, heading east from the Edgar Wallace, reaching

**The Devereux**

the ⬛ **Devereux** in a matter of yards. This place was formerly the Grecian Coffee House, opened in 1702, and frequented by Isaac Newton and Edmund Halley. Robert Devereux's mansion, Essex House – inherited from his stepfather Robert Dudley, an intimate friend of Elizabeth I – also stood in the vicinity. Devereux himself fell from grace and was beheaded in 1601 for high treason. The pub itself is an early-Victorian listed building, intimate and pleasantly decorated with an oak-panelled bar and carved wooden corbels. As regards beers, there are now five handpumps, with changing offerings, though both Fuller's London Pride and Sharp's Doom Bar make frequent appearances.

Leaving the pub, go through the gates opposite into the precincts of the Middle Temple (if the Temple gates are closed, later in the evening, go back to the Edgar Wallace and turn right to arrive on the Strand, then turn right again). The name of the Temple derives from the Knights Templar, a religious order of military monks formed in 1119 to protect pilgrims en route to the Holy Land. Their red

**The Knights Templar**

cross on a white background can be seen in the grounds. The most interesting parts of the Temple today are the church, first built by the knights and consecrated in 1185; and the Middle Temple Hall (with its adjacent gardens) further east. However, much of the Temple was destroyed in the Blitz and the majority of what we see today is a post-war reconstruction, in classical Georgian style.

Walk through the arch opposite, dated 1677, across the small square, Brick Court, and through Pump Court arch to reach Temple Church. Unless visiting the church (worthwhile, but there's an admission charge), you've booked a trip to Middle Temple Hall and Gardens, or you wish to amble around the rest of the Inn, turn sharp left (north) here, keeping left of the church to exit on Fleet Street. Before continuing the pub tour you may enjoy a short detour to view Prince Henry's Room, a fine Jacobean building pretty much above the exit from the Temple, with a splendid plasterwork ceiling in the wood-panelled first-floor room. Admission is free, but it may be worth phoning ahead. If there is time, wander

across the street to the church of St Dunstan's-in-the-West with its distinctive 1830s octagonal tower and lantern. The clock tower adjacent is far older and was erected in thanksgiving for deliverance from the Great Fire of 1666. The splendid clock is presided over by Gog and Magog, who strike the bell every hour.

The imposing **3 Old Bank of England** is across the road just left of the exit from the Temple. This impressive Grade I-listed building, itself dwarfed by the Law Courts immediately behind, has been a pub only since 1995 but was erected in 1886–8 as the Law Courts' branch of the Bank of England. It was designed in the then-trendy Italianate style. Ironically, an historic pub, the Cock, was moved across Fleet Street to make way for the new bank. History abounds here as this was also the spot where Demon Barber Sweeney Todd and his partner in crime, Mrs Lovett, prepared their pies containing the victims of his barbershop massacres – if you believe the legend. Read about this on the steps on the way into the pub. Inside, Fuller's have spent a small fortune: there are new paintings and murals, and large columns rise up to the high ornate plaster ceiling, from which hang three very large brass chandeliers. The central stillion itself almost reaches the ceiling. For a good view you can climb to a gallery, where there is further seating. Along with the Counting House in Cornhill, this pub must rank as one of London's very best bank conversions, and you can enjoy the place with a glass from the full range of Fuller's beers.

Leaving the Old Bank, look across to the erection in the middle of Fleet Street, with a griffin atop. This marks the site of the old Temple Bar, the western gate to the City of London. It now stands in Paternoster

Square by St Paul's. Its narrow portals became an obstruction to traffic, but not before it had assumed some notoriety. As Charles Dickens wrote in *A Tale of Two Cities*, severed heads of criminals were 'exposed on Temple Bar with an insensate brutality and ferocity worthy of Abyssinia or Ashantes' – presumably *pour encourager les autres* to behave…

Take Bell Yard, the alleyway immediately to the west of the building, and walk up alongside the edge of the Royal Courts of Justice,

**Middle Temple Lane**

the nation's main civil courts. This imposing Victorian Gothic building, designed by G.E. Street, was opened by Queen Victoria in 1882 and is faced with Portland stone. At the top of Bell Yard runs Carey Street, named in memory of the wealthy 17th-century nobleman and landowner Nicholas Carey. Once home of the bankruptcy courts and known colloquially as 'Queer Street' (although this archaic reference is now obscure), the street has also had connections

with glitterati from Thomas More to David Bowie, who worked briefly here. There are also two more pubs, very different but both well worth a visit.

A few yards to the right you'll see the imposing **4 Knights Templar**, a fine Wetherspoon's bank conversion. Whilst not quite in the same league as the Old Bank in terms of adornment, it's still mightily impressive. The once-dazzling orange décor has mellowed a bit now… On the beer side of things, the usual Wetherspoon's choices sit alongside several interesting guest beers, all dispensed from a long array of handpumps – you won't want for choice (or quality) here. Naturally it gets very busy at peak times.

Now retrace your steps in the other direction along Carey Street, passing the gated entrance to Lincoln's Inn (see below) to one of London's classic old pubs, the **5 Seven Stars**. Originally built at the end of Elizabeth I's reign in 1602, it is one of the

**The Seven Stars with former guv'nor Tom Paine on the bar**

**Vaulted undercroft below the Chapel of Lincoln's Inn**

few buildings to have escaped the Great Fire in 1666, and recently renovations have revealed genuine 400-year-old timbers. However, the current timbered ground-floor frontage probably dates from the mid- to late-Victorian period. The exterior betrays the pub's expansion to the right. The etched and gilded glass in the doorways advertises 'General Counter' and 'Private Counter', but this small pub is now a single space. Inside you'll see some lovely old mirrors and woodwork. The atmosphere today owes all to landlady Roxy, truly one of the femmes formidables of the London pub scene and, like her food, the stuff of legends. Following the sad demise in 2011 of Tom Paine, the pub's resident ruff-wearing moggy, his successor Ray Brown assumed

ownership in the same manner in no time at all! More importantly, on the five handpumps there's a reliable range of beers with the ever-present Dark Star Hophead and offerings from Adnams, alongside other guests. The Seven Stars is another of the seemingly endless acquisitions by Fuller's, but at least the reputation for a wide guest list and well-kept ales is, to judge from recent history, safe in their hands.

If the New Square gate to Lincoln's Inn was open, retrace your steps again and turn left into the Inn. If it is closed, go on past the Seven Stars to the corner of Serle Street and turn right; the gate into the Inn from Serle Street is open longer on weekdays, so it may still be possible to go in and look at the Inn if you wish. The Inn is closed to the public at weekends. Unlike the Temple, Lincoln's Inn miraculously escaped wartime destruction so retains its old buildings; the whole place is a haven of tranquillity, and is indubitably the most attractive of the four Inns. Don't miss, about halfway up, the handsome Hogarth Chambers, the 15th-century Old Hall beyond, and Lincoln's Inn chapel adjacent. It

**Lincoln's Inn**

**The Soane Museum**

**The Ship Tavern**

was the bells here that were immortalised by John Donne, a one-time preacher at Lincoln's Inn: 'never send to know for whom the bell tolls; it tolls for thee'.

When you've seen enough, aim for the exit through the Serle Street gate (across to your left, by the unmistakable Great Hall). This gives out onto London's largest square, Lincoln's Inn Fields. If you're passing here at night (when the gates are locked and you'll need to walk round the square to the diagonally opposite corner), you'll maybe come across the queues of homeless waiting for the soup kitchen, a relic of the days when the square was a night-time home to rough sleepers. By day it's a tranquil place with numerous imposing plane trees presiding over the lawns. Several notable buildings face it, and two worthy of mention are: the Old Curiosity Shop, still quite quaint looking, in the south-western corner; and, rather grander, the Soane Museum on the

**The Holborn Whippet**

north side. The celebrated architect (Sir John Soane, 1753–1837) designed the house to live in, but also as a setting for his antiquities and objets d'art; and he established the house as a museum to which 'amateurs and students' could have access. Today it's one of London's most worthwhile attractions, and it's still free.

Having arrived at the far (north-west) corner one way or the other, take Gate Street, which runs off to the right towards High Holborn. Where it narrows into little more than an alleyway, you'll find our next stop, the

**6 Ship Tavern**. It stands on a site that has been licensed for getting on for 500 years, and, although still pretty small, it was apparently once just half the size! Inside, the latest refurbishment has been done very well to enhance the pubby feel. The decor features prints of early 20th-century ships. The beer range is probably better than ever too, with six handpumps on the bar. The two

Theakston's offerings are probably a remnant of the pub's days as a William Younger's house, but in addition expect St Austell Tribute, Deuchars IPA and a couple of changing guests. Food is available all day, both down below and upstairs in a more formal setting.

The last official stop on this lengthy pub trawl offers a complete contrast to the last two entries. Turn right out of the Ship and take the next narrow alleyway, New Turnstile,

**Temple Brew House**

through to High Holborn, just short of the Underground station and the junction with Kingsway/Southampton Row. Negotiate the traffic lights to end up on the diametrically opposite corner, and head up Southampton Row for just a couple of minutes. You'll come upon Sicilian Avenue. This unusual little pedestrian street, developed as long ago as 1905 in a very elegant Italianate style, is an interesting setting for the second venture of the people who brought you the Euston Tap.

The **7 Holborn Whippet** is thankfully bigger than the Tap but is still hardly spacious, although clever use has been made of what they have. The fittings are in the main modern, minimalist and functional, but it has an agreeable vibe to it. The retro dividing door with 'public bar' on the glass is a nice touch. Like the Euston Tap, there's an excellent and ambitious beer range, with half a dozen cask ales and even more 'craft' keg offerings; expect to see some of the best new British brewers like Arbor, Bristol and Magic Rock. There's also a good foreign beer range. The draught beers are dispensed from a clever brick pillar with lots of taps sticking out of it.

The name? Well, they claim that this was once an area renowned for its whippet racing. Mmm, I think that's a bit of a cock-and-bull story myself…

You know where the Underground station is.

## PUB INFORMATION

**1 EDGAR WALLACE**
40 Essex Street, WC2R 3JF
020 7353 3120
**Opening hours:** 11-11; closed Sat & Sun

**2 DEVEREUX**
20 Devereux Court, WC2R 3JJ
020 7583 4562
**Opening hours:** 11-11; closed Sat & Sun

**3 OLD BANK OF ENGLAND**
194 Fleet Street, EC4A 2LT
020 7430 2255 • www.oldbankofengland.co.uk
**Opening hours:** 11-11; closed Sat & Sun

**4 KNIGHTS TEMPLAR**
95 Chancery Lane, WC2A 1DT
020 7831 2660
**Opening hours:** 8-11 Mon-Wed; 11-11.30 Thu & Fri; 11-5 Sat; closed Sun

**5 SEVEN STARS**
53-54 Carey Street, WC2A 2JB
020 7242 8521 • www.thesevenstars1602.co.uk
**Opening hours:** 11-11; 12-10.30 Sun

**6 SHIP TAVERN**
12 Gate Street, WC2A 3HP
020 7405 1992 • www.theshiptavern.co.uk
**Opening hours:** 11-11 (midnight Thu-Sat); 12-10.30 Sun

**7 HOLBORN WHIPPET**
25-29 Sicilian Avenue, WC1A 2QH
020 3137 9937 • www.holbornwhippet.com
**Opening hours:** 12-11.30; 12-10.30 Sun

Try also:

**8 TEMPLE BREW HOUSE**
46 Essex Street, WC2R 3JF
020 7936 2536 • www.templebrewhouse.com
**Opening hours:** 12-11 (11.30 Thu; midnight Fri & Sat); 12-10.30 Sun

# Covent Garden & Theatreland

**WALK 4**

The West End district of Covent Garden is one of London's success stories. In the 1970s, it was threatened with a dismal office-led redevelopment after the departure of the fruit and vegetable market, but a spirited campaign by local residents managed to fight off the developers. Our walk starts on land reclaimed from the Thames in Victorian times, before circumnavigating the old Covent Garden market hall, piazza and associated buildings. These include the expanded Royal Opera House; the Theatre Royal, Drury Lane; Inigo Jones's St Paul's church; and the London Transport Museum. The pubs include several worthy of their place in CAMRA's inventory of 'Real Heritage Pubs'. If you are not a regular visitor to London, you may well want to spend some time sightseeing in this interesting area. If you can, this is a route to do outside the peak evening periods.

▶ **Start/finish:** ⇌ ⊖ Charing Cross or ⊖ Embankment

▶ **Distance:** 1.5 miles (2.4km)

▶ **Key attractions:** London Transport Museum; Covent Garden Market; St Paul's Covent Garden; Royal Opera house; Theatreland

▶ **THE PUBS:** Coal Hole; Nell of Old Drury; Cross Keys; Lamb & Flag; Salisbury; Harp

▶ **Timing tip:** Watch out for the limited hours (including mid-afternoon and all-day Sunday closure) at Nell of Old Drury.

**The Cross Keys with its golden cherubs holding the keys of St Peter**

**The Coal Hole**

Start at Charing Cross station and, unless it's evening, look for the exit by the Beer House close to platform 1. This will lead down, via steps, to Villiers Street below. The most pleasant route to the first pub stop is via the Victoria Embankment Gardens to the right, but these close at dusk; if they're shut, the easiest alternative is simply to head up onto the Strand (see map) and walk to the right. The gardens were created in 1874 on the reclaimed land following Joseph Bazalgette's construction of the Victoria Embankment between 1865 and 1870. One striking curio is the York Water Gate. Built for George Villiers, Duke of Buckingham, in 1626, the gate served as the riverside entrance for his mansion, York House, which stood between the Strand and the River Thames. It was one of several waterside steps, which are now some distance from the river. 'Strand' is in fact the German word for 'beach': the road broadly followed the north bank of the Thames at one time.

Either leave the gardens on the left (north) by the statue of Robert Raikes, the founder of the Sunday Schools movement, in which case the onward route is directly opposite. Or, alternatively, walk along to the far end of the gardens and exit onto quiet Savoy Place, the tradesman's entrance to the famous hotel, commissioned by Richard D'Oyly Carte of Gilbert & Sullivan fame and designed by Thomas Collcutt. Walk back to your left and look for Carting Lane, then walk up the sloping street towards the steps that lead up onto the Strand.

By now you'll be upon the first pub stop of the walk, the **Coal Hole**. With a name commemorating the coal-heavers of the Thames, this is part of Collcutt's Savoy complex but was opened in 1904 as the New Strand Wine Lodge. The name is still visible on the front fascia. Here, Art Nouveau features mingle with elements of the 'Olde England' revival. There is a good deal of dark panelling, leaded windows and original decoration. Under the beamed ceiling a plaster frieze depicts maidens picking grapes, and there is a decorated fire surround towards the rear, where the gallery is a converted office. These days the pub is in the Nicholson's chain, and in addition to the house Pale Ale (brewed by St Austell) you can expect to find an excellent choice of up to 10 ales, with plenty of guests alongside favourites like London Pride. The small basement snug is used as a wine bar.

From the Coal Hole make your way across the Strand and up Southampton Street opposite. Ahead lies a cobbled square, home to the old Covent Garden market building dating from the 1830s, and now a mecca of entertainment, shops and cafés. It was saved after a spirited campaign in the 1960s, when residents and workers took on the planners and won, although ironically the gentrification of the area and the exodus of the old fruit and vegetable market has since driven out the former community.

GLASS DETAIL THE SALISBURY

Bear right around the market building – unless you fancy a bit of sightseeing (for instance, Inigo Jones's handsome church of St Paul's is at the other end of the piazza) – passing the London Transport Museum in the south-eastern corner of the square. Take

the first turn right (Russell Street) and cross straight over Bow Street by the Marquess of Anglesey. Take the next right by the corner of the Theatre Royal (Catherine Street), and a few yards

NELL OF OLD DURY

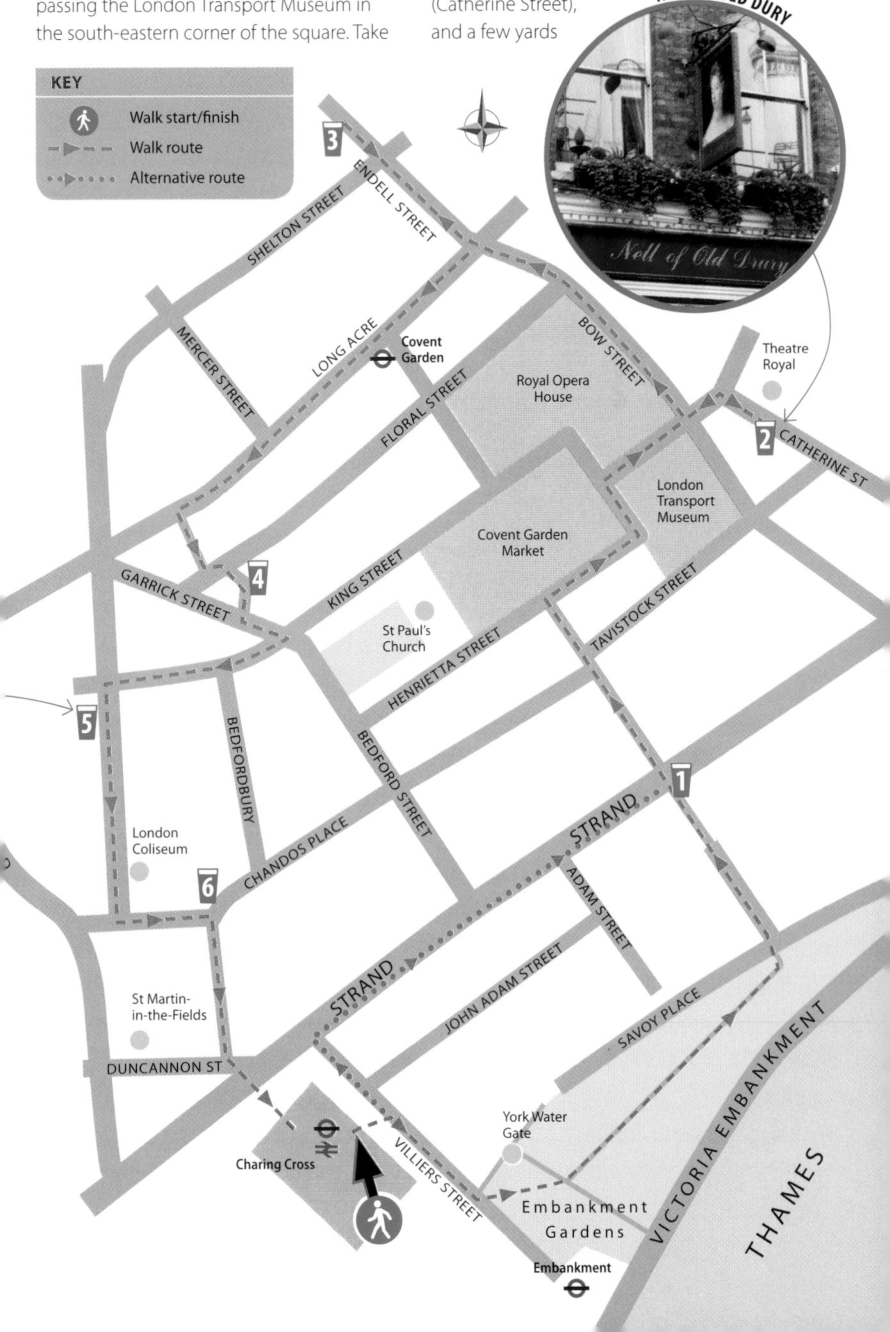

Nell of Old Drury

**KEY**

🚶 Walk start/finish

– – ▶ – – Walk route

•••▶••••• Alternative route

SHELTON STREET
ENDELL STREET
MERCER STREET
LONG ACRE
Covent Garden
FLORAL STREET
Royal Opera House
BOW STREET
Theatre Royal
CATHERINE ST
London Transport Museum
GARRICK STREET
KING STREET
Covent Garden Market
TAVISTOCK STREET
St Paul's Church
HENRIETTA STREET
BEDFORDBURY
BEDFORD STREET
London Coliseum
CHANDOS PLACE
STRAND
ADAM STREET
St Martin-in-the-Fields
DUNCANNON ST
STRAND
JOHN ADAM STREET
SAVOY PLACE
York Water Gate
Charing Cross
VILLIERS STREET
Embankment Gardens
VICTORIA EMBANKMENT
THAMES
Embankment

3
2
4
5
6
1

**The striking exterior of the Cross Keys**

across the very distinctive exterior of the next call, the **3 Cross Keys**. It's striking not just for its elaborate decoration (notably the two golden cherubs holding the crossed keys of St Peter, keeper of the gates of Heaven) but also on account of a heavy covering of foliage. The two together make quite an impression, even before entering. Inside is a fascinating collection of bric-a-brac, ranging from copper kettles to musical instruments and even a diving helmet. There are also brewery mirrors, a large collection of portraits and pictures, including a good watercolour landscape, and two notable clocks. Leased by East London brewers Brodie's, this pub has a good range of its beers and at least one guest. There's a range of food served during the day.

To continue on this anti-clockwise circuit around the market, retrace your steps down to Long Acre and turn right. Head along this shopping street for a few minutes looking out for Stanfords, the famous map and book shop, at No. 14. If you want to drop in, leave by the rear door (or, alternatively, take the passage left immediately beyond the shop), emerging into narrow Floral Street. Bear left here and take the narrow alley, Lazenby Court, a few yards on the right, to arrive at another

down here on your right, opposite the striking façade of the theatre, is the dinky little **2 Nell of Old Drury**. It's a handsome building with a distinctive bow window and a clientele consisting largely of tourists, after-work drinkers and, of course, theatregoers. Because of this it gets busy at certain times. Expect Adnams Broadside and a changing guest on draught.

Return to Bow Street, turning right by the Marquess of Anglesey. This street is probably best known as the home of the first formal police station in London, although the colloquial term 'Bow Street Runners' refers to a forerunner force (before the founding of the Metropolitan Police) attached to a nearby magistrates' office.

Where Bow Street reaches Long Acre, continue more or less straight ahead into Endell Street and walk up here until, at the point where it narrows and becomes one-way, you come

**The Salisbury is a late Victorian gem**

**Lamb & Flag**

famous London pub via the back passage, as it were. Watch your head as you go through the archway with the **4** **Lamb & Flag** on your immediate right.

Entering the pub this way, rather than from Garrick Street at the front, makes it easier to appreciate the late 17th-century origins of this pub, with well-worn boards and panelling, and a lot of atmosphere to savour if you call at one of the few quiet times. The rear room is particularly characterful. Don't miss the array of little brass plaques named for various customers, not all of them celebrities. The pub has now been acquired by Fuller's and offers a wide range of its own beers as well as guests on the eight handpumps. Sandwiches and snacks can be had downstairs, whilst more substantial, good-value meals are available in the Dryden Room upstairs (see box).

Looking back at building upon exit via the main front door, the front space with the two doorways has been opened out in recent times. There was a small lounge to the left, hence the sign above pointing right to the public bar. The smart brick frontage is, of course, a relatively modern addition. Finally, those with a penchant for pub names will maybe recognise the flag as the red cross of the Knights Templar, a military order of monks and the founders of the Temple (see Walk 3), carried on the Pascal Lamb of God.

Walk down the lane to Garrick Street and, crossing over, bear right by the Round House and along brick-paved New Row.

At the end, almost opposite, you will see the splendid exterior of the **5** **Salisbury** across the street. From a pub architecture perspective the Salisbury is the high point of the walk and it is pleasing to see the pride the management takes in the pub's heritage. Rebuilt in 1892, and then called the Salisbury Stores (note the double 'S' in the etched windows), this building fully conveys the sense of glamour of the late Victorian pub. The exterior is pretty stunning and repays close inspection before venturing in. Inside, something of the divided-up plan survives with the small, screened snug on St Martin's Court. The original counter survives and you can mark the position of a now-vanished partition by noting the change from wood to marble. The bar-back is also very fine, as is some, though not all, of the glass. Perhaps the tour de force is the row of bronze Art Nouveau nymphs holding electric lamps. The regular beers come from familiar brewers: St

## THE DRYDEN CONNECTION

The poet John Dryden was beaten to within an inch of his life outside the Lamb in 1679 for writing uncomplimentary words about Charles II's mistress. This violence would become a regular feature of the pub's life as the years went on. In the early 19th century, the pub gained the nickname the 'Bucket of Blood' because of the bare-knuckled prize-fights outside and in the rear room. In fact the whole area was a notorious slum in which fights were commonplace. Today the only fight you will be involved in is the one to get to the bar if you arrive at the wrong time!

**The Harp is one of the beer highlights of the route**

whilst the traditional cider and perry drinker is also catered for. The Harp has lovely stained glass windows, which open in good weather, whilst the interior has stools around the wall below a wide shelf, above which is a collection of paintings. Upstairs is a smaller lounge, which, like the main bar, is often full of appreciative patrons, so don't automatically expect a seat. In fact the crowds often spill out onto the pavement, such is the pub's popularity.

Public transport options upon leaving include numerous buses from Trafalgar Square (return to the bottom of St Martin's Lane and aim for the church), or head down to Charing Cross station by taking the lane opposite the Harp.

Austell Tribute, Timothy Taylor Landlord, and Wells Bombardier; there are guests, too. Food is available until mid evening, though here in the heart of Theatreland there are plenty of other eating options, some maybe less busy.

Leaving the Salisbury, turn right down St Martin's Lane past the rejuvenated Coliseum theatre to the junction at the end, with the National Portrait Gallery and St Martin's church right and ahead, respectively. We turn left, along William IV Street as far as the next junction, where Chandos Place bears half left, and a few yards along is the excellent **6 Harp**. This small, narrow pub, which has little Irish about it despite the name, is as good as it gets for the real ale drinker in London, as the impressive array of CAMRA and other awards testify. During the stewardship of the legendary Binnie Walsh the Harp achieved the ultimate accolade of winning the 2011 national CAMRA Pub of the Year award – the first and only time a London pub has done so. Following her retirement Fuller's bought the Harp in 2014 and wisely have done very little to alter either the place (save for improving the gents' facilities somewhat!) or the beer portfolio, and it still functions as a de facto alehouse with most of the ten handpumps offering a changing range of guest beers. There's also a range of bottle-conditioned and keg craft beers,

## PUB INFORMATION

**1 COAL HOLE**
91-92 Strand, WC2R 0DW
020 7379 9883 • www.nicholsonspubs.co.uk/
thecoalholestrandlondon
**Opening hours:** 10-11 (midnight Fri & Sat)

**2 NELL OF OLD DRURY**
29 Catherine Street, WC2B 5JS
020 7836 5328 • www.nellofolddrury.com
**Opening hours:** 12-3, 5-11.30; 12-midnight Sat;
closed Sun

**3 CROSS KEYS**
31 Endell Street, WC2H 9BA
020 7836 5185 • www.crosskeyscoventgarden.com
**Opening hours:** 11-11

**4 LAMB & FLAG**
33 Rose Street, WC2E 9EB
020 7497 9504 • www.lambandflagcoventgarden.co.uk
**Opening hours:** 11-11; 12-10.30 Sun

**5 SALISBURY**
90 St Martins Lane, WC2N 4AP
020 7836 5863
**Opening hours:** 11-midnight (1am Fri); 12-1am Sat;
12-10.30 Sun

**6 HARP**
47 Chandos Place, WC2N 4HS
020 7836 0291 • www.harpcoventgarden.com
**Opening hours:** 10-11.30 (midnight Fri & Sat);
12-10.30 Sun

# Through Soho – the heart of the West End

Originally farmland, and then a hunting ground, legend has it that Soho got its name from hunters crying out 'Soo hoo!' as they rode through the fields. The rich finally gave up on Soho after a cholera outbreak in 1854. It's a colourful area that has had a long association with immigrants, the music scene and, during the mid-twentieth century in particular, the brothels and sex shops attracted by the relatively cheap rents. Today it's full of cafes, bars and restaurants and retains much of its bohemian atmosphere; and the area around Old Compton Street is still the city's main gay district. This route also takes in one of my favourite Central London gardens. The selected pubs are, in the main, Victorian buildings, some of which retain some fine internal fittings, making the route a worthwhile one for lovers of architecture as well as good beer, although the latter is generally pricey.

- **Start:** Piccadilly Circus
- **Finish:** Tottenham Court Road
- **Distance:** 1.2 miles (2 km)
- **Key attractions:** Phoenix Garden (www.thephoenixgarden.org); Soho Square; Charing Cross Road bookshops
- **THE PUBS:** Crown; Ship; Dog & Duck; Three Greyhounds; Angel; Flying Horse
- **Timing tips:** A good route at any time of day or year, with the pubs open all day, but the usual warnings apply about avoiding the busy evenings unless you don't mind crowds. A daytime tour will enable you to enjoy the Phoenix Garden, while the evening alternative route via Stacey Street and Flitcroft Street (see map) is rather dark and quiet, so you may wish to avoid if alone.

Soho Square with its gardener's hut

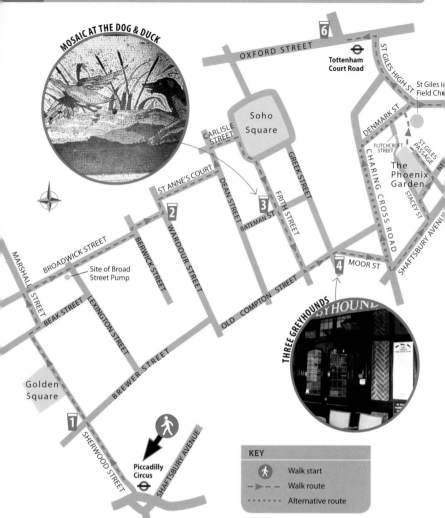

MOSAIC AT THE DOG & DUCK

OXFORD STREET

Tottenham
Court Road

Soho
Square

St Giles in
Field Ch

DENMARK ST

FLITCHCROFT
STREET

The
Phoenix
Garden

CARLISLE
STREET

GREEK STREET

ST ANNE'S COURT

DEAN STREET

FRITH STREET

BATEMAN ST

CHARING CROSS ROAD

STACEY ST

SHAFTESBURY AVEN

BROADWICK STREET

BERWICK STREET

WARDOUR STREET

Site of Broad
Street Pump

MOOR ST

MARSHALL STREET

BEAK STREET

LEXINGTON STREET

OLD COMPTON STREET

THREE GREYHOUNDS

GREYHOUN

BREWER STREET

Golden
Square

**KEY**

SHERWOOD STREET

Piccadilly
Circus

SHAFTESBURY AVENUE

🚶 Walk start

- - ▶ - - Walk route

•••••••• Alternative route

Start at Piccadilly Circus Underground station and use exit 1, which brings you out with the onward route, Sherwood Street, directly ahead and the traffic island with its famous statue behind you. Chances are that, even if you're not a Londoner, you'll be familiar with the statue of Eros atop the Shaftesbury Monument Memorial Fountain, erected in 1893 to commemorate Lord Shaftesbury, the Victorian politician and philanthropist. It was apparently the first statue in the world to be cast in aluminium and has become something of a London icon.

Walk up narrow Sherwood Street, and you hardly have time to get into your stride before encountering the first pub stop: the **1 Crown**. Located on Brewer Street – which was briefly the home of famous Scottish philanthropist David Hume and also the site of the Hickford Rooms, once the main concert halls of London – this Nicholson's pub occupies a very handsome building on a corner site. As with most Nicholson's houses, the external and internal décor is smart, but respectful of the gravitas of the building. The floorboarded L-shaped drinking area wraps

**The handsome façade of the Crown**

**The Ship is one of Soho's best pubs**

around the servery and offers a range of seating areas, mainly circular, brass-topped tables and comfy bench seating. Alongside the three regular ales, the house Pale (brewed by St Austell), Fuller's London Pride, and Windsor & Eton's Knight of the Garter, there are three rotating guests. Upstairs, alongside the facilities, is the more formal Hickford Room, used as a restaurant.

Head directly north from the Crown up Lower James Street, passing the rather disappointing Golden Square on your left. Dickens had it about right in *Nicholas Nickleby* when he noted it 'not exactly in anybody's way to or from anywhere'. Except, of course, we are very much on our way somewhere, for Dickens didn't enjoy the choice of ales we have now, nor of course could he have realised that close by here Carnaby Street would become the centre of London fashion in the swinging sixties. To take a peek, it's a short detour left and first right when we reach the T-junction with Beak Street, but looking rather sorry for itself these days. Culture vultures note that Canaletto lived briefly at No. 41 (see the blue plaque), but our route bears right, then left at the Old

**Plaque on Broad Street**

Coffee House, which appears in Walk 6 and is certainly worth a visit if you have the stamina (see description on page 52). Try not to be put off by the awful ground-floor exterior: what a contrast to the Crown! It's much better inside.

We're now heading up narrow Marshall Street, and turning right into Broadwick Street we're heading towards the centre of Soho. Passing the John Snow pub on the right, there's an interesting little piece of history here. The pink granite kerbstone marks the site of the Broad Street pump where Dr Snow, in an early example of applied geography, demonstrated with a map that an outbreak of cholera in Soho was the result of contamination of the water from this pump. Prior to this it was thought that cholera was an airborne disease. The pub itself has been very nicely restored even down to replaced screens by Samuel Smith, and you may wish to have a peek inside – but be aware that this is the pub that gained some notoriety in 2011 when a gay couple was ejected from the premises after allegedly kissing inside, prompting some entertaining protests, which have wide coverage on the internet.

**The distinctive exterior of the Dog & Duck**

**One of Denmark Street's famous music shops**

Continue along Broadwick Street towards the Dutch-gabled pub at the end, the Blue Posts. It is claimed that the name referred to posts marking the boundaries of the Soho hunting ground, but mapping their locations hardly adds credence to this story; and the alternative explanation – that they were places where sedan chairs, an early form of taxi if you like, could be hired – may be more plausible. Today there are still five pubs in the district that carry this unusual name. The exterior of this one, with its Watney's lamps and frosted windows, looks very sixties and, indeed, you may well be tempted in for a quick visit. Rest assured that the demon ales produced by this one-time bête noire of CAMRA are no longer to be found inside! To your right is Berwick Street with its market, but, to continue the trail, carry on along Broadwick Street keeping the Blue Posts on your right, to reach Wardour Street in a few yards.

This is one of Soho's main thoroughfares and is remembered by many for the golden years of the Marquee Club at No. 90, which hosted many of the great names of rock music from the sixties to the eighties. Closer to hand, indeed almost opposite, is the next official pub on the walk, the **2 Ship**. This is one of Soho's best pubs and, fittingly for the area, is very keen on its music. Those who belong to

the aforementioned Marquee era can wallow in nostalgia here, for music from that period is frequently played, sometimes rather loudly. The place has an attractive interior with etched glass and mirrors, though most of what you see in is a post-war restoration following considerable wartime damage. This is a Fuller's house, so of course expect its range of beers.

Just north (turn right on exit) of the Ship is St Anne's Court, and cutting through this narrow passage leads out onto Dean Street. Turn left, and at the next junction (with Carlisle Street by the Nellie Dean of Soho, which itself has a range of real ales) bear right (the home of *Private Eye* is a few yards down on the left) to reach Soho Square. The attractive oasis was laid out in the late 17th century, but it is best known for the attractive gardener's hut at the centre, though this isn't as old as it looks. It's believed that the current structure was a 1920s folly built primarily to conceal an electricity sub-station. Head anti-clockwise (turn right) around the square and take the next exit, which is Frith Street. On the first junction, 100 yards down, stands what is arguably Soho's best pub, at least as regards its décor, the **3 Dog & Duck**.

Dating back to 1897, this splendid little pub has a distinctive exterior with polished granite facings, which probably date from a

1930s makeover. Don't miss the floor mosaic as you go into the fine interior, which has some notable Victorian tile work (look out for the yellow tiles sporting the two animals, underneath the large advertising mirrors). The Victorian pub would undoubtedly have had several divisions, as evidenced by the former doorways, and was probably opened out in the thirties when some of the internal fittings were renewed. A semi-enclosed snug at the rear still remains. This is another pub that has now passed into the Nicholson's chain, and as such it has a wider range of ales than before, with the usual Nicholson's regulars and some interesting guests on the half-dozen handpumps.

Continue down Frith Street passing the famous Ronnie Scott's jazz club on the right, and take the first left, Old Compton Street. There's no chance of missing the next pub, the **4** **Three Greyhounds** on the next corner, as it has a striking four-storey mock Tudor exterior. The name probably references the old hunting ground here. Inside it's far smaller than you might expect, but despite this there are no less than four separate doorways (not all used today), so the original layout must have been very intimate! This is yet another Nicholson's house now, and offers the usual St Austell-brewed house beer and Fuller's London Pride alongside a couple of interesting guests kept in good condition.

Turn right out of the pub and, keeping Ed's American Diner on your left, walk down to Cambridge Circus in 50 yards. Cross Charing Cross Road and continue down the left (north) side of Shaftsbury Avenue, but only for another 100 yards or so, before taking Stacey Street, the first left. In daylight hours the wonderfully informal little Phoenix Garden, which is a short way along on the right, can be taken in en route. To get to the entrance, take first right and then left, keeping the garden on your left. The Phoenix Garden opened in 1984 and was created by the local community working together as the Covent Garden Open Spaces

Association. The site was bombed during the Blitz of London, and post-war the damaged buildings were cleared and it was used as a car park. This is the last of several similar gardens on vacant plots once managed by the association, and it's a lovely little oasis of tranquillity full of wild flowers and secluded seats. Continue by bearing left out of the garden and taking the path through the

## "Denmark Street… a short street full of colourful shopfronts"

ROBERT GALBRAITH, THE CUCKOO'S CALLING

edge of the churchyard to emerge on St Giles High Street by the church of St Giles.

If it's after dusk and the garden is closed, another route to St Giles High Street is to walk up to the end of Stacey Street and right via another alleyway, Flitchcroft Street; or, for a more frequented and better-lit alternative, walk instead up the Charing Cross Road northwards and bear right down Denmark Street (see map). In each case just a few yards to the right from the frontage of the parish church is the **5** **Angel**. Now that one of the sixties-style frosted windows has been replaced with clear glass, the place is no longer quite the secret it once was: one can now see into the main bar, and a very

**Phoenix Garden is a lovely oasis**

**The enclosed side entrance to the Angel**

traditional affair it is too, as you'd expect from Samuel Smith. A recent spruce-up has changed little else in this three-room pub, which still retains two separate street entrances. Perhaps the highlight is the small rear saloon, accessed via the unusual enclosed side carriageway, which also leads to a secluded little rear patio. There's also a tiny rear garden, which closes quite early in the evening. As with all Sam Smith's pubs, the sole real ale is Old Brewery Bitter; unpretentious food is also available.

The final stop on this route involves negotiating the road network around and under Centre Point to reach the junction of Tottenham Court Road and Oxford Street. The tower block itself, one of London's earliest and still one of the more iconic (indeed it was listed in 1995), was completed in 1966 and is perhaps the most well-known work of architect Richard Seifert. Disruption from Crossrail works continues but you need to pick your way to the crossroads by Tottenham Court Road Underground station, for right adjacent, on the north-west corner of the junction, stands the ⑥ **Flying Horse**. This, the last-remaining pub on Oxford Street, was rebuilt in 1892 in a Flemish Renaissance style to the designs of architects Saville & Martin. At this time it was renamed the Tottenham, so Nicholson's recent reversion to the original is welcome. They have also revamped the basement to extend the drinking area. The interior is a long,

narrow space and retains much to admire, despite some opening out, as its Grade II* listing testifies. There is some impressive tile and mirror work, especially in the rear part, where there is a tiled frieze with swirling foliage, an ornate mahogany-surround fireplace, mirror and mahogany panelling. Far better are the glazed paintings representing the seasons; and the carved mahogany panelling with large mirrored sections and small bevelled mirror sections at the top. J K Rowling, writing under the pseudonym Robert Galbraith, describes the pub in her novel *The Cuckoo's Calling*. Expect Sambrook's Junction Ale, Nicholson's house Pale Ale (brewed by St Austell) alongside several guests, and a similar food regime to other Nicholson's houses earlier in this walk.

## PUB INFORMATION

**1 CROWN**
64 Brewer Street, W1F 9TP
020 7287 8420 • www.nicholsonspubs.co.uk/
thecrownbrewerstreetlondon
**Opening hours:** 10-11 (11.30 Fri & Sat); 12-10.30 Sun

**2 SHIP**
116 Wardour Street, W1F 0TT
020 7437 8446 • www.shipsoho.co.uk
**Opening hours:** 12 (1 Sat)-11; closed Sun

**3 DOG & DUCK**
18 Bateman Street, W1D 3AJ
020 7494 0697 • www.nicholsonspubs.co.uk/
thedogandducksoholondon
**Opening hours:** 10-11

**4 THREE GREYHOUNDS**
25 Greek Street, W1D 5DD
020 7494 0953 • www.nicholsonspubs.co.uk/
thethreegreyhoundslondon
**Opening hours:** 11-11.30 (midnight Fri & Sat);
12-10.30 Sun

**5 ANGEL**
61-62 St Giles High Street, WC2H 8LE
020 7240 2876
**Opening hours:** 12-11; 12-10.30 Sun

**6 FLYING HORSE**
6 Oxford Street, W1D 1AN
020 7636 8324 • www.nicholsonspubs.co.uk/
theflyinghorseoxfordstreetlondon
**Opening hours:** 10-11 (midnight Fri & Sat)

# West One – Regent's Park to Soho

This linear walk takes us from the southern end of Regent's Park towards Oxford Circus, finishing up in Soho. Expect to find good-quality pub interiors, alongside some fine Georgian and Edwardian architecture, especially along and to the west of the north–south axis of Great Portland Street. The first pub is one of London's hardest to find, whilst the architectural highlight is undoubtedly the fine Argyll Arms, where the trail crosses the shopping mecca of Oxford Street. Regent's Park, part of architect John Nash's plan for this area commissioned by the then Prince Regent (later George IV) in the early 19th century and now home to London Zoo, lies directly to the north of our start point and offers a great opportunity to stretch your legs before tackling the pubs.

▶ **Start:** ⊖ Great Portland Street or ⊖ Regent's Park

▶ **Finish:** ⊖ Oxford Circus or ⊖ Piccadilly Circus; or buses from Regent Street

▶ **Distance:** 1.2 miles (2 km)

▶ **Key attractions:** Regent's Park and Zoo; Royal Institute of British Architects; Oxford Street; Liberty's; Soho

▶ **THE PUBS:** Dover Castle; Cock; Argyll Arms; Clachan; Shaston Arms; Old Coffee House

▶ **Timing tip:** Watch out for the Sunday closure of some of the pubs, but on the other hand, if you don't mind messing with the order of the pubs, the Argyll opens for breakfast (and beer!) at 8am.

**The Dover Castle**

Start at Park Crescent, which lies immediately south of Regent's Park Underground station on the Bakerloo Line and 100 yards west of Great Portland Street station on the Metropolitan, Circle and Hammersmith & City lines. Park Crescent was originally conceived by architect John Nash as a formal entrance to Regent's Park, but only the southern half was ever completed, and it is cut off from the park by the busy Marylebone Road. Walk down past its handsome terraces to Portland Place, which leads south from Park Crescent. This is a wide and majestic avenue, one of London's best, lined with houses in the Adam style. Clearly not in this style, but certainly noteworthy, is the headquarters of the Royal Institute of British Architects (RIBA) at No. 66 on the corner of Weymouth Street. The interior of this Portland stone building is open to the public and well worth a visit.

After all this culture, refreshment is close at hand. Cross Portland Place, turning right into Weymouth Street and first left into Weymouth Mews, where halfway down on the right is the well-hidden **1 Dover Castle**. Dating back to 1750, it has apparently held a licence since 1777. The somewhat bland exterior is more than compensated for within, where the old wood-panelled interior, whilst partially opened out, retains its appealing atmosphere and there is some etched glass from its partitioned days. Comfortable seats and leatherette benches are the order of the day, and there's an open fire in the main room. The rear snug is a gem and has something of the atmosphere of a gentlemen's club. If you are a visitor to London, consider yourself lucky to have found the place: it's one of the most concealed of all London pubs, and many

**Dividing screens inside the Cock**

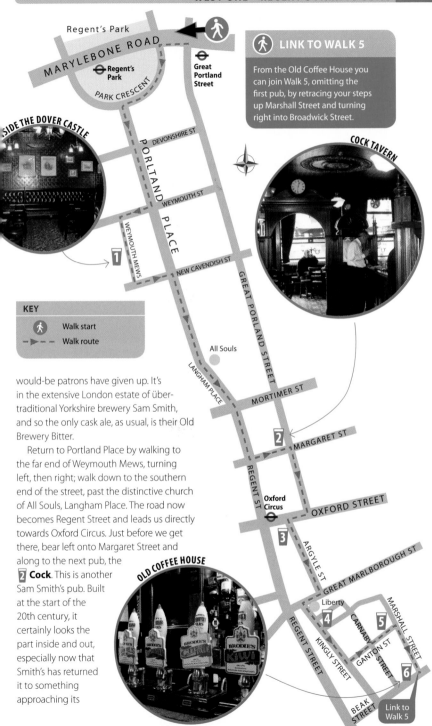

Regent's Park

MARYLEBONE ROAD

Regent's Park

Great Portland Street

PARK CRESCENT

INSIDE THE DOVER CASTLE

PORTLAND PLACE

DEVONSHIRE ST

WEYMOUTH ST

WEYMOUTH MEWS

NEW CAVENDISH ST

**1**

**LINK TO WALK 5**

From the Old Coffee House you can join Walk 5, omitting the first pub, by retracing your steps up Marshall Street and turning right into Broadwick Street.

COCK TAVERN

**KEY**

👤 Walk start

- - ▶ - - Walk route

All Souls

GREAT PORTLAND STREET

LANGHAM PLACE

MORTIMER ST

**2** MARGARET ST

REGENT STREET

Oxford Circus

OXFORD STREET

**3**

ARGYLE ST

GREAT MARLBOROUGH ST

OLD COFFEE HOUSE

Liberty

**4**

KINGLY STREET

CARNABY ST

GANTON ST

**5**

MARSHALL STREET

**6**

BEAK STREET

Link to Walk 5

would-be patrons have given up. It's in the extensive London estate of über-traditional Yorkshire brewery Sam Smith, and so the only cask ale, as usual, is their Old Brewery Bitter.

Return to Portland Place by walking to the far end of Weymouth Mews, turning left, then right; walk down to the southern end of the street, past the distinctive church of All Souls, Langham Place. The road now becomes Regent Street and leads us directly towards Oxford Circus. Just before we get there, bear left onto Margaret Street and along to the next pub, the **2 Cock**. This is another Sam Smith's pub. Built at the start of the 20th century, it certainly looks the part inside and out, especially now that Smith's has returned it to something approaching its

**Handpumps on the bar of the Clachan**

original splendour. Accordingly, much of what you see is not original, but the result of a Victorian-style refit. The attractive tiled floor, and the screens inside dividing the rooms are good examples of this, as are the 'snob screens': the array of little swivelling glass panels on the bar counter. These were present on a number of Victorian bar counters and were installed to afford punters more privacy. Very few originals survive. For all that, the comfortable interior is very well done and makes up for the paucity of cask beer choice, which, as usual in Sam Smith's pubs, is Hobson's choice, the Old Brewery Bitter.

**The Clachan's imposing façade**

Come out of the pub and walk straight down to Oxford Street, about 100 yards away. Wading through the shoppers, cross the road and turn right for a few yards before heading left into the pedestrianised Argyll Street just before the traffic lights. Note the distinctive Leslie Green tiled former entrance to the Underground station on the corner. Just a few yards further down is a pub that surely must be the architectural highlight of this walk, the **3** **Argyll Arms**. It's named after

one of the Duke of Marlborough's generals who was also a local landowner. Given its location so close to the bustle of Oxford Street, the survival of the stunning exterior and interior of this pub, built in 1868 and remodelled circa 1895, is quite remarkable.

The striking exterior, with those distinctive curved windows, leads to a mirror-lined and terrazzo-floored corridor. In turn, compartments open up on the right with splendidly etched and cut screenwork. These small compartments are now very rare in pubs and are not to be missed here; these are the best originals of their kind left in London. The bar-back is original, and note the tiny landlord's office halfway down. To the rear of this large pub is a spacious room where the staircase is worth looking at for its ironwork. Nicholson's have gone to town on the beer range here over the past few years: there's a fine array of no fewer than 16 beer engines, in two sets (one set is in the rear room), and, although they are not all continually in use, you can expect five changing guests along with three regulars. An all-day food menu complements the beers.

Continue down Argyll Street to Liberty's half-timbered building at the bottom. This imposing edifice was constructed in 1922–3, coinciding with the Tudor revival's influence on pub design. It was made of timbers from *HMS Impregnable* and *HMS Hindustan* and still houses the famous Arts and Crafts movement store, which was founded in 1875. Turn right and then first left into Kingly Street. Here, well hidden in this quiet little side street parallel with nearby Regent Street, is the imposing façade of the **4 Clachan**. This is another late Victorian rebuild, circa 1898, which has managed to keep some of its original fittings, including some rich wood-carving and structural ironwork. Look for the pretty tiling, including a floor mosaic advertising the pub's unusual name, in the entrances. Note also the cosy raised seating area at the back of the pub, which could conceivably once have been the landlord's parlour. The pub was formerly known as the Bricklayers and owned by Liberty, which had plans to turn it into a warehouse. Once again it's in the Nicholson's

**The Shaston Arms**

**Liberty's impressive half-timbered frontage**

chain with up to seven rotating guests supporting the regulars, London Pride, Truman's Runner and Sharp's Doom Bar.

From the Clachan, walk further down Kingly Street as far as the Blue Posts pub on the corner of Ganton Street, noting the rather handsome exterior with its leaded and stained glass. Turn left to reach and cross the pedestrianised Carnaby Street, now only a shadow of its former Swinging Sixties self. Just a little further on the left and sporting a loud red paint job is the next port of call, the **5 Shaston Arms**. Stepping inside this inviting and intimate little pub, with its screened drinking booths and dark woodwork, one could be forgiven for thinking that this was one of London's hidden vintage pubs. In fact, it has been a pub for less than 20 years, having been skilfully converted via a wine bar from shop premises. There are modern booths along one side, and a back room with skylight, so it's a bit bigger than it appears from outside. It is part of the Hall & Woodhouse estate, so you'll find Badger Bitter and Tanglefoot, plus a H&W seasonal ale, on handpump.

**The cosy interior of the Old Coffee House**

Today the cosy interior retains an old bar counter (with hatches to service the beer engines) and even vestiges of an old spittoon under the foot rail. Large old brewery mirrors adorn the rear walls along with all manner of other ephemera. The real pull of the place, however, is the beer, as this is, at the time of writing, one of only three Brodie's tied pubs (the others both feature in this book). As such expect an extensive range of their beers, five on handpump and another five on keg. If you like your beers well hopped and zesty, you've come to the right place. Food is available here if you're planning to eat at the final stop on this walk.

Leaving the Shaston, turn left and then take the right turn into Marshall Street. Continue south, crossing Broadwick Street to reach the final pub of this walk on the following corner with Beak Street. The **6 Old Coffee House** looks frankly awful from outside with what looks to me like some seventies restaurant-style window job at ground-floor level, but don't let that put you off. Inside the place could hardly be more traditional-looking, and definitely is an old pub, although the name stems from the 18th-century tradition of using coffee houses as political and business meeting places.

For the nearest Underground stations, retrace your steps to Oxford Circus for the northern termini, or walk down Lower James Street, almost opposite the pub, for about five minutes in the same direction to reach Piccadilly Circus. Regent Street and buses are two minutes away to the right along Beak Street.

## PUB INFORMATION

**1 DOVER CASTLE**
43 Weymouth Mews, W1G 7EH
020 7580 4412
**Opening hours:** 12-11; closed Sun

**2 COCK**
27 Great Portland Street, W1W 8QE
020 7631 5002
**Opening hours:** 12-11, 12-10.30 Sun

**3 ARGYLL ARMS**
18 Argyll Street, W1F 7TP
020 7734 6117 • www.nicholsonspubs.co.uk/
theargyllarmsoxfordcircuslondon
**Opening hours:** 8-11.30 (midnight Fri & Sat);
12-10.30 Sun

**4 CLACHAN**
34 Kingly Street, W1B 5QH
020 7494 0834 • www.nicholsonspubs.co.uk/
theclachankinglystreetlondon
**Opening hours:** 10-11 (11.30 Fri & Sat);
10-10.30 Sun

**5 SHASTON ARMS**
4 Ganton Street, W1F 7QN
020 7287 2631 • shastonarms.co.uk
**Opening hours:** 12 (12.30 Sat)-11; closed Sun

**6 OLD COFFEE HOUSE**
49 Beak Street, W1F 9SF
020 7437 2197
**Opening hours:** 11-11; 12-11 Sun

# Political London – Westminster & St James's

**WALK 7**

▶ **Start:** ⊖ Westminster

▶ **Finish:** ⊖ Piccadilly Circus

▶ **Distance:** 2 miles (3.2 km)

▶ **Key attractions:** Westminster Abbey; Houses of Parliament & Palace of Westminster; Cabinet War Rooms; St James's Park; Buckingham Palace; St James's Palace

▶ **THE PUBS:** St Stephen's Tavern; Speaker; Sanctuary House; Red Lion (Craven Passage); Golden Lion; Red Lion (Duke of York Street)

▶ **Timing tips:** Several of the pubs are closed on Sundays. St Stephen's Tavern opens up at 10am, so an early start on a sunny day is feasible and allows time to take in some sightseeing in between the pubs. The route through Dean's Yard is closed at night, so this is a route for daylight hours.

A very good walk for the beer tourist, offering plenty to see in addition to the interesting pubs. Many of the sights will be familiar but there will probably be something new here even for many Londoners. Starting at the very heart of the capital, close to some of its most iconic sights, the route winds into St James's, one of London's richest areas and one of its first true suburbs. From the latter part of the 17th century onwards, it was laid out in grid fashion as an exclusive residential area and remained as such until after World War II. Today it's more associated with commerce, although many of the gentlemen's clubs survive here alongside some well-known London institutions such as Christie's the auctioneers. Unlike Westminster, St James's is a relatively unfrequented area for visitors, but as our route finishes with one of London's best small pub interiors you're unlikely to be disappointed – unless you turn up on a Sunday!

**St James's Park and Horse Guards Parade**

Start the walk by the Bridge Street exit from Westminster Underground station. The first thing that greets you upon emerging from the station is the magnificent 'Big Ben' opposite, correctly named St Stephen's Clock Tower but renamed the Elizabeth Tower in 2012 in honour of Queen Elizabeth II's Diamond Jubilee. Behind this are the massed tourist sights of Westminster Hall, Westminster Abbey and Charles Barry's classic gothic Palace of Westminster.

Once you've drunk in that little list, attention can turn to the first pub stop of the day, a few yards along to the right; and the **St Stephen's Tavern** has an interior that is not out of place in such exalted company. Surprisingly the pub had been closed for over a decade before it was acquired by Hall & Woodhouse and reopened in 2003 after an expensive refurbishment. Built in 1875, it takes its name from the clock tower across the road. The interior has been well restored with much to attract the eye; for example, the high bar-back with some very fine mirrors,

**Westminster Abbey**

an ornate coffered ceiling with chandelier, some attractive light fittings and a Victorian bar counter. Some of the window glass has survived too, particularly the very appealing 'Public Bar' door glass in the Bridge Street entrance. The exterior appearance is pretty good, too, as befits such a key location, with one of those wonderful big lamps hanging over each of the two main entrances. All sorts of the great, good and not so good have drunk here from the 'other places' across the road (and indeed there's still a bell in here to summon inmates back to the chamber for votes), but these days you're far more likely to be sharing the bar with tourists. Up to four beers from the Hall & Woodhouse portfolio, including Tanglefoot and a seasonal guest, are on tap.

The onward route involves crossing Bridge Street at the Parliament Square lights and walking alongside the (now heavily guarded) entrance to the Palace of Westminster, then crossing again to walk alongside first St Margaret's parish church, itself with a long history stretching back to the 12th century; and, behind, Westminster Abbey. I'm not even going to try to encapsulate the history of this

**The atttactive light fittings in St Stephen's Tavern**

building – there are plenty of good guides available, but leave adequate time to justify the admission fee if you're planning to take in the Abbey en route.

Walk along to the tall, slender Westminster Scholars War Memorial facing the West Front of the Abbey and look for a sentry box beside an archway in the castellated frontage on the left – this is normally open during daylight hours, so head through here into secluded Dean's Yard, which hosts the buildings of Westminster School and most of the remaining precincts of the former monastery of Westminster. The green in the centre is where the pupils have a right to

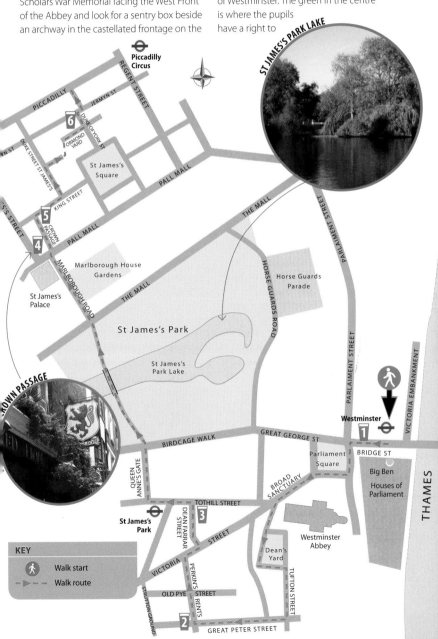

ST JAMES'S PARK LAKE

CROWN PASSAGE

**KEY**

🚶 Walk start

– – ▶ Walk route

play football, and indeed they have some claim to have invented the game as we know it today. Aim for the smaller archway at the diametrically opposite corner of Dean's Yard, leading out into Tufton Street straight ahead.

Walk up as far as Great Peter Street, and turn right to follow it across Marsham Street and for a further 200 yards until you spot the distinctive

**2 Speaker** on the corner of the oddly named Perkin's Rents. This friendly one-bar corner pub, whose exterior appearance has a bit of the Edinburgh tenement about it, is a peaceful haven for locals, civil servants and MPs. There are caricatures of past prime ministers and lesser MPs on the walls. It has built a reputation for well-kept and interesting beers, three changing guests supporting Taylor Landlord and Young's Bitter. A decent range of Belgian bottled beers is available too alongside homemade food, from sandwiches to a daily main meal. No music or TV will intrude upon your conversation in this pleasant haven.

If you're after some food on the go, I would strongly recommend continuing up Great Peter Street to Strutton Ground, the second on the right, with its sandwich bars and cafés. Otherwise head up Perkin's Rents, directly north from the pub, to meet Victoria Street. This was part of an area known as the Devil's Acre (a term first coined by Dickens) in Victorian London, on account of the appalling housing conditions and outbreaks of cholera and typhoid.

Cross over carefully and head up Dean Farrar Street between the office blocks a little to your right. Fork right almost immediately and walk along to the next junction, where sitting grandly on the corner is the **3 Sanctuary House**. The name derives from the almonry of Westminster Abbey which was here or hereabouts. Almoners were monks who were vested with the duty of providing food, drink and shelter to the poor and ailing. Since 1997 this has been a Fuller's hotel sitting atop a well-regarded pub serving a wide range of its ales, staples and seasonals. The décor is traditional with polished wood floors, benches and bar stools, and bar meals are available most hours.

Walk up Tothill Street to the left after leaving the Sanctuary House, towards St James's Park Underground station under the bulk of 55 Broadway, one of the few celebrated buildings in London to be known principally by its address. It was built by noted architect Charles Holden (he of Underground stations on the Northern Line and elsewhere; see Walk 24) as the headquarters for the Underground Group, the forerunner of the London Underground. Bear right here at the Old Star public house into Queen Anne's Gate, and then use the pedestrian crossing to St James's Park.

St James's Park is the oldest of London's royal parks and started life as a hunting ground for Henry VIII, though the present park was

**The Speaker**

**The Red Lion, Duke of York Street**

landscaped by John Nash in the early 19th century. Walk straight across to the bridge, which affords attractive views of the London Eye to the right, and Buckingham Palace to the left through the trees. Keep on the same bearing to the exit and cross the Mall, which, unless it's Sunday when it's closed to traffic, will be busy, so use the controlled crossing. Take the street opposite, Marlborough Road, past St James's Palace, most of which is closed to the public as it is Prince Charles's private London pad. The palace was also the principal London residence of monarchy until Buckingham Palace was selected by Queen Victoria in 1837. Across the street is Queen's Chapel, one of Inigo Jones's classical churches.

All this culture and you may be ready for the next drink, so at the end of Marlborough Road as you emerge onto Pall Mall (named for a French precursor to croquet), look for an archway opposite in Quebec House. This is Crown Passage and home to an atmospheric little alleyway of shops and a pleasant pub, the **4 Red Lion**. The frontage of the pub suggests a venerable age, perhaps the 18th century, and a rather presumptuous sign reads 'London's last village pub'. The cosy, panelled interior, however, is probably a legacy of the 1930s

and, although the pub is very small, it would have been subdivided at one time as the two doorways suggest. All in all it is a civilised place away from the tourist trail. Adnams Southwold Bitter and St Austell Tribute are the offerings at the bar. Don't expect to dine here, but sandwiches are available.

Upon leaving the Red Lion and continuing up Crown Passage, you emerge onto King Street. A few doors down to the right there is the second of three lions on this walk, this time the **5 Golden Lion**. Built by the prolific pub architects Eedle & Meyers, in 1897–9, it sports a very attractive façade with bow windows, whilst the interior is small, solid and handsome, with a sturdy bar counter and gantry, wooden floors and seating on stools. Young's, London Pride and Greene King IPA were available as well as Harveys Sussex Best Bitter on my last visit. As you leave the pub look across the street and you'll spot the home of Christie's, the famous auctioneers, who have been here since 1823.

Before taking the next turning on the left, Duke Street St James's, if you continue on the south side of the road as far as No. 33 and look across the street, you should spot London's oldest blue plaque, at first-floor level on No. 1C. It commemorates the brief residence here

**Rich internal fittings at the second Red Lion**

in 1848 of Napoleon III, first President of the French republic and its last Emperor.

Cross the street and head up Duke Street St James's as far as the narrow entrance into Mason's Yard on the right by No. 12. This tiny square is now dominated by the newest of the White Cube galleries, on the site of a former electricity sub-station. Earlier the square was home to the Indica bookshop and gallery (at No. 23), which in its colourful history was where John Lennon met his future wife Yoko Ono for the first time at an art exhibition in 1966. As you head from the narrow exit to Mason's Yard in the far corner, by No. 9, the house on the right of the alley, No. 13, was, despite its unprepossessing appearance today, the location of the former Scotch of St James club, which attracted regulars like the Rolling Stones, The Who and Eric Clapton, not to mention being the venue that Jimi Hendrix first played after arriving in London, also in 1966.

The covered alley leads out into Ormond Yard, and at the end bear left to arrive at the final pub on this walk, yet another lion. This **6 Red Lion** is one of the most splendid of the surviving Victorian pubs in London, and indeed in Britain. Although the building was constructed in 1821, both the pub's frontage and its interior are later in date. This is a veritable late-Victorian cathedral of glass,

mirrors and woodwork. The richness of the mirrors here are particularly impressive, as they glint and sparkle in the light. Yet, despite the size, it is clear that the building had several internal divisions in the past, hence three doors at the front, each of which would have led into a separate compartment. A quasi-corridor leads to the rear room, which is separated from the small front space by an island servery. It can get quite crowded at lunchtimes and early evenings; but it quietens down later on. Since being acquired by Fuller's, it offers a wide range of their beers including a rotating seasonal. The extensive menu is available on the pub's website. A real London classic to finish this route!

To get to transport, bear left on exit and turn right onto Jermyn Street by St James's church. This street has long been and indeed still remains an epicentre of gentlemen's fashion, with shirts a speciality. The cut-through almost opposite leads a few yards up to Piccadilly, with the Underground station about five minutes walk away to the right.

## PUB INFORMATION

**1 ST STEPHEN'S TAVERN**
10 Bridge Street, SW1A 2JR
020 7925 2286 • ststephenstavern.co.uk
**Opening hours:** 10-11.30; 12-10.30 Sun

**2 SPEAKER**
46 Great Peter Street, SW1P 2HA
020 7222 1749
**Opening hours:** 12-11; closed Sat & Sun

**3 SANCTUARY HOUSE**
33 Tothill Street, SW1H 9LA
020 7799 4044 • sanctuaryhousehotel.co.uk
**Opening hours:** 8-11; 8-10.30 Sun

**4 RED LION**
23 Crown Passage, SW1Y 6PP
020 7930 4141
**Opening hours:** 11 (11.30 Sat)-11; closed Sun

**5 GOLDEN LION**
25 King Street, SW1Y 6QY
020 7925 0007 • www.goldenlion-stjames.co.uk
**Opening hours:** 11-11; 12-5 Sat; closed Sun

**6 RED LION**
2 Duke of York Street, SW1Y 6JP
020 7321 0782 • redlionmayfair.co.uk
**Opening hours:** 11.30-11; closed Sun

# Back-street Belgravia

It's difficult to believe that Belgravia's smart streets of stuccoed houses occupy land once known as the 'five fields', a marshy wasteland which was a hangout of highwaymen and other ne'er-do-wells. The crossing of the River Westbourne (the same steam that a little to the north was dammed to form the Serpentine) was known as the Bloody Bridge after their activities. The area was drained and laid out for the Earl of Grosvenor in the 1820s by Thomas Cubitt (1788–1855), one of the earliest and most important of London's speculative builders. Today an average house on fashionable Chester Square will set you back about £7m. Belgravia's residents don't like unnecessary change, including tacky refurbishments; so the pubs on this top-quality stroll are much the same as they were when the first edition of *London Pub Walks* came out – generally classy, tastefully decorated and urbane.

▶ **Start:** ⇌ ⊖ Victoria

▶ **Finish:** ⊖ Sloane Square

▶ **Distance:** 1.7 miles (2.5 km)

▶ **Key attractions:**
Hyde Park; Albert Hall; Victoria & Albert Museum; Knightsbridge shopping; Belgrave Square

▶ **THE PUBS:** Horse & Groom; Grenadier; Nag's Head; Star Tavern; Antelope; Duke of Wellington; Fox & Hounds. Try also: Wilton Arms

▶ **Timing tip:** The Horse & Groom is not open at weekends, so plan accordingly.

**The lovely old-fashioned Nag's Head**

**The Grenadier, on a quiet back street in Belgravia**

Exit Victoria station, if possible, by the side exit to Buckingham Palace Road, or turn left and left again from the front exit. Carefully cross the busy road and head down Lower Belgrave Street, towards Belgrave Square. When Thomas Cubitt – who also laid out Kemp Town in Brighton and built Osbourne House on the Isle of Wight for Queen Victoria – developed the area from the 1820s onwards, he was building for the well-connected, the success of which is testified by the high blue plaque quotient today; but in so doing he excluded pubs from everywhere in Belgravia except the mews, those little backstreet alleys hidden from immediate view. So it's no surprise that our first few pubs here are mews pubs off the beaten track.

Pass Eaton Square with St Peter's church on your right. Originally designed in a classical style by the architect Henry Hakewill in about 1825, the church was the victim of an arson attack in 1987 which destroyed the roof and the interior. It was re-dedicated in 1992 following a widely praised restoration. Bear right immediately beyond St Peter's, and left into cobbled Wilton Mews. You'll see the first pub of the day coming into view across the next junction. The **🍺 Horse & Groom** was opened in 1864 with the then clientele being the stable and mews workers of the gentry. Today it's a pleasant Shepherd Neame house with a small wood-panelled bar; outside tables appear in decent weather. Expect Shep's Master Brew and Spitfire, plus a seasonal guest. There's a full food menu including sandwiches. The pub is reputed to have been a favourite haunt of Beatles manager Brian Epstein.

Continue along Groom Place, following it round to the first left, and left again into Chapel Street. This in turn leads in a few yards to Belgrave Square with its profusion of mature trees. Turn right and, at the end of the square, cross the roads and continue directly ahead into Wilton Crescent before taking another mews turning, Wilton Row, first right. Following this quiet little street brings you to one of the city's most sequestered pubs, the **🍺 Grenadier**. Licensed from around 1820, it is quite likely that Wellington's guards from the nearby

**The foliage-bedecked Wilton Arms**

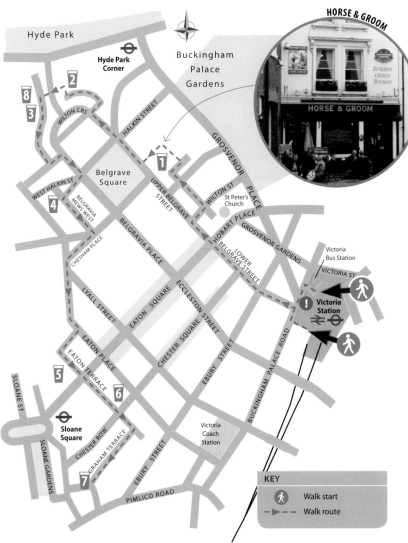

barracks used the place, but whether the Iron Duke himself did is open to question, since he was prime minister by 1828 and had switched military matters for politics before this time. Certainly an old photograph in Mark Girouard's *Victorian Pubs* suggests a far humbler past than the smart building of today. The small front bar with its well-worn floorboards and atmospheric seating would have originally been divided up, as the side door suggests, and the once private rooms

to the side and rear of the bar counter are now dining rooms, though without loss of character. Note the now very rare pewter bar top, and the old-fashioned handpulls, now redundant. Those on either side, however, offer four ales: Taylor Landlord, Fuller's London Pride, and two guests, often including Woodforde's Wherry. Food is available throughout the day.

Leave the pub by the side alley, Barrack Yard, and keep left into another mews. If

**Adnams beers are on offer at the Nag's Head**

you follow this round to the left again, you should be able to exit onto Wilton Place. If, for any reason, the gates are closed, simply return to Wilton Crescent and turn right and right again into Wilton Place. Cross over into Kinnerton Street, another mews, and almost directly ahead is the **8** **Wilton Arms**, which is worth a visit if you have time and capacity. It's another Shepherd Neame house, open daily, with Master Brew, Spitfire and the brewery's seasonal guests.

Just a few yards down the street to the left, however, is an altogether rarer beast, the **3** **Nag's Head**. This is a lovely old-fashioned pub, which was built in the 1830s and first licensed as a beer house shortly afterwards. The name reminds us that horses and carriages for the rich of Belgravia were stabled in the mews, and this would have been a basic beer house for the stable boys and footmen who lived hereabouts. There are wood-panelled walls, floorboards, a fireplace with a range, and perhaps the lowest bar counter in London. As with so many pubs, new drinking areas have been brought into use by extending into once private quarters; in this case the pub has been extended up to a rear mezzanine and down into the basement, but without detriment to its quirky character. That character derives from the guv'nor, who has been here a long, long time. It's Belgravia's only genuine free house, but Kevin favours Adnams beers: you have a choice of three. There's an interesting collection of old penny-arcade machines,

but I'm glad to say, no modern ones in this staunchly traditional boozer. Finally, I'm happy to say that Kevin operates a zero-tolerance policy for mobile phones or other electronic gadgetry – you have been warned!

Continue down Kinnerton Street to Motcomb Street and turn left to the junction with Wilton Terrace. Before turning right down to the other corner of Belgrave Square, note the blue plaque on the first house left, indicating that Earl Mountbatten of Burma and his wife, Edwina, lived here. Turn right again at the square into West Halkin Street before taking the mews on the left, coming upon the **4** **Star Tavern** almost immediately, a pleasant surprise indeed. The attractive frontage is matched by a welcoming interior, although I preferred the shabby benches to the plusher post-refit ones. Again it's an early 19th-century building that once would have been divided into several rooms. It is now popular with a range of customers and retains an upstairs bar as well as the main drinking areas below. Since 1951 it's been a Fuller's house, so expect their beers. It's one of CAMRA's 'famous five', having appeared in every edition of the *Good Beer Guide* to date. Legend has it that this was also the place where the Great Train Robbers planned their heist.

**The attractive Star Tavern**

**The Duke of Wellington has pavement seating**

Continue down the mews to the German Embassy at the end and reach Chesham Place. If you've had your fill by now, you can return to Victoria rail and tube stations in 10 minutes by turning left then right and continuing straight down Belgrave Place. However, to continue our tour, turn right and at the junction half left into Chesham Street, merging into Eaton Place and almost immediately taking the next right into West Eaton Place. Follow the road round, and in a couple of minutes you will reach the **5 Antelope**.

On the outskirts of Belgravia and close to Sloane Square, the Antelope was, like the Nag's Head, also built for the household staff working in the grand houses, though there had apparently been a pub here before Cubitt developed the area. Note the two separate entrances, a sign that it was originally divided into several bars. Some vestige of this layout

**The Antelope**

can still be seen inside, although some of the areas, like the room on the left, have only recently been converted into use from private quarters. The rear area has an attractive tiled fireplace and floorboards. Fuller's beers are on offer, plus one guest. A recent development is a new upstairs dining room with food served until 3pm at lunchtimes and 9.30 in the evenings.

Leaving the Antelope, you can see the next stop across the street ahead of you, so there's not much opportunity to walk off any excesses! Continue down the street across the main road and reach the **6 Duke of Wellington**, on a prominent corner site, with benches outside. This is yet another early Victorian pub, but reportedly it was originally opened as a library for employees of the Belgravian gentry. The modernised interior, with several prints of the Iron Duke around the walls, now has a single drinking

**Floral display at the Fox & Hounds**

area around a horseshoe bar. The television can be rather obtrusive if switched on but the pub is a pleasant enough locals' pub, with a range of up to five well-kept beers from the Shepherd Neame portfolio.

To finish, continue down Eaton Terrace as far as Graham Terrace, the next road on the right, and turning here you will see the  **Fox & Hounds** just ahead. Or, at least, you may need to look behind a splendid floral display, as I did on my last visit. In 1999, this former Charrington's pub was the last pub in London without a spirits licence. This quaint custom dated back to the Beer Act of 1830 and was at one time very common, put into place with the hope of luring the populace away from spirits.

Credit where it's due: Young's, who currently own the pub, have, in my opinion, improved the ambience with their most recent refurbishment, creating a homely and cosy atmosphere in the long, narrow interior. Would that their other refits had been as sensitive as this. Another welcome development is the availability of a guest beer on one of the pub's three handpumps.

From here, the easiest public transport option is to walk to the other end of Passmore Street and take bus 11 or 211 to Victoria. Alternatively continue to the end of Graham Street and turn right into Holbein Place; it's then a walk of about five minutes to Sloane Square Underground station.

## PUB INFORMATION

**1 HORSE & GROOM**
7 Groom Place, SW1X 7BA
020 7235 6980 • www.thehorseandgroombelgravia.com
**Opening hours:** 11.30-11; closed Sat & Sun

**2 GRENADIER**
18 Wilton Row, SW1X 7NR
020 7235 3074
**Opening hours:** 12-11

**3 NAG'S HEAD**
53 Kinnerton Street, SW1X 8ED
020 7235 1135
**Opening hours:** 11-11; 12-10.30 Sun

**4 STAR TAVERN**
6 Belgrave Mews West, SW1X 8HT
020 7235 3019 • www.star-tavern-belgravia.co.uk
**Opening hours:** 11 (12 Sat)-11; 12-10.30 Sun

**5 ANTELOPE**
22-24 Eaton Terrace, SW1W 8EZ
020 7824 8512 • www.antelope-eaton-terrace.co.uk
**Opening hours:** 12-11 (11.30 Fri & Sat); 12-10 Sun

**6 DUKE OF WELLINGTOn**
63 Eaton Terrace, SW1W 8TR
020 7730 1782
**Opening hours:** 11-11; 12-10.30 Sun

**7 FOX & HOUNDS**
29 Passmore Street, SW1W 8HR
020 7730 6367 • www.rampubcompany.co.uk/
visit-pubs/fox-and-hound
**Opening hours:** 12-11

**Try also:**

**8 WILTON ARMS**
71 Kinnerton Street, SW1X 8ED
020 7235 4854 • www.shepherdneame.co.uk/pubs/
belgravia/wilton-arms
**Opening hours:** 11-11; 12-10.30 Sun

# Notting Hill, Bayswater & Portobello Market

**WALK 9**

As late as the 1950s, Notting Hill was still described by some as a slum, while the insalubrious bedsits of the area became home to West Indian migrants. The Pembridge Road area saw Britain's first race riots in 1958, in response to which the now-celebrated Notting Hill Carnival was born. Today the area has been gentrified to a great degree, especially in the posher south-eastern side of Notting Hill, touching Kensington and Bayswater, where this walk takes us. Despite the high tourist quotient around Bayswater, there are still a good number of pubs where a decent pint comes before fancy food. That said, you'll be able to eat well at most of the places on this rewarding walk.

> **Start:** Notting Hill Gate
>
> **Finish:** Padington
>
> **Distance:** 2 miles (3.2 km)
>
> **Key attractions:** Kensington Gardens; Whiteley's shopping centre; Portobello Road Market; Hyde Park; Notting Hill shops
>
> **THE PUBS:** Uxbridge Arms; Windsor Castle; Churchill Arms; Cock & Bottle; Prince Edward; King's Head. Try also: Phoenix
>
> **Timing tip:** The world famous Portobello Road Market is at its best by far on a Saturday, so why not combine a visit to the market (arrive by 10am if you can) followed by the pub walk?

**Antique shop on Portobello Road**

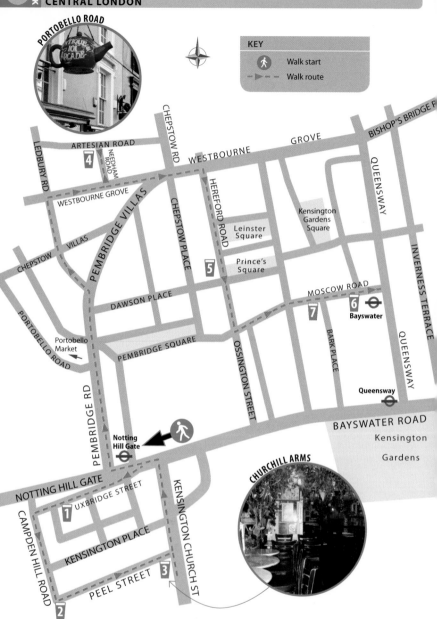

PORTOBELLO ROAD

KEY

🚶 Walk start

Walk route

CHURCHILL ARMS

If you're up for the market first, it's a good option to do a shortened tour by heading down to the Cock & Bottle from Portobello Road and taking it from there. If you're doing the whole round, there's an option to use the bus halfway through the route.

🚶 Start at Notting Hill Gate Underground station and exit onto the southern side of the road. If you've arrived before noon, there are plenty of cafés, bric-a-brac shops and other attractions along Notting Hill Gate, and on Pembridge

Road, which also leads to the Portobello Road Market. To start the day's drinking, head south down the narrow, short Farmer Street right at the junction, opposite Pembridge Road, and bear right into Uxbridge Street. Here, just yards away from busy Notting Hill Gate, is the secluded **1** **Uxbridge Arms**, a smart little wood-panelled Enterprise Inns house unknown to the vast majority of the trippers heading for the market. It's very comfort-ably furnished, but the reliable quality of the beers here is what draws drinkers. Expect a choice of three: currently Fuller's London Pride, Wadworths 6X, and St Austell Tribute. You can sit outside in good weather on this quiet street.

Continue down to the end of Uxbridge Street and turn left into pleasant Campden Hill Road. It's a mere five minutes' walk to the next stop: the attractive **2** **Windsor Castle** occupies a bold corner plot. A good-

**Windsor Castle**

quality 1930s refit has survived fairly well: this divided the interior layout into three main rooms, a layout more typical of the Victorian pub. In fact the mahogany bar-back in the 'Campden Bar' is the sole survivor from the Victorian era. If you can get here at a quiet time, you can walk around and admire the timber panelling and screens, and some curious low doorways between the separate rooms, which were probably inserted for cleaners. The public area has been extended, notably by a new restaurant at the rear with views of the pub's pleasant little garden; but the character of the old core of the pub has not been compromised too much. Sadly though the attractive painted pub sign has been replaced in the latest refurbishment by a miserably poor substitute… philistines. On the plus side, they have expanded their beer range further: regulars are Taylor Landlord, Windsor & Eton's Knight of the

**Timber panelling and screens inside the Windsor Castle**

Garter, with four rotating guests from the M&B list in support. If you're out for the day and want to eat properly, this is as good as anywhere to do it, unless you love Thai food, in which case hold your horses.

Coming out of the Windsor Castle, drop straight down adjacent Peel Street, with its attractive Campden Houses estate of flats on the left, to reach Kensington Church Street at the bottom. Now, turn right and walk along to the next corner, where, sporting what must surely be the best display of plants adorning any London pub, sits the **3** **Churchill Arms**.

A real local institution, this grand old pub caters for a loyal and appreciative clientele, although at Fuller's bar prices you'd need to well-heeled to be a regular here. It was built in the Victorian era but given a complete internal refit around 1930. The separate rooms have been merged into a U-shaped drinking area, but there is a characterful little room on the way to the restaurant. The walls are panelled and there are a couple of pretty tiled fireplaces. The snob screens on the bar are interesting. They were widespread in the 19th century, conferring the privacy Victorians wished for; but it's very possible that these are reproductions from the mid-20th century. Outside, competing with the wonderful floral display is a decent new pub sign of the eponymous war leader but ironically the place's name predates him: his grandparents apparently used the pub though! As mentioned, this is a Fuller's house and usually offers its whole range of beers, but a good proportion of the clientele also come to enjoy the popular Thai restaurant at the right-hand side of the

**The Churchill Arms**

pub. Food is served in an atmospheric rear conservatory, which has a glass roof hidden in a mass of foliage, the plants creating a splendid jungle-like canopy. If you wish to join the diners on your route, it may be advisable to book ahead.

Having almost reached the halfway point of this tour, you may well feel like a longer stroll to walk off any surplus before drawing a second wind. It's a little over three-quarters of a mile to the next stop. However, if you prefer a far shorter walk, the bus stop is 40 yards to your right upon exiting the Churchill. Take bus 328 (every few minutes) to the Artesian Road stop in Chepstow Road (see map) and walk down to the first corner. If you're walking, head back to Notting Hill Gate using your map; then take Pembridge Road/ Gardens as far as Chepstow Crescent, turn left up here, keep on until you reach Westbourne Grove, turn right, first left into Needham Road and the **4** **Cock & Bottle** is on the far corner.

**The ornate bar back at the Cock & Bottle**

Of early Victorian origin, this attractive corner pub on a handsome terrace retains traces of its former multi-room layout, together with some snob screens, although these are modern. The jewel here, though, is the splendid bar-back with its unusual shape and remarkably ornate detailing. What a pity, though, that the illuminated stained glass panels depicting swans (in commemoration of the pub's former name) have been removed in the latest refurbishment by the new management: another act of unnecessary vandalism. Fortunately the handsome chequered tile floor and proper old-fashioned urinal in the gents has survived: I still think we need all these listed before they are lost! On the beer front, Truman's Swift and Sambrook's Wandle Ale are the current regulars, with two guests, usually something from nearby Portobello, and Adnams. It remains a decent drinkers' pub although the emphasis on food has

become much more pronounced with a new, pricey menu.

Return to Westbourne Grove and turn left, passing the upmarket shopping parade and taking the second right into Hereford Road, which puts us firmly into Bayswater with its hotels and general air of affluence. Just past Leinster Square, and still on Hereford Road, we arrive at our next port of call, the spacious **5** **Prince Edward**, on the right. Considering the location, and the fact that tourists from nearby hotels make up a good deal of its trade, the pub is still fairly unpretentious. The drinking area is arranged around an island bar, and dining (the kitchen is open throughout the day) tends to take place in the rear area. The more unspoilt part fronting Needham Road retains a wooden dado. This is a Hall & Woodhouse pub and the normal offerings are its K&B Sussex, Badger Best, and Tanglefoot.

Suitably fortified, it's once again an easy walk to the next pub. Continue down Hereford Road to Moscow Road. This street may have been named in honour of Tsar Alexander's visit to England in 1814. Turn

**The Cock & Bottle is an attractive corner pub**

pub inside and out, as befits a location just a stone's throw from Queensway, the interior is spacious and comfortable, with not too much sunlight, just as a proper pub should be. Note the three sets of doorways suggesting the former partitions. The pub has passed from Fuller's to the Greene King/Spirit Group and is part of the Taylor Walker badged portfolio (such is the opacity of pub takeovers these days!). Expect a couple of GK beers with the new Taylor Walker 1730 also a regular. This beer is brewed by Westerham Brewery to an old recipe, celebrating the Westerham connection of the old Taylor Walker Brewery that, in 1948, it bought the town's Black Eagle brewery. There are a couple of guests, quite frequently these are Jennings Cumberland Ale and Sharp's Doom Bar. Moreover, if you can show a valid CAMRA membership card, you'll get 10% off the pump prices. You can eat in here until 10pm.

left and a five-minute stroll brings us to two pubs close together on the right. If you've the capacity for both you could try the recently spruced-up **7 Phoenix** which, although a Greene King house, has guest ales included on its four handpumps so you may get something interesting; and there's a list of craft bottled beers. Otherwise pass along a few doors directly to the **6 King's Head**. A smart but tasteful-looking corner

Bayswater Underground station is just down on Queensway at the end of Moscow Road.

## PUB INFORMATION

**1 UXBRIDGE ARMS**
13 Uxbridge Street, W8 7TQ
020 7727 7326
**Opening hours:** 12-11; 12-10.30 Sun

**2 WINDSOR CASTLE**
114 Campden Hill Road, W8 7AR
020 7243 8797 • www.thewindsorcastlekensington.
co.uk
**Opening hours:** 12-11; 12-10.30 Sun

**3 CHURCHILL ARMS**
119 Kensington Church Street, W8 7LN
020 7727 4242 • www.churchillarmskensington.co.uk
**Opening hours:** 11-11 (midnight Thu-Sat);
12-10.30 Sun

**4 COCK & BOTTLE**
17 Needham Road, W11 2RP
020 7229 1550 • www.cockandbottlew11.com
**Opening hours:** 12-11 (11.30 Fri & Sat)

**5 PRINCE EDWARD**
73 Princes Square, W2 4NY
020 7727 2221 • theprince-edward.co.uk
**Opening hours:** 10-11 (midnight Fri & Sat);
11.30-10.30 Sun

**6 KING'S HEAD**
33 Moscow Road, W2 4AH
020 7229 4233 • www.taylor-walker.co.uk/pub/
kings-head-bayswater/c1196
**Opening hours:** 11-11; 12-10.30 Sun

Try also:

**7 PHOENIX**
51 Moscow Road, W2 4AL
020 7229 0647 • phoenix-pub.co.uk
**Opening hours:** 11-11; 12-10.30 Sun

# Gems around Smithfield

This is a walk full of interest in a lesser-known part of London. It circumnavigates the great structure of Smithfield Market, still the largest meat market in the land, and passes the great ecclesiastical treasure of St Bartholomew's church. There are other notable landmarks, not to mention a variety of excellent pubs. Most of these are closed at weekends, so it's a walk to enjoy during the week.

WALK
10

▶ **Start:** ⊋ ⊖ Farringdon, or ⊖ Chancery Lane

▶ **Finish:** ⊋ ⊖ Farringdon

▶ **Distance:** 1.4 miles (2.3 km)

▶ **Key attractions:** Smithfield Market; Old Bailey; St Bartholomew's church; The Charterhouse (www. thecharterhouse.org)

▶ **THE PUBS:** Olde Mitre; Viaduct; Hand & Shears; Red Cow; Jerusalem Tavern

▶ **Timing tip:** Note the weekend closure of most of the pubs.

**St Peter's brewery's only London house, the Jerusalem Tavern**

Start at Farringdon station on Thameslink National Rail and the Underground. Upon exit from the station, turn right and walk down to the Farringdon Road by the John Oldcastle. The name of this Wetherspoon pub recalls the eponymous tavern that once stood in the former grounds of Sir John's nearby mansion. Oldcastle is thought to have been the model for Shakespeare's character Falstaff. Turn left, then first right onto Charterhouse Street, before turning right again into the curious Ely Place with its gated and guarded entrance. To get to this point from Chancery Lane Underground station, head eastwards down High Holborn to Holborn Circus, and Ely Place is the first turning left after crossing into Charterhouse Street.

The first pub on this walk is one of the hardest to find in London, although since Fuller's acquired it they have taken to placing advertising boards at the end of the tiny alley where it lies hidden, removing much of the mystique! Turn into gated Ely Place and aim for the passageway between numbers 9 and 10. In fact, given its history, the 🍺 **Olde Mitre**

might well feel like a separate kingdom. The original tavern is said to have been built in 1546 for the servants of the nearby palace of the Bishops of Ely, and technically the pub was for years part of the county over which they presided. Until the late 1970s Cambridgeshire was the licensing authority for the pub! The nearby palace, the oldest Roman Catholic church in the city, was demolished in 1772 along with the pub, although the latter was rebuilt soon afterwards. The preserved trunk of a cherry tree, which allegedly marked the boundary of the Bishop of Ely's property, can still be detected in the corner of the small front bar of this very atmospheric hostelry.

The interior you see today, replete with wood panelling throughout, dates back to an interwar refitting; and the larger back room has a cosy snug. A rare outside gents' toilet completes the scene. In addition to Fuller's beers, the six handpumps dispense several guest ales, usually including Deuchars IPA and other Caledonian beers; and Adnams Bitter. Expect a draught cider too. The popular and long-serving licensee, 'Scotty' to the regulars, is now enjoying a well-earned retirement but apart from that little else has changed much, and the pub continues to collect awards and plaudits almost annually. Not to be missed!

If you continue on the narrow passageway upon leaving the Olde Mitre, you emerge onto Hatton Garden, centre of the London jewellery trade. Turn left to reach Holborn Circus, with St Andrew's church, rebuilt by Wren after the Great Fire, on the busy intersection. Be careful crossing Charterhouse Street before turning next left on the continuation of High Holborn, now named after the viaduct over Farringdon

**Tucked away down an alley, the Olde Mitre is one of the hardest pubs to find in London**

OLDE MITRE

⊖ **Chancery Lane**

HOLBORN

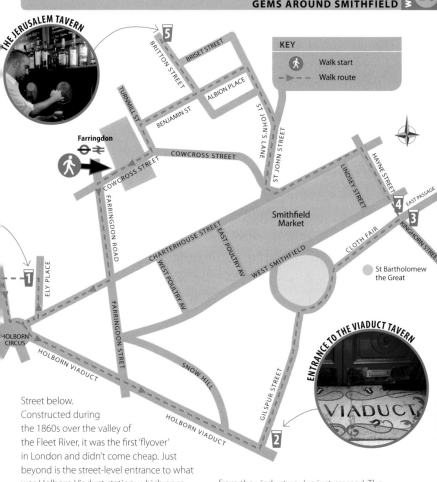

THE JERUSALEM TAVERN

**KEY**

🚶 Walk start

▶ Walk route

5

BRITTON STREET

BRISET STREET

ALBION PLACE

TURNMILL ST

BENJAMIN ST

ST JOHN'S LANE

ST JOHN STREET

**Farringdon**
🚶 ➡

COWCROSS STREET

COWCROSS STREET

LINDSEY STREET

HAYNE STREET

EAST PASSAGE

4

3

KINGHORN STREET

FARRINGDON ROAD

Smithfield
Market

CHARTERHOUSE STREET

EAST POULTRY AV

WEST SMITHFIELD

CLOTH FAIR

St Bartholomew
the Great

ELY PLACE

1

WEST POULTRY AV

FARRINGDON STREET

HOLBORN
CIRCUS

HOLBORN VIADUCT

SNOW HILL

GILSPUR STREET

ENTRANCE TO THE VIADUCT TAVERN

VIADUCT

2

HOLBORN VIADUCT

Street below.
Constructed during
the 1860s over the valley of
the Fleet River, it was the first 'flyover'
in London and didn't come cheap. Just
beyond is the street-level entrance to what
was Holborn Viaduct station, which once
had a connection to the Metropolitan line
at Farringdon before becoming a terminus
until the re-opening of Snow Hill tunnel in
the 1980s and the Thameslink Project. Just
beyond, on the next corner, you'll see the
impressive Central Criminal Court on the
southern side of the street, with its gilded
statue of Justice with her sword and scales.
Until 1902, this was the site of the infamous
Newgate prison.

Time for another stop, and right
opposite stands the handsome Grade II-
listed **2 Viaduct Tavern** with its impressive
curved frontage. Although remodelled at
the turn of the century, the pub dates back
to about 1870, taking its name of course

from the viaduct you've just crossed. The
four doorways suggest a once typically
divided Victorian pub, although predictably
the partitions have gone. However, many
of the other original features have survived,
the most prominent being the three large
Victorian paintings of Rubenesque maidens,
each representing a facet of London life:
agriculture, commerce, and the arts. The
latter painting was either shot or, according
to some stories, bayoneted by a drunken
soldier in World War I, and still carries the
wound. Nowadays, the paintings are glazed
to prevent further damage to the canvas.
Between each of the paintings is one of
several cherubic face reliefs that are a feature
throughout the pub. Look out for the cut and

**The small central bar of the Hand & Shears**

gilded glasswork, especially towards the rear of the pub, where a little publican's office, once common but now a rare survivor, can also be seen. The widely circulated story that the pub's cellars were once cells of Newgate prison has now been discredited. Historians now agree they were cells of the former Giltspur Street Comptor (a small prison), which closed in 1853, above which the pub was built in c.1870. A blue plaque marking the former existence of the Giltspur Street Comptor is attached to a wall close to the Viaduct Tavern. Meanwhile the former cells can still be visited today. The pub is another fairly recent acquisition of Fuller's brewery so expect its beers including a seasonal guest.

Walk north up Giltspur Street towards Smithfield Market. This is a famous spot in the history of London, with a market having existed here since the 12th century. Older still was the famous Bartholomew Fair, which was a cloth fair originally founded to fund the famous Bart's hospital nearby. The site was also used for jousting and was notorious as a place of execution during the Reformation. In the 19th century, Smithfield established itself as the largest meat market in England and the current market hall with its ironwork and glass roof was built to a design by Sir Horace Jones in 1868. Like most London markets it's only a shadow of its former self, but at least it's not yet a chintzy boutique mall or a collection of wine bars.

To the right of the small open space in front of the market hall, down a narrow passage to the right of the Butcher's Hook & Cleaver, is what remains of the splendid church of St Bartholomew the Great. A detour to visit the church is highly recommended. The Priory church was founded in 1123 by Prior Rahere as part of a monastery of Augustinian Canons, but was dissolved in 1539 and the nave of the church demolished. What remains is the impressive chancel, parts of the transepts and one side of the cloisters. The interior must surely still be the most atmospheric of all London's parish churches.

Fortified spiritually, we can now walk down the narrow and attractive Cloth Fair just a bit beyond to the right, where the poet John Betjeman used to live, before we encounter the **3** **Hand & Shears** on a corner site. This handsome pub has kept an interior that is still faithful to the style that countless unassuming London pubs would have once had, but is now a significant Central London surviving example of what is basically a Victorian layout. The woodwork is plain and simple; and, remarkably, there are still three separate bar areas plus a small snug partitioned off by simple screenwork. The plain floorboards and wooden panelling are entirely in keeping with this delightfully simple former working men's beer house.

**The handsome exterior of the Hand & Shears**

**The ornate roof of Smithfield market**

Staple beers are from Courage, and Adnams is often among the limited guest range – but you're here as much to take in the atmosphere as the beers.

Anyway, a step across the street and you'll have more beers than you can shake a stick at: to get there, simply cross the road and go through the archway to arrive immediately at the **4 Old Red Cow** on Long Lane. A pub that has seen a few ups and downs over the years, it was given a very welcome facelift a few years ago, especially on the beer front. The exterior is tastefully smartened up but it's far smaller inside than first impressions might suggest, and you may have to fight your way to the small bar, but for once it'll be well worth it. Expect four cask ales, which could be from anyone, anywhere, but likely to be interesting; however, it's for their 'craft' keg beers that the Cow is gaining a good reputation via one of the best selections in the area. Arbor, Camden Town, Magic Rock and Kernel are among the well-regarded brewers who make regular appearances here. The informative website gives an up-to-date lowdown on the latest beers on, with tasting notes and an opportunity to suggest guest brews; and they now feature a brewery of the month and showcase its beers. Check the pub's Facebook page to see what's on at the moment. There is an upstairs

bar, again hardly large, and sometimes hired out privately, but worth a look if it's rammed down below. The kitchen is open all day, but food is on the pricey side.

Cross into Hayne Street opposite. Emerge by Charterhouse Square and cross the road to walk along the left of the square, maybe detouring again to look at the enticing group of buildings on its northern side. This Oxbridge-looking building is Charterhouse, founded as a Carthusian monastery in 1370. It passed through successive owners after dissolution by Henry VIII, coming into the possession of Thomas Sutton in 1611. He it was, being fabulously wealthy, who established both the Charterhouse Hospital for aged men and Charterhouse

**Old Red Cow**

School for the education of the sons of the poor. By the early 19th century, Charterhouse had become a leading public school. Interestingly, the writer William Makepeace Thackeray (1811–63) was not impressed by his education there; he wrote that he 'was lulled into indolence and when I grew older and could think for myself was abused into sulkiness and bullied into despair'. Although the public school with which the name is perhaps associated most closely moved out to Surrey in 1872, the building still functions as an almshouse. Guided tours are Tuesdays, Wednesdays, Thursdays and every other Saturday (£10 per person) at 2.15pm. Call 020 7253 9503 for details or book via the website.

Returning to the task at hand, head through the gate at the north-western corner of the square and pass the Fox & Anchor, a recently smartened-up fin de siècle building with its Art Nouveau exterior, including some fine Doulton tiling. On account of the very high beer prices, I'm not going to recommend it in this book, but wealthy readers could sneak in without me knowing…

Continue down to Charterhouse Street opposite the northern side of the meat market, turn sharp right into St John Street, and then branch into narrower St John's Lane, consulting your map if need be. Turn left into Albion Place, and right at the end into Britton Street. Here is the final pub in this walk, the little **5** **Jerusalem Tavern**. The name comes from the Priory of St John of Jerusalem, founded in 1140, which once stood in St John's

### LINK TO WALK 13

To join the latter part of Walk 13, turn right from the Jerusalem Tavern and walk up to the Clerkenwell Road. Turn left, and continue for 5–6 minutes, crossing the Farringdon Road, and turn right into Eyre Street Hill for the Gunmakers, or left into Leather Lane for the Craft Beer Co.

Lane, but the building itself has been a pub for only about 15 years. It was built in 1719–20 by Simon Mitchell, originally as a merchant's house. The interior, reached via a lobby room, has lots of atmosphere and displays some 18th-century panelling. Note also the 'four seasons' tile panels from the same period in the front lobby. The other noteworthy thing here is the beer: this is the only London house of the St Peter's brewery of Suffolk whose fine ales are dispensed in curious fashion: air pressure brings the beer from conventional casks stored in the cellar through taps set into false 'casks' attached to the wall. The brewery's bottled ales are also available here.

Turn back towards Albion Street, but bear right opposite into Benjamin Street to reach Farringdon station in less than five minutes.

**The Jerusalem Tavern**

### PUB INFORMATION

**1** **OLDE MITRE**
1 Ely Court, Ely Place, EC1N 6SJ
020 7405 4751 • www.yeoldemitreholborn.co.uk
**Opening hours:** 11-11; closed Sat & Sun

**2** **VIADUCT TAVERN**
126 Newgate Street, EC1A 7AA
020 7600 1863 • viaducttavern.co.uk
**Opening hours:** 8.30am-11; closed Sat & Sun

**3** **HAND & SHEARS**
1 Middle Street, Cloth Fair, EC1A 7JA
020 7600 0257 • www.thehandandshears.co.uk
**Opening hours:** 11-11; closed Sat & Sun

**4** **OLD RED COW**
71-72 Long Lane, EC1A 9EJ
020 7726 2595 • theoldredcow.com
**Opening hours:** 12-11 (midnight Fri & Sat);
12-10.30 Sun

**5** **JERUSALEM TAVERN**
55 Britton Street, EC1M 5UQ
020 7490 4281
**Opening hours:** 11-11; closed Sat & Sun

# Aldgate to Shoreditch via Brick Lane

**WALK 11**

Brick Lane is one of the most famous streets in the East End. Its name comes from the brick and tile makers who used to live in the area, but the area has been home to successive waves of immigrants, from Huguenot silk weavers to the Bangladeshi migrants of the 1970s. Hand in hand with this story goes the history of anti-racist struggle, culminating in the 'Battle of Brick Lane' in 1978 and the murder of garment worker Altab Ali. Happily things are far more harmonious today. No book with this subject could fail to pay respect to the huge Truman Brewery, which was in business on Brick Lane until its closure in 1988. The regeneration of the former Truman Brewery represents the latest example of socio-economic change here. The walk traverses Brick Lane and calls at a remarkably varied mixture of pubs and bars, which epitomise the changing geography of the East End.

▶ **Start:** ⬤ Aldgate East

▶ **Finish:** ⬤ Shoreditch High Street

▶ **Distance:** 1.7 miles (2.8 km)

▶ **Key attractions:** Whitechapel Market; Whitechapel Gallery; Brick Lane; Christ Church; Fournier Street; Spitalfields City Farm; Old Truman Brewery

▶ **THE PUBS:** Dispensary; Pride of Spitalfields; Carpenters Arms; King's Arms; Well & Bucket.

▶ **Timing tips:** The Dispensary is closed at the weekend, and the Carpenters Arms only opens its doors at 4pm from Monday to Wednesday.

Brick Lane

**The Dispensary is housed in a former hospital**  **Old Truman Brewery, Brick Lane**

Start at well-connected Aldgate East Underground station. You need the southern side of busy Whitechapel Road, unless it's a weekend when our first stop is closed, and you're heading straight for Brick Lane; so look for the correct exit to save negotiating the busy street. It's not far to the first pub stop: Leman Street is the one-way street running south from the junction, and it's less than a five-minute walk before you come across the first building of any antiquity hereabouts.

The 🍺 **Dispensary** is housed in a handsome former hospital built in 1858 as home to the Eastern Dispensary, a philanthropic institution with roots almost a century earlier still, and one of the first endeavours to provide medical treatment for the poor in East London. As the bold inscriptions on the front elevation make very clear, all this relied upon voluntary contributions. The listed building was re-opened in 2006 following a sympathetic renovation retaining much of the gravitas of the original: the

**Brick Lane**

tiled entrance gives onto a couple of small rooms to the right, a Portland stone staircase, and the main bar, left, which is smaller than one might have expected but which leads to a mezzanine floor set out primarily for diners. The real attraction for us is the beer range, with the house beer (by Nethergate) supported by four interesting guests, usually including a dark beer. There's a wide food menu served at lunchtimes and in the evenings.

Bear left on exit from the pub, turning into Goodman's Stile. The name relates, one assumes, to nearby Goodman's Fields, which in turn is named for Roland Goodman, who once farmed the land here for a local nunnery. Cross over Commercial Road into narrower White Church Lane, which brings you out on Whitechapel Road with the little garden on the corner now named Altab Ali Park in memory of the victim of the 1978 race riots. Use the controlled crossing and head up Osborn Street opposite; this becomes Brick Lane. The area around Brick Lane was noted for its

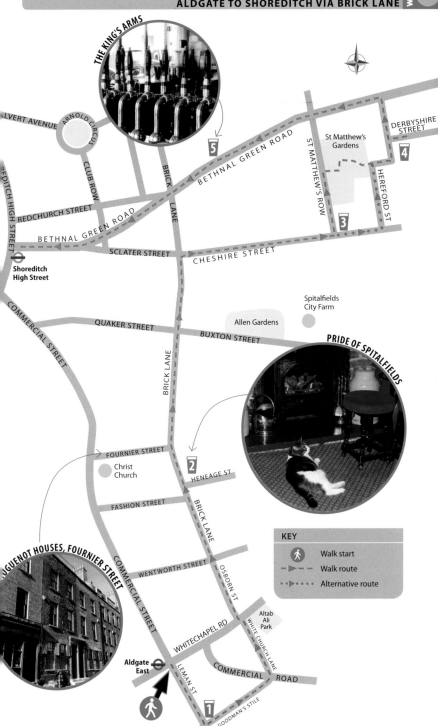

THE KING'S ARMS

LVERT AVENUE

ARNOLD CIRCUS

DERBYSHIRE STREET

St Matthew's Gardens

**5**

BETHNAL GREEN ROAD

BRICK LANE

ST MATTHEW'S ROW

HEREFORD ST

**4**

CLUB ROW

REDITCH HIGH STREET

REDCHURCH STREET

BETHNAL GREEN ROAD

**3**

SCLATER STREET

CHESHIRE STREET

**Shoreditch High Street**

Spitalfields City Farm

COMMERCIAL STREET

QUAKER STREET

Allen Gardens

BUXTON STREET

BRICK LANE

PRIDE OF SPITALFIELDS

FOURNIER STREET

Christ Church

**2**

HENEAGE ST

FASHION STREET

BRICK LANE

UGUENOT HOUSES, FOURNIER STREET

WENTWORTH STREET

COMMERCIAL STREET

OSBORN ST

Altab Ali Park

WHITE CHURCH LANE

KEY

🚶 Walk start

– – – – Walk route

•••••• Alternative route

WHITECHAPEL RD

**Aldgate East**

LEMAN ST

COMMERCIAL ROAD

**1**

GOODMAN'S STILE

79

**The Carpenters Arms**

**Christ Church on Fournier Street**

clothing industry during much of the 20th century, but much of this been replaced by the restaurants and cafés of 'Banglatown'. These days you may have to wave away numerous enthusiastic Bangladeshis keen to usher you in to eat, or indeed you might want to return here once the drinking is done. One architectural gem to look out for is on Fashion Street, the second turning on the left: the Moorish Market was an ambitious indoor market, a sort of early mall, opened by one Abraham Davis in 1905 with more than 60 shops. It didn't really take off, but the remarkable building survives and is now an educational institution.

Just beyond this, on the other side of Brick Lane, the next pub is well hidden and, if you don't know it, quite a surprise in view of the all the multi-ethnic commerce along Brick Lane. The **2 Pride of Spitalfields** is just a few yards down Heneage Street, a turning on the right. From the outside, the snowy white paintwork of this classic local makes it look like a bit of Greece transported to Banglatown; but inside it's as traditional as you could expect, and deservedly a firm favourite. The friendly and efficient service is a big plus as it often gets very busy, but it's worth almost any wait to sample the well-kept ales. The guv'nor keeps four beers as regulars: Fuller's London Pride and ESB, alongside Crouch Vale Brewer's Gold and Sharp's Doom Bar. The fifth handpump is allocated to a guest beer but,

appropriately for the locale, that's often from the nearby 'phoenix' Truman microbrewery. The walls are lined with interesting pictures of bygone East End life. There's food on weekday lunchtimes only.

There's plenty of interest as you continue northwards along Brick Lane. Don't miss Fournier Street, the next left as you continue northwards. Named after Huguenot refugee George Fournier, the houses date mainly from the 1720s and, ironically since the successive waves of immigrants were too poor to change them, they now form one of the best preserved collection of early Georgian townhouses in Britain, and these days some of the most desirable listed residences in London: you'll need at least £2 million to buy into the street and join neighbours like Tracy Emin and Gilbert & George.

**The Pride of Spitalfields**

**The stripped-back but welcoming King's Arms**

The next sight to see is the Old Truman Brewery, presided over by the chimney still bearing the name of the old brewery. The 10-acre site has undergone extensive regeneration with a mix of businesses, retailers, galleries and a market moving in. If you want to visit the Spitalfields City Farm, it's on Buxton Street, to the right, otherwise Brick Lane continues north, passing under the new bridge carrying the London Overground railway. Look out for Cheshire Street on the right shortly beyond, and head down here away from the bustle of Brick Lane.

A good five minutes' stroll will bring you across the border into Bethnal Green, and to the next pub on this walk; and it's one with a bit of history. On the corner with St Matthew's Row, the **3 Carpenters Arms** was once the most notorious pub in London, bought by infamous gangsters Reggie and Ronnie Kray and run by their mother, Violet. Closed for years, the place was rescued by current landlords Eric and Nigel, former customers, who saved it from property developers intent on turning it into flats. They have repositioned the pub to suit the new demographic and

turned it into a good beer destination. The three cask ales (Taylor Landlord, and two changing guests) are complemented by a variety of keg beers which includes a changing and often interesting guest; and a wide range of bottled beers, which are advertised on the blackboard. For such a small pub there's a surprisingly good and varied menu: check the website for typical fare. There's a pleasant little rear courtyard which might offer some space if the two pub rooms are busy.

Walk up St Matthew's Row towards the eponymous church (at night, or if the church garden gates are locked continue via Hereford Street – check your map) and walk through the pretty St Matthew's Garden around the church. It has an interesting history, having been consumed by fire in 1759 and left roofless by bombing in 1940. The gate at the far end of the churchyard leads into Sale Street, hardly 50 yards long, swinging 90 degrees to the left and becoming Buckfast Street. Along on the right here is the **4 King's Arms**. This is yet another reinvented old East End pub which reopened in 2013 with a bold new external sign providing a focus for the

**The newly-refurbished Well & Bucket**

remaining fragments of the once-splendid tilework, it re-opened in 2013. Great new artwork adorns the wall; and a splendid modern wall mirror hangs in convincing Victorian gin-palace style. The reborn pub has an island bar, comfortable seating all around, dim lighting and a back yard for outdoor drinking. There's also a vibrant little cocktail bar hidden away in the cellar. Four handpumps have been installed and the pub always has an interesting and varied selection of beers including some from local micros. Other interesting offerings are available on the keg taps and in the fridge. Fresh oysters are the pick of the food menu. Be warned that it's already proving popular and can be quite crowded at peak times.

Plenty of buses stop nearby, and Shoreditch High Street station on the Overground is not far down the street to the right.

handsome street corner building. Inside the décor is in line with other hipster-friendly pubs in the area, with plenty of woodwork and fairly minimalist fittings, but the place is welcoming and comfortable for all that. In summer large windows open and street tables offer a pleasant alternative 'seating experience'. You'll get a very good choice of beers here, with up to six cask ales and more than twice that number of keg taps. If you want to splash out there's also an interesting list of expensive world bottled beers. Food consists mainly of grazing plates of cheeses and charcuterie with Scotch eggs.

There's plenty of more down-to-earth stuff at the end of Buckfast Street on the Bethnal Green Road, which is the direction of onward travel. Heading to your left along the busy road and crossing to the northern side at a safe and convenient spot it's barely 300 yards to the final call on this walk, the **5** **Well & Bucket**. The pub was established in an era when the local population still collected their water from the public well in Bethnal Green Road, hence the name. However, the lingering presence of cholera in the area made drinking beer a much safer option than drinking water! Part of the Truman estate, it was later acquired by Belhaven, but after falling out of pub use for some 15 years it was acquired by pubco Barworks; and after extensive restoration of what was left of the interior, including the

## PUB INFORMATION

 **DISPENSARY**
19A Leman Street, E1 8EN
020 7977 0486 • www.thedispensarylondon.co.uk
**Opening hours:** 11.30-11; closed Sat & Sun

 **PRIDE OF SPITALFIELDS**
3 Heneage Street, E1 5LJ
020 7247 8933
**Opening hours:** 10-1am (2am Fri & Sat); 10-Midnight Sun

 **CARPENTERS ARMS**
73 Cheshire Street, E2 6EG
020 7739 6342 • www.carpentersarmsfreehouse.com
**Opening hours:** 4-11.30 Mon-Wed; 12-11 Thu; 12-12.30am Fri & Sat; 12-11 Sun

 **KINGS ARMS**
11 Buckfast Street, E2 6EY
020 7729 2627 • thekingsarmspub.com
**Opening hours:** 12-11.30 (midnight Fri & Sat); 12-11.30 Sun

 **WELL & BUCKET**
143 Bethnal Green Road, E2 7DG
020 3664 6454 • www.wellandbucket.com
**Opening hours:** 12-midnight (12.30am Fri & Sat); 12-11 Sun

# Central excursion by 'beer bus'

When the railway companies were building their lines into London in the nineteenth century, they were forbidden to drive their tracks into the heart of the city, which is why many of the termini today lie in a line along the axis of the Euston & Marylebone Roads. Happily this axis is the route followed today by bus 205, which not only links the stations, it connects a ribbon of good quality, interesting drinking holes. More than one of the pubs has noteworthy architectural and/or heritage features, whilst the beer range is, as usual in London these days, surely wide enough for even the most discriminating imbiber.

## WALK 12

- **Start:** ⇌ ⊖ Paddington
- **Finish:** ⇌ ⊖ Old Street
- **Distance:** Less than a mile on foot
- **Key attractions:** Madame Tussauds, London Planetarium; London Zoo & Regents Park
- **THE PUBS:** Victoria; Barley Mow; Albany; Euston Tap; Parcel Yard; Old Fountain. Try also: Thornbury Castle
- **Timing tip:** The Old Fountain is closed at the weekend, but as an alternative weekend finish try the Wenlock Arms, (see page 99) 5 minutes from the bus.

**The revamped King's Cross station**

**The Victoria at Paddington**

of London pub interiors. The rounded, stuccoed exterior is appropriately tasteful for the locality, but what sets the place apart architecturally are the interior fittings which seem to have survived the late Victorian frenzy of redecoration and replacement and, if we believe the date on the clock, go back to 1864. Pride of place probably goes to the glass and mirror work, especially the gilded glass set in the wonderful bar back and screen on the back wall. The interior décor gets it right with smart floorboards and a variety of comfortable seating areas. Do not miss a trip upstairs to both the theatre bar (which although more modern has an agreeable ambience), and the very impressive library room with its leather seats and an atmosphere redolent of a gentlemen's club. The beers are from Fuller's, and a varied food menu is served throughout the day. All in all just the sort of place to set you up for an enjoyable day's drinking!

Exit Paddington station onto Praed Street, and look for the road leading off at the left-hand (south-east) corner of the station – London Street, as the first part of the route is on foot. Head down past the parade of shops, by which time you may see a stern picture of our longest serving monarch staring lugubriously at you in the distance. She might have been cheered by the pub which takes her name, however, for the **1 Victoria**, at the corner of Strathearn Place, is a high-quality rarity in the context

### LINK TO WALK 14

If you alight two stops before the Old Fountain, at Windsor Terrace, it's a five minute walk to the excellent Wenlock Arms (see Walk 14), which you can do as a stand-alone extra pub or continue and visit the other pubs along the Regent's Canal.

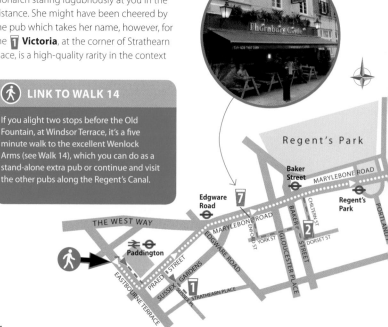

Walk back to the bus stop, on the northern side of Praed Street, and take the next 205 for a few stops alighting right outside Baker Street station. However, if you want to take in an extra pub, get off at Marylebone station (the stop before) and crossing the road by the lights head directly into Enford Street opposite where you'll find the **7 Thornbury Castle**. It's no oil painting outside and fairly modern and plain within, but with a very good range of up to six interesting beers sourced in the main from regional micros. From here it might be as quick to stay on the south side of the street with your map and look for Chiltern Street (see below).

If you're staying on the bus, alight at Baker Street station where, if you value your life, you are advised to take the subway to reach the southern side of the Marylebone Road in safety: it's inside the station entrance. Then walk down Chiltern Street for a few minutes, and Dorset Street is the third on the right. The **2 Barley Mow** is a few yards along. It was built

The 'pawnbrokers' boxes at the Barley Mow

in 1791 and as such claims to be the oldest pub in Marylebone. It's certainly remains a very traditional pub which has a comfortable, well-worn feel throughout. The pub is rightly renowned for a pair of small all-wooden drinking cubicles, now unique in London. Some claim they were used for pawnbroking transactions but in reality they're very probably simply another example of the Victorian passion for privacy! Look out also for the little rear room with some very

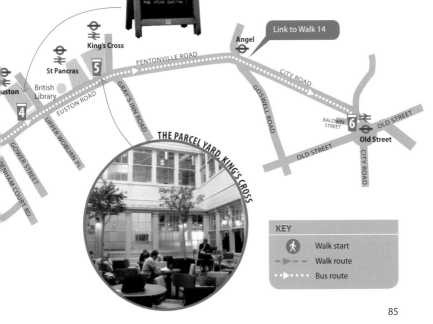

**The Euston Tap has almost 30 changing cask and keg beers**

old panelling. In keeping with the trend throughout London the beer range is much improved since the first edition of this book was published: Fuller's London Pride has a constant presence, with changing beers on the other five handpumps, Mighty Oak and Sharp's being among the more favoured breweries along with Fuller's seasonals. Food-wise it's toasted sandwiches until 4pm, with a daily special – a hot meal – available all day.

Retrace your steps to the bus stop, and continue by the next 205 the short distance, three stops, to Euston Road/Great Portland Street. Again it's the south side of the road we want and this time using the crossing is mandatory. Once across the street bear to the left of the Underground station island and you'll see the **3** **Albany** on the left, at the northern end of Great Portland Street itself. In a handsome Victorian building built of London's famous yellow stock bricks, the single split level bar room with its textured ceiling is well-endowed by natural light via wide arched windows. It's yet another pub which has recently been given the modern makeover and is now run by enthusiastic young management who

are serious about their beer. Four real ales rotate regularly, and you'll find national favourites like Taylor Landlord and Doom Bar alongside more interesting offerings from say Thornbridge or Sambrook's. In support is a lengthy list of draught keg offerings including beers from Sierra Nevada, Camden and BrewDog; as well as some Belgian and other interesting bottles in the fridge. A generally lively and youthful crowd occupies the eclectic furniture, and it can be busy and noisy, but it's a far better port of call for the imbiber than it was in its Firkin days. As you might expect, it takes its food seriously and this is probably the best eating option on this particular route. Check the website for menus.

Return to the same bus stop, and it's only three more stops on the 205 until you alight at Euston station. Just at the entrance to the bus stances is the next bar on the route (they get very touchy if you call it a pub), the **4** **Euston Tap**. With almost 30 changing cask and keg options, this is the ultimate beerhound's Tardis, and my favourite of several decent drinking options a stone's throw from Euston station. It occupies one of the small pavilions which once flanked the station's late lamented Doric Arch,

**The Albany**

**The stunning new roof in King's Cross station**

demolished in 1962 in surely one of the worst acts of British railway vandalism. At least these two little survivors (the other, under the same ownership, is now a cider bar) are now being put to imaginative and productive use after years of neglect! Be warned, it's tiny inside, and not given to comfort: there are at least some seats 'upstairs' but these, along with the diminutive toilets, are only accessed via some rather perilous spiral stairs which, given the strength of some of the beers, must be a health and safety hazard! The Tap's web and social media sites provide updates on the latest beers, but frankly whenever you turn up there'll be more than enough choice to satisfy.

**The Parcel Yard**

It's back on the bus for the short hop down to King's Cross, and, at the time of writing, the newest of the rash of railway station bars which are springing up all over the country. The nearby Betjeman Arms has been open at the revamped St Pancras for a while now, but I am plumping for the **5 Parcel Yard** in adjacent King's Cross. To access it, you need to traverse the splendid new concourse with its magnificent metal lattice roof, spreading in a half-cylinder span of 52 metres. For once Network Rail has spent some money to come up with something which stands comparison with the Victorian railway era. The pub is up a flight of steps at the far end of the concourse: it's a clever renewal of Thomas Cubitt's original GNER parcel office of 1852, a bright, spacious, and functional bar with several separate spaces retaining a good deal of the original materials; you can even look out onto the platforms from the further rooms. The pub is one of the few Grade I-listed pubs in London, and Fuller's deserve credit for producing something which is a worthy complement to the wider setting. In this context one is more

**The Old Fountain**

forgiving about the stratospheric prices than might otherwise be the case! You can expect the entire Fuller's range of beers (including seasonals) on the bar as well as one or two guests; and there's a fairly extensive food menu, viewable on the website.

Once back on the next 205 eastwards, you can relax for a while as the final pub of the sextet is some nine stops away: the bus passes Angel and heads down the City Road before you need to alight at Old Street Station. Baldwin Street is directly across the busy artery but you'll need to walk the few yards down to the junction to cross safely. Head into the short side road and you'll spot the **6 Old Fountain** a few yards along on the right. Sporting a distinctive external paint job and some handsome leaded windows this otherwise unassuming-looking local has become a real destination for beer aficionados, winning the local CAMRA Pub of the Year award in 2011. The pub sign is interesting: the pub apparently took its name from one of the local medicinal springs, and at one time the emblem, a portcullis surmounted by a ripple design was widespread. This free house has been in the same family for a long time, and has two bar rooms, with a new roof garden for those warmer days. The comprehensive beer range (Fuller's London Pride plus seven changing guests) comes mainly from local and regional microbreweries; the pub is noted for new brews and an extensive range of local bottled beers. Food is available at lunchtimes, and in the evenings until 10. Check the website for beer festivals.

Getting home, Old Street on the Underground is just a step away, or you can stay with the 205 for Liverpool Street station; the 135 bus from East Road will take you to Shoreditch for the London Overground.

## PUB INFORMATION

**1 VICTORIA**
10A Strathearn Place, W2 2NH
020 7724 1191 • www.victoriapaddington.co.uk
**Opening hours:** 11-11; 12-10.30 Sun

**2 BARLEY MOW**
8 Dorset Street, W1U 6QW
020 7487 4773
**Opening hours:** 12-11; closed Sun

**3 ALBANY**
240 Great Portland Street, W1W 5QU
020 7385 0221 • www.thealbanyw1w.co.uk
**Opening hours:** 12 (11 Sat)-midnight; 12-10.30 Sun

**4 EUSTON TAP**
West Lodge, 190 Euston Road, NW1 2EF
020 3137 8837 • www.eustontap.com
**Opening hours:** 12 (11.30 Sat)-11.30; 12-10 Sun

**5 PARCEL YARD**
King's Cross Station, N1 9AL
020 7713 7258 • www.parcelyard.co.uk
**Opening hours:** 8am-11; 9am-10.30 Sun

**6 OLD FOUNTAIN**
3 Baldwin Street, EC1V 9NU
020 7253 2970 • www.oldfountain.co.uk
**Opening hours:** 11-11; 12-11 Sun

Try also:

**7 THORNBURY CASTLE**
29A Enford Street, W1H 1DN
020 7402 2189 • www.thornburycastle.uk.com
**Opening hours:** 12-11; closed Sat & Sun

# From King's Cross into Clerkenwell

**WALK 13**

Clerkenwell takes its name from the Clerk's Well in Farringdon Lane. Like many other inner London suburbs it was transformed by the Industrial Revolution. Brewing made use of the good water, while precision instruments, notably clock and gunmaking, became local specialities: Hiram Maxim invented the first machine gun in nearby Hatton Garden. Perhaps Clerkenwell's most interesting claim to fame is its strong communist connections, with both Marx and Lenin having lived and worked at some point around Clerkenwell Green. King's Cross too is seeing huge changes, and if you have the time an hour spent walking around the new landscape north of the station would be well spent.

▸ **Start:** ⇌ ⊖ King's Cross/St Pancras

▸ **Finish:** ⇌ ⊖ Farringdon

▸ **Distance:** 1.8 miles (2.9 km)

▸ **Key attractions:** King's Cross canalside regeneration; Charles Dickens Museum (www.dickensmuseum. com); Karl Marx Memorial Library; British Museum; British Library (www.bl.uk); Old Clerkenwell village; St James's church; Spa Fields; Exmouth Market; Leather Lane Market

▸ **THE PUBS:** Queen's Head; Calthorpe Arms; Union Tavern; Old China Hand; Exmouth Arms; Craft Beer Co. Try also: Gunmakers.

Queen's Head

**Calthorpe Arms**

**King's Cross/St Pancras**

GRAY'S IN

suggest the usual Victorian internal subdivisions, but today only the far door is in operation, leading into a single bar, a long, narrow room. Sensitive restoration has made the most of the heritage features, notably the floor and wall tilework. The place now has its own microbrewery, although the output from this is not always on sale on the three handpumps. Nonetheless you can expect an interesting choice from other micros, with a dark beer usually available. Draught cider fans are also well catered for, and there's a supporting range of 'craft' and bottled beers. There's a small patio at the rear used by smokers. It might be a little early in the day to think about food if you're doing the whole route, but sharing platters and snacks are available.

From the Queen's Head, return to Gray's Inn Road and bear left. Walk past the Calthorpe Community Garden and in a further five minutes or less you'll reach the **2 Calthorpe Arms**. Alternatively you could catch the bus (17, 45, 46) a couple of stops to Guildford Street. A Young's local in a Victorian building with a solidly attractive corner frontage in brick and tile, the Calthorpe made a small piece of history, being once used as a temporary magistrates' court after the first recorded murder of a policeman on duty, back in 1830. On the handpumps, the Bedford-brewed Ordinary and Special bitter, plus two guests. By Young's standards, the interior is still pretty traditional, and even the tasteless carpet is blending in now it's been worn in a bit!

However you arrive at the transport hub of King's Cross/St Pancras, and whether or not you have the time to work up a thirst with a leisurely walk around the remarkable new landscape of the King's Cross redevelopment, start the beer walk by making your way down to the front exits on the Euston Road, admiring the tremendous gothic St Pancras Renaissance Hotel of Sir George Gilbert Scott, now restored to its former glory and function, having survived years of dereliction and attempts to demolish it by British Rail. The new Eurostar terminal has been the impetus for a wholesale regeneration of what was a rather seedy area.

Cross Euston Road and bear right at the busy junction along the Gray's Inn Road, past the cheap eateries that still line the road here, and the rather grander Willings House, built for an advertising company but now a budget hotel. The third turning on the left is Acton Street and here's our first call of the day, the **1 Queen's Head**. It's a handsome Victorian pub inside and out. The appealing central bay window is flanked by two pairs of double doors, which

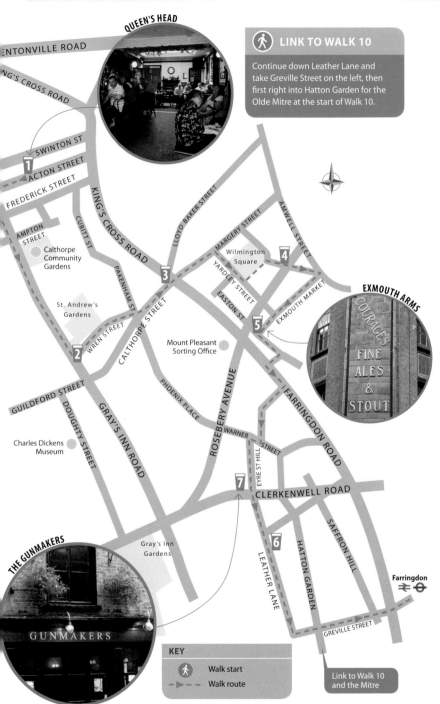

QUEEN'S HEAD

ENTONVILLE ROAD

NG'S CROSS ROAD

**LINK TO WALK 10**

Continue down Leather Lane and take Greville Street on the left, then first right into Hatton Garden for the Olde Mitre at the start of Walk 10.

SWINTON ST

**1** ACTON STREET

FREDERICK STREET

KING'S CROSS ROAD

AMPTON STREET

LLOYD BAKER STREET

MARGERY STREET

AMWELL STREET

Calthorpe Community Gardens

CUBITT ST

Wilmington Square

**4**

St. Andrew's Gardens

PAKENHAM ST

**3**

YARDLEY STREET

EXMOUTH MARKET

EXMOUTH ARMS

CALTHORPE STREET

EASTON ST

**5**

COURAGES FINE ALES & STOUT

WREN STREET

Mount Pleasant Sorting Office

**2**

GUILDFORD STREET

PHOENIX PLACE

ROSEBERY AVENUE

FARRINGDON ROAD

DOUGHTY STREET

GRAY'S INN ROAD

Charles Dickens Museum

WARNER STREET

EYRE ST HILL

**7**

CLERKENWELL ROAD

THE GUNMAKERS

Gray's Inn Gardens

LEATHER LANE

**6**

HATTON GARDEN

SAFFRON HILL

Farringdon ≷ ⊖

GUNMAKERS

GREVILLE STREET

**KEY**

🚶 Walk start

- - - Walk route

Link to Walk 10 and the Mitre

**The Union Tavern sits on a prominent corner site**

You are very close to the Charles Dickens Museum here, which has benefited from a £3 million restoration and upgrade, and is particularly to be recommended. To get there, cross into Guilford Street opposite and take the first left into Doughty Street. The Museum is at No. 48. When the great author moved to this house in 1837, it must have been on the very northern fringe of the city – he lived here for only two years but wrote *Nicholas Nickleby* and *Oliver Twist* whilst here. It's the only one of some 15 London addresses he had to have survived intact.

To continue the walk from the Calthorpe, head away from the Gray's Inn Road on Wren Street with pretty St Andrew's Gardens opposite; continue ahead as it merges into Calthorpe Street. At the junction with the

**Charles Dickens Museum**

Farringdon Road, on a prominent corner site, is the **3 Union Tavern**. Following the closure and loss of the nearby Pakenham Arms, the Union has stepped up to the plate with a sensitive refurbishment and a much improved beer range. Heritage features abound here, from the mosaic in the lobby to some glazed screenwork and good cut glass and wall mirrors. Even the Victorian porcelain in the sparklingly clean gents has survived, I'm pleased to say.

A kitchen has been added offering good, keenly priced food; but the main attraction is a set of four handpumps offering a changing range of well-kept beers, predominantly from London micros (Hackney, Belleville, etc).

Lovers of interesting architecture should make the short detour up Lloyd Baker Street from the Union Tavern to look at the estate of unusual and interesting houses laid out by Thomas Lloyd Baker around 1820. Handsome Granville Square on the left up here was the scene of Arnold Bennett's novel *Riceyman's Steps*.

The walk continues along Margery Street, the next left turn a few yards south down the Farringdon Road. Then take the first right into Yardley Street and skirt round attractive Wilmington Square to the south east corner where short Tysoe Street leads down to the Rosebery Avenue. On the corner here is the **4 Old China Hand**. Despite the name it's a pretty traditional place which boasts that all of its drinks are British. The interior, with chunky furniture and floorboards has lost some of its quirky charm from its O'Hanlon's days, but the beer range is arguably better than ever now with four handpumps offering a changing range of interesting beers from micros. In addition, the impressive bottled beer and cider list is large enough to warrant an extensive menu. There's no food available but customers can bring their own, so you could lunch here with something from a street food stall on nearby Exmouth Market.

Tysoe Street continues for forty yards across the Rosebery Avenue: head down here on leaving the China hand, and bear right into lively Exmouth Market, with the next pub stop, the **5 Exmouth Arms**, on the next corner. With a handsome tiled exterior dated 1915, the Exmouth Arms epitomises the changes that have taken place in the district: the market has lost its earthiness and is now attracting a younger, trendier crowd with a lot more money. The pub itself is no longer a down-to-earth market boozer, but the recent refurbishment has left it with a good mix of 'traditional' and 'trendy'. What's not in doubt is that the beer range and quality has taken a sharp turn upwards: four casks from small British ale breweries and around 80

The tiled exterior of the Exmouth Arms

bottled beers, as well as a wide range of more than a dozen decent craft beers on keg. The management deserve credit for making this pub a destination, and it's now very popular among the local workers and residents, so much so that you may find it pretty full at times. All in all it's a welcome addition to the area's pub stock.

Moving on, walk down to and cross Farringdon Road. Turn left, passing the Eagle, which is credited with being probably the

## MOUNT PLEASANT SORTING OFFICE

Mount Pleasant probably takes its name from the higher ground hereabouts overlooking the valley of the River Fleet, which is now, of course, buried underground. In 1877, the former Clerkenwell prison on this site was closed and the Post Office acquired the land, although some of the old prison buildings survived until 1930. Operations grew rapidly, first with parcels, and later with the transfer of the London Letter Post Office here in 1900.

By 1914 the volume of post had reached almost six billion items a year! This was what stimulated the construction of the Post Office Underground Railway in that year. The site was rebuilt following extensive war damage and, although mechanisation, electronic recognition and new technology have reduced the volume of mail and the number of workers, it's still Britain's largest sorting office and covers an area of 7.5 acres.

**Leather Lane market and the Craft Beer Co**

first 'gastropub', before turning right into Bakers Row. Now at the end of this short street turn first right, then left, and in a short step you'll be walking up the hill, past the  **Gunmakers** which is worth a stop if you have the stamina, but not at the expense of the final full entry on the route. It's slipped back a little as a beer destination and despite its small size focuses heavily

on food, but there are three handpumps and several 'craft' beers in support. Carry on up the hill and cross the Clerkenwell Road directly into Leather Lane. The down-to-earth street market operates until about 3pm on weekdays; but open for longer on the first corner is one of London's big beer destinations, the  **Craft Beer Co**.

One of a small but growing chain of beer houses, the Craft has had a recent exterior makeover which has brought this former Victorian corner pub, sporting some lovely green tiles, back to its best. And inside, there's no argument that this place offers one of the finest selections of beers, on draught and in bottle, that you'll find in any pub in London. Expect up to sixteen cask ales plus many more on keg. Moreover, they are interesting and well kept; the chances are that if you are a beer geek, you'll already know all about this place. It can get very busy, and you may have to stand, but you're bound to find something to your taste here.

To get to transport, continue down Leather Lane and take Greville Street on the left to reach Farringdon (Underground & Thameslink); or continue right to the end of Leather Lane for High Holborn buses and Chancery Lane Underground a few yards to the right.

## PUB INFORMATION

**1 QUEEN'S HEAD**
66 Acton Street, WC1X 9NB
020 7713 5772 • queensheadlondon.com
**Opening hours:** 12-midnight (11 Mon); 12-11 Sun

**2 CALTHORPE ARMS**
252 Grays Inn Road, WC1X 8JR
020 7278 4732 • www.rampubcompany.co.uk/visit-pubs/calthorpe-arms
**Opening hours:** 11-11.30; 12-10.30 Sun

**3 UNION TAVERN**
52 Lloyd Baker Street, WC1X 9AA
020 7278 0111 • www.uniontavernlondon.com
**Opening hours:** 11-11; 12-10.30 Sun

**4 OLD CHINA HAND**
8 Tysoe Street, EC1R 4RQ
020 7278 7678 • www.noordinarypub.com
**Opening hours:** 12 (2 Sat & Sun)-2am

**5 EXMOUTH ARMS**
23 Exmouth Market, EC1R 4QL
020 3551 4772 • exmoutharms.com
**Opening hours:** 11-midnight (1.30am Fri & Sat); 11-10.30 Sun

**6 CRAFT BEER CO**
82 Leather Lane, EC1N 7TR
07530 211437 • thecraftbeerco.com/pubs/clerkenwell
**Opening hours:** 12-11; 12-10.30 Sun

Try also:

**7 GUNMAKERS**
13 Eyre Street Hill, EC1R 5ET
020 7278 1022 • www.thegunmakers.co.uk
**Opening hours:** 12-11; closed Sat & Sun

# Regent's Canal I: Islington to Hoxton

**WALK**
**14**

The Regent's Canal was built to link the Grand Junction Canal at Paddington with the Thames at Limehouse. The celebrated architect John Nash, one of the canal's movers and shakers, was a chum of the Prince Regent, later King George IV; and it was he who allowed the use of his name for the canal. Beset by various financial and technical problems, it was opened as far as Camden in 1816, and east to Limehouse in 1820. It cost £772,000 to build, which was twice the original estimate. It is this second, eastern half that today has become a very good linear ribbon for good pubs, so much so that this and the next route celebrate some 12 of the best. If there's a drawback to this route, it's that there's not really much walking between pubs at all; in fact the first one is right by the Underground station! The varied selection of pubs offers a wide beer range these days but can be on the pricey side, so take plenty of money!

> **Start:** ⊖ Angel
> **Finish:** ⊖ Haggerston or ⊖ Old Street
> **Distance:** 1.9 miles (3 km)
> **Access:** Northern Line, or buses (30, 73, 205, 214, 476) from bus stop E at Kings Cross/St Pancras
> **Key attractions:** Islington Museum; Angel Gallery; Regent's Canal
> **THE PUBS:** Brewhouse & Kitchen; Charles Lamb; Earl of Essex; Island Queen; Narrow Boat; Wenlock Arms; Baring
> **Timing tip:** If you like a bit more space between your pubs, consider taking in the two Regent's Canal routes in one day, selecting every second pub according to your preferences. Note that some of the pubs don't open until 3pm on weekdays.

**Barges moored on the Regent's Canal**

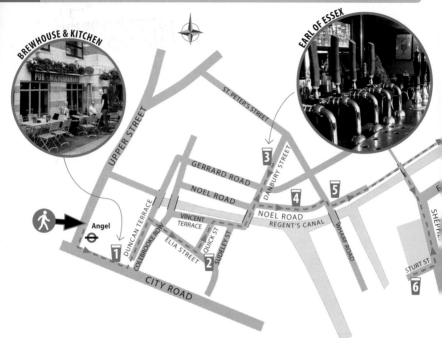

Start at Angel Underground station on the Northern Line, or bus it eastwards from Kings Cross/St Pancras, and exit onto Islington High Street. The pubs here and on Upper Street are best left to the crowds; instead bear round to the left out of the station onto the City Road where you'll find the first stop before you have even had a chance to get into your stride. The relatively new Islington branch of the **1** **Brewhouse & Kitchen** chain sits on the corner of Torrens

**Regent's Canal by the Prince of Wales**

Street; the décor and general appearance is modern, with large windows and a spacious bar room with a variety of seating. In keeping with the rest of the chain most of the cask beers on sale are produced on the premises. But the beer menu, including keg and 'craft' offerings, is extensive and classified into styles, so you should find something to your taste. The food menu, should you be looking to eat already, is also expansive.

Now some walking, but not that much! Set off down the City Road but only as far as the pretty Duncan Terrace gardens about 100 yards down on the left. If open you can walk through the gardens, leaving on the eastern side by the junction with Elia Street. The handsome garden is one segment of a series of linked and linear public spaces known as the New River Walk, built over the route of the historic New River, a constructed water channel completed in 1613 from Hertfordshire to provide a clean water supply to London. On the right hand side of the gardens, the first street leading off is Elia Street. This pleasant and quiet backwater is home to

**Charles Lamb – a backstreet gem**

the **2** **Charles Lamb**, appropriately named since of course the famous English writer and essayist is probably best known for his *Essays of Elia*. Feeling far further away from the bustle of Upper Street than it really is, this little backstreet gem has been carefully and traditionally refurbished and is often very busy with appreciative visitors from near and far. You'll get a decent choice of beers here, with Dark Star Hophead the regular, supported by three guests. They take their food seriously here too (best to check the

**Brewhouse & Kitchen**

website for times), but not to the extent that drinkers feel sidelined or segregated.

Leaving the pub bear right up Quick Street to join Vincent Terrace with the Regent's Canal making its first appearance on the walk, in a cutting across the road. West of this point the canal enters the Islington Tunnel, three quarters of a mile long and one of three tunnels on the canal. It was opened in 1819 with a steam-chain tug introduced in 1826 to reduce bottlenecks caused by boatmen manually 'legging' through it, and this service continued until the 1930s. Turn to the right, passing the Prince of Wales, closed for major refurbishment at the time of writing. If you want to walk down to the towpath, you can do so at the end of the road here by the bridge, but otherwise and/or thereafter the onward route crosses the bridge and heads directly north with the next pub already in your sights, just 150 yards or so up Danbury Street. The **3** **Earl of Essex** is quite a different beast from the preceding pubs, and, following renovation in 2012, has barged into the reckoning as a beer destination in an area not short of competition. With its central island bar counter and more varied and intimate seating, the Earl feels more inviting than some other modern refurbishments, and they've retained quite a number of features

**The Island Queen – a restored Victorian Gem**

that provide links with the past. Look out for the handsome old bar-back complete with gilded lettering and a couple of old Watney red barrels (diminutive and empty, I'm pleased to say!); and some surviving etched glass, as well as the external glazed tiles.

The star turn here, though, is the extensive and interesting beer list although the Earl does major on keg and 'craft' beers rather than cask. That said there should be around four of the latter available when you call in, along with cider. A prominent wall board shows you the latest offerings at a glance. Unusually for the area there's a pleasant secluded garden at the rear.

Retrace your steps as far as Noel Road, just before the canal bridge, and turn left down this tree-lined street to reach the

**4 Island Queen** in no distance at all. This is a restored Victorian gem, named after the monarch and her fondness for the Isle of Wight. Despite losing some of its original screenwork and having been modernised,

**Inside the Earl of Essex**

it nonetheless retains a distinctive and attractive identity. The frontage still has three doorways and some impressive curved windows, though sadly the glass is now all clear. Inside, the impression is one of height, space and grandeur around the central island bar area with its elegant stillion. To the left you can see how originally a porch would have led in from the door entrance: to the right note the mosaic floor. A separate room survives, divided by a nice screen but minus its door, and there is a corridor to the upstairs rooms. Etched glasswork by Morris of Kennington, who were responsible for the wonderful glass in the Princess Louise, High Holborn (see Walk 2), survives here and the lincrusta (heavily embossed paper) ceiling is another feature. There are now four beers available, with Taylor Landlord (very popular with the regulars) and Sharp's Doom Bar on as fixtures, supported by two changing guests. The pub offers a pleasant ambience for eating as well as drinking – see the website for all the menus.

Playwright Joe Orton lived at 25 Noel Road with his lover Kenneth Halliwell for the last few years of their lives, and was a regular in the Island Queen; it's ironic that the council has erected a blue plaque on his former abode. This was the same council that pressed for severe prison sentences against the two men, when they were found guilty of defacing local library books in 1962!

At the far end of Noel Road, right by the bridge crossing the canal, stands the

**5** **Narrow Boat**. In many ways this über-smart gastropub is the very epitome of the gentrification of the area, but in this case it's all about location, for the pub makes the most of its site alongside the canal. Wide sliding doors afford a view out across the water, and in good weather the pair of balconies offer the best seats in the house, right above the canal towpath. Downstairs, there's access to canalside seats. Since Young's acquired the Narrow Boat they have widened the beer choice, at least two of their own beers being complemented by Sharp's Doom Bar and up to three changing guests with a clear local flavour – the likes of Redemption are among the most frequently seen. Food? Well, you'll not go hungry here, with everything from snacks and sandwiches upwards; the problem might be bagging a table to eat at.

**A Canal lock at the City Road Baisin**

To continue the walk, rejoin the towpath and continue eastwards as far as the next footbridge in about 200 yards. Cross the canal onto Shepherdess Walk, and right into Sturt Street. In an area of change with council blocks standing cheek-by-jowl with new apartments, the **6** **Wenlock Arms** at the far end of the street looks increasingly incongruous, a Victorian remnant somehow clinging on against a sweeping tide of modernity. In fact, many cask ale drinkers will be familiar with this pub as it has a long and proud record as an award-wining alehouse; but the latest chapter in the Wenlock's fight against adversity ended only recently after attempts to sell the site for redevelopment were thrown out by Hackney Council. Instead a couple of flats now occupy the upper floor and the future of the pub looks assured

for now, a rare happy ending story. So the Wenlock continues to serve a wide range of eight changing and well-kept ales from all parts, alongside a range of imported beer and real cider. Being accredited in CAMRA's LocAle scheme you should find something from the London area on the bar too. The old fashioned benches and slightly tatty décor all

**Wenlock Arms**

add to the charm of this great pub, unspoilt by progress, except perhaps for the welcome refurbishment of the facilities! Note also the 'Private Bar' floor mosaic in the Wenlock Road entrance. Besides its solid support for the cause of good cask beer, it is also well known for jazz, usually on Thursday evenings.

Return to the canal and continue along the towpath to the next bridge, which carries New North Road across the canal. Leave the canal again here and take Baring Street, which runs parallel to the canal on the north

**The curved frontage of the Baring**

side. A loop of the road forks off to the left but you'll probably spot the  **Baring** before you reach the fork. Occupying a curving five-bay frontage in a Victorian building, this is yet another pub that has been gentrified to an extent, but it still retains a more traditional, community feel than some other makeovers. The long bar that wraps round at the right-hand end gives access to a garden area at the rear. Shepherd Neame Spitfire is the regular beer – supported by two changing guests, at least one of them a LocAle. In addition there's a wide range of keg beers, and an extensive menu if you want to finish off the walk with a meal. Sometimes the TV can intrude as major sporting events are advertised and shown.

From the Baring, the best homeward transport options are buses 21, 76 and 141 from Baring Street down to Old Street on the Northern Line for Underground services; or return to the canal and make for Haggerston station on the Overground, about half a mile.

### 🚶 LINK TO WALKS 15 AND 19

Return to the canal and continue east to pick up Walk 15 between Howl at the Moon and the Fox, or leave the canal at the De Beauvoir Road bridge and take the next left for the Stag's Head on Walk 19.

## PUB INFORMATION

 **BREWHOUSE & KITCHEN**
Torrens Street, Angel, EC1V 1NQ
020 7837 9421 • www.brewhouseandkitchen.com/islington
**Opening hours:** 7.30am-11 (midnight Fri) Mon-Thu; 11-midnight Sat; 11-10 Sun

**CHARLES LAMB**
16 Elia Street, Islington, N1 8DE
020 7837 5040 • www.thecharleslambpub.com
**Opening hours:** 12 (4 Mon & Tue)-11; 11-11 Sat; 12-10.30 Sun

 **EARL OF ESSEX**
25 Danbury Street, Islington, N1 8LE
020 7424 5828 • www.earlofessex.net
**Opening hours:** 12 (2 Mon)-11.30 (12.30am Fri & Sat); 12-11 Sun

 **ISLAND QUEEN**
87 Noel Road, Islington, N1 8BD
020 7354 8741 • www.theislandqueen.co.uk
**Opening hours:** 12-11.30 (midnight Fri & Sat)

 **NARROW BOAT**
119 St Peters Street, Islington, N1 8PZ
020 7400 6003 • thenarrowboatpub.com
**Opening hours:** 11-11 (midnight Fri & Sat)

 **WENLOCK ARMS**
26 Wenlock Road, Islington, N1 7TA
020 7608 3406 • wenlockarms.com
**Opening hours:** 3-11 (midnight Thu); 12-1am Fri & Sat; 12-11 Sun

 **BARING**
55 Baring Street, Hoxton, N1 3DS
020 7359 5785 • thebaringpub.co.uk
**Opening hours:** 3-11; 12-11 Sat & Sun

# Regent's Canal II: Hoxton to Mile End

The second part of the Regent's Canal epic involves quite a bit more walking than the first, especially between the Dove and the Eleanor Arms (about 1½ miles). As such, it's an attractive option to do this route by bicycle, which is permitted (although pedestrians have priority) on the canal towpath. As a walk it's just as rewarding as the first, more so in some respects for the variety of canal-side land use and the traverse of a changing area of London. The pubs, a mixture of the resolutely traditional and the very new, reflect the social changes that are occurring in the area. There's an opportunity to cut across Victoria Park, surely the most notable of the open spaces of East London. The Geffrye Museum, specialising in the history of the English domestic interior, is right by Hoxton station and, as it opens at 10am (closed Mondays, except Bank Holidays), offers a good cultural opportunity at the outset.

**Start:** Hoxton

**Finish:** Mile End Road, for Mile End

**Access:** London Overground; bus 243 from Waterloo/Farringdon/Old Street

**Distance:** 4.7 miles (7.5 km)

**Key attractions:** Hoxton Street market (hoxtonstreet-market.co.uk); Victoria Park; Broadway Market; Geffrye Museum (www.geffrye-museum.org.uk)

**THE PUBS:** Howl at the Moon; Fox; Dove; Eleanor Arms; Palm Tree

**Timing tips:** Saturday is the best day for this walk as the Fox only opens at 4pm on weekdays; although you could consider reversing the route, ending up at the Fox which is just a short step from Haggerston station. Additionally, the long-standing Hoxton Street market is at its busiest on Saturday; and Hackney's Broadway food market is also in full swing. Finally, hours at the Palm Tree are sometimes erratic: if you arrive and find it closed, knock and it may be opened to you!

The Dove

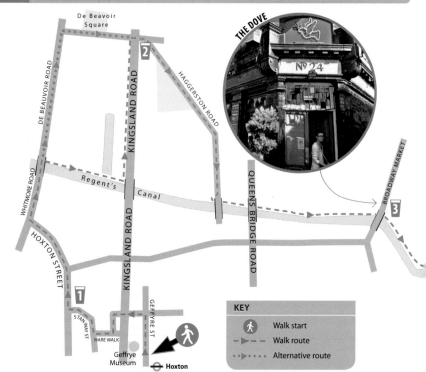

Start at Hoxton station on the London Overground, and emerge from the station on the west side of the railway, with the rear garden of the Geffrye Museum directly ahead. Walk to the right (northwards) and bear left at the first junction to reach the Kingsland Road in 100 yards. Left again here and, unless you're visiting the museum (entrance along on the left), cross the road and take the narrow lane, Hare Walk, between the modern flats just a few yards along on the right. At the end, turn right again and follow this road round to the junction with Hoxton Street, where you'll come across the market and the first pub of the day, **1 Howl at the Moon**. It's another story of a successful conversion of a disused pub in a once run-down but now revitalised area. A single spacious room looks out onto the street, and with the market taking place right outside there's often plenty to look at. You'll have a choice, usually, of three changing beers, with Hammerton's session

beer N1 a favourite at the moment. Other guests typically have a local provenance. The beers are complemented by English food at reasonable prices.

**Howl at the Moon**

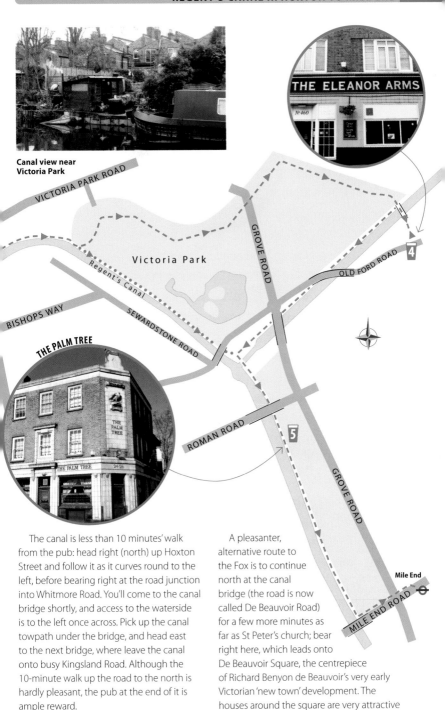

**Canal view near Victoria Park**

THE ELEANOR ARMS

THE PALM TREE

The canal is less than 10 minutes' walk from the pub: head right (north) up Hoxton Street and follow it as it curves round to the left, before bearing right at the road junction into Whitmore Road. You'll come to the canal bridge shortly, and access to the waterside is to the left once across. Pick up the canal towpath under the bridge, and head east to the next bridge, where leave the canal onto busy Kingsland Road. Although the 10-minute walk up the road to the north is hardly pleasant, the pub at the end of it is ample reward.

A pleasanter, alternative route to the Fox is to continue north at the canal bridge (the road is now called De Beauvoir Road) for a few more minutes as far as St Peter's church; bear right here, which leads onto De Beauvoir Square, the centrepiece of Richard Benyon de Beauvoir's very early Victorian 'new town' development. The houses around the square are very attractive with interesting features, such as shaped gables, sculptured chimneys and windows with lozenge-patterned leaded lights. Keep directly east onto St Peter's Way, which brings you out on the Kingsland Road directly opposite the Fox!

The **2** **Fox** continues the theme of intelligent renewal, which has become a feature of the best pubs in this area of inner London. This large Victorian pub, despite being geographically challenged insofar as it's midway between Shoreditch and Dalston, has put itself firmly on the map since its re-opening in 2012, with a tempting range of beer and food. Bar staff seem well informed about their beer, which includes an interesting range in cask on seven handpumps, with a strong emphasis upon local suppliers, so expect the likes of Hackney, London Fields and Brodie's to be much in evidence. The same can be said for the keg beers (Thornbridge Jaipur is a favourite but supported by some other strong contenders

**The Fox**

from home and abroad), whilst in the fridge there's an extensive range of bottles from around the world – so you'll not want for choice here no matter how long you might stay. The food (all sorts including sharing plates and Sunday roasts) is taken very seriously too, and as such it's a very good option if you intend to eat whilst undertaking this route. The main bar room is spacious and open, and in summer a very appealing alternative is to head upstairs to the roof terrace, which offers sheltered tables amongst leafy planters. *Time Out* rightly concluded that 'This is how to reopen a pub and appeal to the progressives and traditionalists alike.'

It would be tempting to settle in here and forget that you have a few miles to cover, but there's a walk now of the best part of a mile to fill the lungs and work off at least some of the calories. Bear right out of the pub and sharp right again (Haggerston Road), and follow the lane down past some lovely old Victorian cottages facing a green, then past the church and an area of more modern housing until you reach the canal again, access to which is via steps on the right before the bridge. Again turn left under the bridge to continue eastwards. The canal-side path traverses an area of post-war flats before you come upon a rare lock – just beyond this, leave the canal temporarily once again at the southern end of Hackney's Broadway Market. Since 2004, a new Saturday food market has been the catalyst for the gentrification of the former run-down area, although Hackney Council has ruffled a few feathers in the process.

Turn left and walk up Broadway Market for no more than 100 yards to arrive at the **3** **Dove** with its distinctive and attractive tiled exterior. Renamed, and made over some time earlier than the street, this bustling free house chimes perfectly with the new vibe in the area, and, although the rambling interior

**The Dove's Michelangelo-inspired ceiling**

**Lock and keeper's cottage on the Hertford Union canal**

is far larger than it looks from outside, you'll be lucky to get a seat at the weekend as it attracts a mixed crowd. There are six cask ales, including three guests, with East London Pale and Crouch Vale Brewer's Gold among the fixtures; but despite this, it's as a destination for Belgian beers, both on draught and in bottle, that the Dove is best known. Reports of service and welcome continue to be very mixed, it has to be said, and prices for some of the beers are very high. The unisex toilets are an unusual feature.

It's a longer walk to the next pub, so return to the canal and continue eastwards (if you're on a bike, Andrews Road runs parallel with the canal as far as Mare Street, the next road junction, and may be easier). A few minutes beyond the Mare Street bridge you'll reach the western gate into Victoria Park; unless you're pushed for time and wish to skip the slightly off-piste Eleanor Arms (in which case continue on the towpath), leave the canal and take the path following the northern perimeter of the park.

At more than 200 acres Victoria Park is the largest in the East End. Laid out in the early years of the monarch's reign, it later became a key amenity for the working classes of the East End. As well as an essential green space, the 'People's Park' became a centre for political meetings and rallies with its own Speaker's Corner to rival that at Hyde Park; here, the largest crowds were to hear socialist speakers such as William Morris.

Cross the Grove Road via the gates by the Royal Inn on the Park, and in less than 200 yards beyond, bear right on the path that passes the striking Grade II*-listed Burdett-Coutts Memorial Drinking Fountain, gift of the wealthy philanthropist and erected in 1862 allegedly at a cost of £6,000, a small fortune in those days. Head on the same bearing to leave the park by the Gunmakers Gate, crossing the canal as you leave the park, and walk the short distance up to the Old Ford Road.

A short step to the left brings you to the **4** **Eleanor Arms**. This East End local

**The traditional interior of the Eleanor Arms**

won't win many prizes for its architecture, but you can rely on a friendly welcome and a well-kept pint here as its frequent appearance in the *Good Beer Guide* testifies. The single room wraps round the bar and the rear area has the pool table and the TV; but there's also a beer garden. Beers are from Shepherd Neame, including seasonals; if the tank is low after the walk across from Hackney, food consists chiefly of filled baguettes. If you're here on a Sunday, you may be lucky enough to catch the regular jazz jam session.

**The curving bar counter of the Palm Tree**

Return to the canal bridge you just crossed and drop down to the towpath; this waterway is actually the Hertford Union, London's shortest canal, which connects the Regent's Canal with the Lee Navigation, a little over a mile to the east. To return to the former, head west (left when reaching the bridge) and walk for about 7–8 minutes. Once back at the junction, head south (left on the Regent's Canal) once again towards Globe Town and Mile End, but not for long, for once under the road bridge, and just beyond a small wetland area to the left-hand side of the towpath, stands the last pub of the day, on its own in the midst of open space that was once housing.

The **5 Palm Tree** is distinctive on account of its unspoilt exterior, branded in the signage and style of the former Truman's brewery, which of course once owned so many pubs in the East End. Truman's distinctive eagle adorns the corner elevation, whilst the company's ceramic work survives right the way round at ground-floor level. Inside there are still two quite separate bar rooms, the main one retaining its curving bar counter and old tiled chequerwork at its foot. Note, too, the dinky little island stillion holding the bottles and optics. The smaller 'posh room' round the back has similar if slightly better-quality fittings, and both rooms have some old tables. Note the framed piece of old etched glasswork in the

rear room: the now long-serving landlady apparently saved this piece from workmen from the brewery, who were smashing the Victorian screens when they moved in. The two beers on tap here are changing and often unusual ales from all over.

Leaving the Palm Tree, it's about a 10-minute walk along the canal to reach the Mile End Road; and if you're not taking a bus from here, the Underground station is about a further five minutes east, to your left.

## PUB INFORMATION

**1 HOWL AT THE MOON**
178 Hoxton Street, Hoxton, N1 5LH
020 7339 9221 • hoxtoncrafthouse.com
**Opening hours:** 12-11 (1am Fri & Sat)

**2 FOX**
372 Kingsland Road, Hackney, E8 4DA
020 7254 8462 • www.thefoxe8.com
**Opening hours:** 4 (12 Sat)-midnight Mon-Fri;
12-11.30 Sun

**3 DOVE**
24-28 Broadway Market, Hackney, E8 4QJ
020 7275 7617 • dovepubs.com
**Opening hours:** 12-11 (midnight Fri & Sat)

**4 ELEANOR ARMS**
460 Old Ford Road, Bow, E3 5JP
020 8980 6992 • www.eleanorarms.co.uk
**Opening hours:** 4 (12 Fri & Sat)-11; 12-10.30 Sun

**5 PALM TREE**
127 Grove Road, Bow, E3 5RP
020 8980 2918
**Opening hours:** 12.30-midnight (2am Sat);
12-midnight Sun

# A gourmet's walk through Southwark & Borough

**WALK 16**

▶ **Start/finish:** ⇄ ⊖
London Bridge

▶ **Distance:** 1.75 miles
(2.8 km)

▶ **Key attractions:** Borough
Market; Southwark Cathe-
dral; Rose Theatre Exhibition;
Clink Prison Museum

▶ **THE PUBS:** Rake; Market
Porter; Lord Clyde; Royal
Oak; George; Southwark Tav-
ern; Sheaf (Hop Exchange).
Try also: Simon the Tanner

▶ **Timing tip:** Pubs around
Borough Market get notori-
ously busy, particularly in
the evenings and at week-
ends, when the otherwise
very worthwhile farmers'
market is in full swing.

Southwark, south of the original London Bridge and
home to Borough Market, has a history dating back to
Roman times. Before the 17th century Puritan purges,
and despite the land being owned by the Bishop of
Winchester, it was a thriving red light district, illegally
until 1611, when brothels were licensed by Royal
decree. Thanks to the coming of the railway and the
gentrification of the riverside, Southwark's character
has changed considerably. The market stems from the
trade that came up to London from Kent, and thence
derives the area's long association with the hop trade.
The thriving food and drink market is the focus for this
walk, which also reaches further afield to make the most
of some fine and varied drinking holes, which between
them offer one of the best beer ranges in this book. The
Charles Dickens is shut with an uncertain future at the
time of writing, hence its removal from this edition; but it
may have reopened by the time you read this.

Borough Market
and the Shard

Start at the recently refurbished London Bridge station, and walk down the hill to Borough High Street, where the bulk of Southwark Cathedral competes with the railway bridges and viaducts for your attention. The cathedral is probably more attractive inside than out, with the early English choir the most admired feature, while the nave is late Victorian.

Alongside the cathedral is the gentrified but still wonderful market, with an atmosphere all of its own thanks to its location under the ironwork holding up the trains above your head. It's well worth factoring in half an hour to the walk to enjoy the stalls and maybe buy some of the goods on show. If it's cheese you're after, Neal's Yard Dairy is in Park Street across the road from the Market Porter (see below).

Our first refreshment call is adjacent to the market and the cathedral in Winchester Walk. Linked to Utobeer, the people running the beer stall in the market, the **1 Rake** has in its relatively short life risen rapidly to take its place among the 'must do' beer bars of London. Another place that is little bigger than the proverbial Tardis, it's especially well known for its remarkable range of bottled beers from around the world; but in addition, there are three handpumps and another

**The Rake offers an array of world craft beers**

six keg taps. The former dispense a changing array of rotating guest beers from quality brewers, with Oakham and Dark Star among the favoured visitors; the taps offer craft world beers. In short, the place is a world tour of beer under one roof, with knowledgeable and enthusiastic staff on hand to offer guidance should you require it. As such it's a big hit with overseas beer tourists as well as us natives, so don't expect the place to yourself; indeed, it's often hard to reach the bar especially if you go at busy times. If you get here soon after midday opening or mid-afternoon, however, you should be alright. In either case the outdoor covered terrace doubles the drinking area, and leads to the gents.

Leaving the Rake, turn left and walk round the edge of the market to the **2 Market Porter**. This well-known and highly popular boozer rarely lacks for customers, so, if and when

**The ever-popular Market Porter**

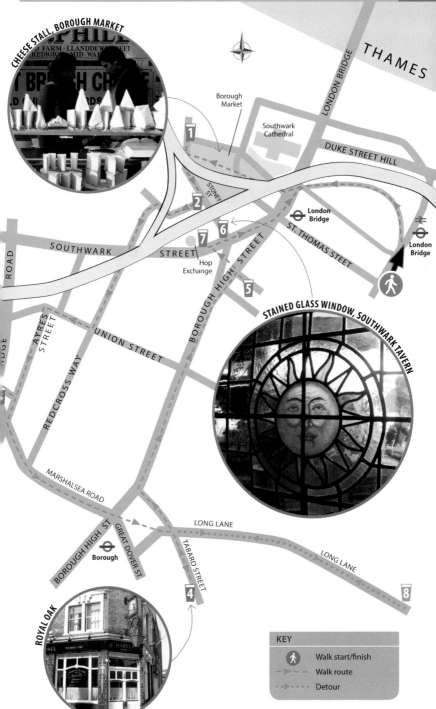

CHEESE STALL, BOROUGH MARKET

THAMES

Borough Market

Southwark Cathedral

LONDON BRIDGE

DUKE STREET HILL

STONEY ST

**London Bridge**

ST. THOMAS STEET

London Bridge

SOUTHWARK STREET

Hop Exchange

BOROUGH HIGH STREET

STAINED GLASS WINDOW, SOUTHWARK TAVERN

ROAD

AYRES STREET

UNION STREET

REDCROSS WAY

MARSHALSEA ROAD

BRIDGE

BOROUGH HIGH ST

GREAT DOVER ST

**Borough**

LONG LANE

LONG LANE

TABARD STREET

ROYAL OAK

| KEY | |
|---|---|
| 🚶 | Walk start/finish |
| – – – | Walk route |
| · · · · · | Detour |

**The robustly traditional Royal Oak**

an impressive display of colourful flowers in summer.

Leave the Market Porter by Park Street, heading away from the market and the crowds, past the Neal's Yard cheese emporium. Head around the corner and first left into Redcross Way. Continue across busy Southwark Street and under the rail bridge as far as Union Street. Here, bear right, but then take the first left, which is Ayres Street. This street was renamed to commemorate Alice Ayres, a Victorian nursemaid who was honoured after rescuing three children in her care from a house fire in 1885, a fire which cost her own life. At the far end of the roads stands one of South East London's most traditional old pubs, the **3** **Lord Clyde**, which presents a striking frontage with its distinctive tiled exterior. This bears the names of both the former owners, Truman Hanbury Buxton, and the erstwhile publican. It's also unusual in that it dates back to a 1913 rebuild, a period from which we have few pubs; and its restrained internal fittings reflect the austerity of that era compared with the glitz of Victorian pub interiors. Unusually, too, this resolutely traditional local retains two separate drinking areas, although there would have originally been more, as is apparent by the number of doorways. The main bar still has its tapering tongue-and-groove counter, bar-back, an original fireplace and some of the original etched glass. The back room has a hatch to the servery. Above all it's a first-rate pub, run by the same family for more than 50 years and which represents the finest traditions of the Great British boozer, serving a top-notch pint in a friendly atmosphere where conversation is the order of the day. There's a good choice of five well-known beers including Young's Bitter, Hog's Back TEA and Adnams Bitter. There's a full lunchtime menu on weekdays, with evening meals Wednesday to Friday.

you get to the bar, you'll have earned your reward – and the reward is a wide choice of ever-changing beers, which are chalked up on the blackboard to the right of the bar. The regular is Harveys Sussex Bitter, but you'll have up to a dozen to choose from in what is a permanent beer festival. The crowds keep on coming to enjoy them, and it's almost become a victim of its own success with the thankfully efficient staff having little time to draw breath at busy times. The interior, whilst much altered, still retains some character, whilst the outside sports

**Trumans tilework at the Lord Clyde**

**Borough Market draws in foodies from all over town**

From the main door of the Clyde, walk the 30 yards or so down to the Marshalsea Road and turn left, passing the Peabody flats before reaching the busy junction by Borough Underground station. The easiest and safest way to get to the next pub is to cross the Borough High Street by the controlled crossing so that you're standing under the tower of the church of St George the Martyr. The church stands on a small island with part of Tabard Street running behind it – the rest of Tabard Street runs away across Long Lane (with the island refuge in the centre) to your right; and that's where we're heading, so cross again and walk up past the older shops and new flats to the next corner, where sits the **4 Royal Oak**. This pub is housed in a mid-Victorian building, which was purchased and re-styled by Harveys of Lewes in 1997, their first London tied house, and still one of only two. The restoration has been done very well, in a robustly traditional style, even down to the two bars being separated by a parody of an off-sales counter. That said, as we go to print, there are rumours that Harveys are gearing up for a modernising refit. My view is that

they would be mad and bad to vandalise this well-loved local which in the eyes of many of its loyal regulars has an interior close to pub perfection. Expect a good range of Harveys fine ales here, including seasonals, with the odd guest. Prices both for food and for beer have, in relative terms, steadily crept up, but it's still a must-do pub and a regular winner of CAMRA awards.

**Southwark Cathedral and the Shard**

**The George is London's last remaining galleried coaching inn**

Return to cross Long Lane and reach Borough High Street, this time walking beyond the church down towards London Bridge. If you're planning to take in **8** **Simon the Tanner** (see box), turn right down Long Lane instead. Borough High Street was used as a primary route into the City of London from the south for over 2,000 years and the place still retains some of its former character. The further part of the High Street, beyond the Union Street junction, is the more atmospheric, with high buildings, narrow frontages and deep plots, some with rear yards, a land-use pattern adopted by the old coaching inns that once lined Borough High Street. Many of the yards are still in existence today, including King's Head Yard, White Hart Yard and George Inn Yard, which all survive in name if not form. Also noteworthy (at No. 67, on the right, just beyond the George), is the frontage proclaiming WH & H Le May's

## SIMON THE TANNER

From Long Lane, it's almost half a mile down the road towards Bermondsey to reach Simon the Tanner. Re-opened after a period of dereliction in 2011, it commemorates the leather trade in its name. The four handpumps offer an excellent and changing menu with beers from some of London's best micros often available while there's a keykeg line of similarly high quality. This listed building is a great addition to the round if you have the time and the stamina, it's just a bit geographically challenged. Even the (C10) bus doesn't help much, although on the way back the stop is closer.

Hop Factors, a reminder of this area's long association with the Kentish hop trade.

If you're a Londoner, chances are you'll know of the **5 George**, London's only surviving galleried coaching inn. If you haven't seen it, it's a must – down the alley at No. 77. The George is only a vestige of its former self, as two sides of this old inn were demolished when the Great Northern Railway was built, and what remains is the south wing. This was not the first time it had been tampered with, as it was rebuilt in 1676 after a devastating fire swept through Southwark. The room at the west end of the building, as one enters the courtyard, is the real jewel, with panelling, fireplace and plain bench seating of considerable antiquity. Note the glazed servery with now rare examples of old fashioned 'cash register'-style handpumps. The

**Glazed tilework at the Southwark Tavern**

ground floor rooms to the east were not originally pub rooms and have, along with the modern bar, been more recently brought into use. The panelled upstairs rooms are also well worth a look. The George is owned by the National Trust and leased to Greene King, so it's beers from the GK stable (including the pub's house ale) on most of the handpumps, although the rare GK XX Mild has been seen here and they usually have a guest as well as some interesting bottles.

Just beyond the George on Borough High Street there's a road junction where Southwark Street joins from the left. Cross the two roads here to find yourself on the busy corner of Stoney Street at the edge, once more, of Borough Market. Look behind you and you'll get a decent view of the Shard, the striking new 95-storey office block that rises above London Bridge station. The last two pubs on this tour are almost adjacent here. The first, on the corner, is the

**6 Southwark Tavern**. It's always been an attractive building with its glazed tilework in favour of the long-defunct Meux brewery, along with leaded windows, hop motifs and a bit of surviving stained glass. Of late the place has been made over internally, but tastefully, and now offers a wide range of beers: Sharp's Doom Bar is a regular but there are usually four interesting guests sourced nationally alongside there's a lengthy list of beers on keg, and a bottled list featuring a decent range of Belgian beers. Besides the main bar there's an atmospheric basement with some small cubicles, well worth looking at.

A few yards further down Southwark Street is the remarkable Hop Exchange. Built in 1867, it provided a single market centre for hop dealers, in much the same way there was a Coal Exchange, Metal Exchange and a Stock Exchange. This is now the only survivor, and even here the building has lost a couple of floors and suffered the ignominy of being

**Inside the Hop Exchange, also home to the Sheaf**

converted into a corporate hospitality suite and offices; but it's still highly impressive, both the external façade and the great hall within. But it's the cellar that will be of greatest interest at this particular time, for here is to be found the ⑦ **Sheaf**. Until a few years ago it was the Wheatsheaf, but following the re-opening of the original Young's Wheatsheaf (minus all its internal features of heritage interest) around the corner in Stoney Street, a name change by

one or the other looked to be on the cards. The Sheaf is accessed down some steep stairs but, thanks to the cast iron supports and barrelled brick roof, retains plenty of original character (unlike its reopened competitor). Part of the Red Car pub group, the Sheaf offers up to 10 beers, with plenty of changing guests supporting (ironically) Young's Bitter, and Fuller's London Pride. With rare (for London) beers appearing here at times it's a good call for beer tickers too. The house beer is brewed by Nethergate. Check the website news section for the current and forthcoming beer menu, not to mention the extensive food menu which stretches from sandwiches to full plates.

London Bridge station is close by. Just retrace your steps, pass the Southwark Tavern, crossing Stoney Street, and the station is on the right.

## PUB INFORMATION

**1 RAKE**
14 Winchester Walk, SE1 9AG
020 7407 0557 • www.utobeer.co.uk/aboutus_rake.html
**Opening hours:** 12 (11 Fri; 10 Sat)-11; 12-8 Sun

**2 MARKET PORTER**
9 Stoney Street, SE1 9AA
020 7407 2495 • www.markettaverns.co.uk/the_market_porter.html
**Opening hours:** 6-8.30, 11-11; 12-11 Sat; 12-10.30 Sun

**3 LORD CLYDE**
27 Clennam Street, SE1 1ER
020 7407 3397 • www.lordclyde.com
**Opening hours:** 11 (12 Sat)-11; 12-6 Sun

**4 ROYAL OAK**
44 Tabard Street, SE1 4JU
020 7357 7173 • www.harveys.org.uk/pubs/the-royal-oak-london
**Opening hours:** 11 (12 Sat)-11; 12-9 Sun

**5 GEORGE**
George Inn Yard, 77 Borough High Street, SE1 1NH
020 7407 2056 • www.george-southwark.co.uk
**Opening hours:** 11-11

**6 SOUTHWARK TAVERN**
22 Southwark Street, SE1 1TU
020 7403 0257 • www.thesouthwarktavern.co.uk
**Opening hours:** 11-midnight (1am Thu & Fri); 10-1am Sat; 12-midnight Sun

**7 SHEAF**
24 Southwark Street, SE1 1TY
020 7407 9934 • www.redcarpubs.com/The-Wheatsheaf
**Opening hours:** 11-11 (midnight Fri); 12-midnight Sat; 12-10.30 Sun

**Try also:**

**8 SIMON THE TANNER**
231 Long Lane, SE1 4PR
020 7357 8740 • simonthetanner.co.uk
**Opening hours:** 12 (5 Mon)-11; 12-10.30 Sun

# Outer London

# Kentish Town locals

This is a short but rewarding ramble in a varied area between Camden to the south and Highgate to the north. It's not an area for tourist sights, but it's easily accessible by train, and nearby are the contrasting attractions of Hampstead Heath and Camden Town. If you're keen to stretch your legs before tackling the pubs then take the Underground, and a map, to Hampstead (or the Overground to Hampstead Heath) and enjoy a stroll across the Heath and Parliament Hill Fields, with fine views across London. This will bring you out at Gospel Oak and the Southampton Arms, from where you can reverse the route. The pubs continue to improve here as in other parts of the city, and this route has the advantage of being compact, that's to say, less walking and more pub time!

▶ **Start/finish:** ⇌ ⊖ Kentish Town; or ⊖ Gospel Oak

▶ **Distance:** 1.7 miles (2.7 km)

▶ **Access:** Northern Line, Barnet branch; Thameslink rail services from Luton, St Albans, St Pancras, London Bridge and Croydon

▶ **Key attractions:** Hampstead Heath & Parliament Hill Fields; Camden Lock and market (1 mile)

▶ **THE PUBS:** Pineapple; Junction Tavern; Southampton Arms; Bull & Last; Bull & Gate. Try also: Assembly House

▶ **Timing tips:** The Junction Tavern doesn't open until 5pm in the week so plan accordingly if you're visiting Monday to Thursday. That said, the excellent Southampton Arms gets very busy indeed in the evenings so there's much to be said for an early start!

**View over London from Parliament Hill**

Starting at Kentish Town station, on both the Thameslink and Northern Line, it's hard to miss the **6** **Assembly House**, as it dominates the road junction by the station with its impressive frontage. This pub is an optional extra primarily for its interior architecture, for despite some pretty aggressive stripping out over the years, there's enough of the former grandeur of this late Victorian drinking palace remaining to testify to its former glories. The best bits today, aside from the bar-back with its decorated glazing, are undoubtedly at the far right-hand end, en route to the former billiard room at the rear. The skylight over the billiard room remains and the surviving glass, French embossed and cut, is some of the best you'll find anywhere in London. This was the work of local firm William James and is a joy to behold. Sadly most of the etched glass on the exterior windows has been lost, a probable mixture of brewery vandalism and past negligence by the local council. Owners Greene King have attempted to reposition the pub in line with the area's gentrification but this is counterbalanced by the large TV screens. Beer-wise they offer up to three guests as well as their in-house range of Greene King beers, so you may pick up something interesting if you pop in.

Whether or not you visit the Assembly House, walk eastwards along Leighton Road and take the first turning left into Leverton Street. Five minutes' walk up here brings us to one of Kentish Town's success stories. A vigorous local campaign in 2001–2 resulted in the listing

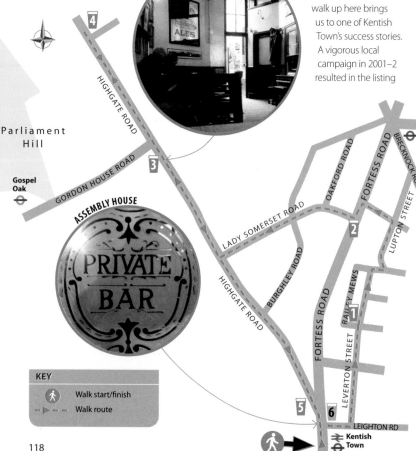

JUNCTION TAVERN

**KEY**

Walk start/finish

Walk route

of the **1 Pineapple** and the defeat of an application to turn it into flats. It's easy to see why local people hold the place in such high regard. Inside there is a central servery surrounded by a horseshoe-shaped drinking area, with a couple of small lobbies en route to a pleasant conservatory and garden at their rear. Look out for the impressive mid-Victorian bar-back with etched and gilded mirror work and two old Bass mirrors on the pub walls. Meanwhile, behind the unpretentious benches, there is

**Bar back at the Pineapple**

some old panelling. This all makes for a very relaxed ambience. Even though it's just a short distance away, this area feels like a different world from the hurly burly of Kentish Town and the Assembly House. Save the *Guardian* crossword until you get here! The beer range has expanded to five, with Sharp's Doom Bar being the regular. The guests are usually from the London area and change regularly in this free house. Two beer festivals a year include one at Easter. The Pineapple was voted local CAMRA Pub of the Year for 2012.

Walk further up Leverton Street and on through the traffic-free area on Lupton Street ahead before turning next left into Ravelly Street, which leads us onto Fortess Road. Just down to the left on the opposite side is the next pub, the **2 Junction Tavern**. At first glance this looks like another casualty of the gastrophication of our pub heritage, and without a doubt it's food and wine that dominate; but enter through the side door and you come into an attractive rear drinking area with lots of wood and, more importantly, an interesting range of beers. On the four handpumps Adnams Broadside and Sharp's Doom Bar are the regular offerings with Battersea micro Sambrook's a frequent presence among the guest list dominated by small London and regional breweries. The pub holds beer festivals in late May and October. The backyard has been converted into a

conservatory and a small but very attractive garden. Be warned, during the week (Monday–Thursday) the pub is only open from 5pm.

Leaving the Junction, it's again a short walk to the next stop. Cut down Lady Somerset Road to the Highgate Road and turn right. Just past the railway bridge look out for the distinctive sign of the **3 Southampton Arms**. Since opening in late 2009 in its current incarnation, this honest unpretentious pub has made a tremendous impression on the London beer scene. It's a tiny pub stripped back to the basic elements of good beer and cider, and simple pub food (Scotch eggs, scratchings, sausage rolls, pork pies, etc); but with friendly, efficient and knowledgeable staff serving one of the best beer selections you'll find in London, it's little surprise it gets so busy. There are at least 10 ales on tap and almost as many ciders, and all of them from independent brewers around the UK; the pub boasts that it doesn't serve any mass-produced fare from the big breweries. The house beer is from Howling Hops, based at the Southampton's sister pub, the Cock in Hackney. With a vintage record player and a real fire for those winter nights, what's not to like? Of all the numerous new alehouses springing up around London, this one is still one of the very best. But, be warned, take cash, they won't appreciate you waving plastic at them in here!

**Southampton Arms**

From the Southampton, continue up the road, past the traffic lights where you should switch sides, to the **4 Bull & Last**. In total contrast to the Southampton, this old corner pub has undergone the more typical North London gastrophication, albeit tasteful, and majors on a serious (and pricey) food menu. The website assures us that the 'young and passionate team' which I noted in the last edition are still here, although the place is a bit more dog and child-friendly than some of us old traditionalists might feel comfortable with. That said it's still worth a visit on account of a changing and interesting beer menu with London micros playing a prominent role; in fact they have had mini-seasons of individual breweries such as London Fields and Redemption of late.

Now, the last stop is right back in the thick of Kentish Town, so you might wish to wait for the frequent 214 to take you back down the hill. Walking, allow ten minutes at least to reach the impressive exterior elevation of the **5 Bull & Gate** on the right just before the road junction, the Assembly House and the station.

 **LINK TO WALK 18**

Bus 214 from outside the Southampton Arms takes you to Highgate village in about five minutes for Walk 18.

Once a coaching inn and apparently named the Boulogne Gate after Henry VIII's victory in France in 1544, the Bull & Gate has been for long a rather down-at-heel building of faded glories. Now however it has been acquired by Young's who have invested in a heavy refurbishment; but this one has I think worked well, and the place has been spruced up whilst enhancing some of the remaining interior heritage. Foremost here is the splendid cut glass on the bar back. The rear room, originally a billiard hall which so many London pubs had as a fixture in the late Victorian period, and which later became a live music venue, is now a smart restaurant. The beer range is as you would expect primarily confined to the Young's/Wells stable

Kentish Town station is just 100 yards away beyond the Assembly House (right upon exit).

## PUB INFORMATION

 **PINEAPPLE**
51 Leverton Street, NW5 2NX
020 7284 4631
**Opening hours:** 12-11 (midnight Fri & Sat);
12-10.30 Sun

**2 JUNCTION TAVERN**
101 Fortress Road, NW5 1AG
020 7485 9400 • www.junctiontavern.co.uk
**Opening hours:** 5-11; 12-midnight Fri & Sat;
12-11 Sun

**3 SOUTHAMPTON ARMS**
139 Highgate Road, NW5 1LE
www.thesouthamptonarms.co.uk
**Opening hours:** 12-midnight

**4 BULL & LAST**
168 Highgate Road, NW5 1QS
020 7267 3641 • www.thebullandlast.co.uk
**Opening hours:** 12-11 (midnight Fri & Sat);
12-10.30 Sun

**5 BULL & GATE**
389 Kentish Town Road, NW5 2TJ
020 3437 0905 • www.bullandgatenw5.co.uk
**Opening hours:** 11-11 (midnight Thu-Sat); 12-10.30 Sun

Try also:

 **ASSEMBLY HOUSE**
292 Kentish Town Road, NW5 2TG
020 7209 0038 • www.metropolitanpubcompany.
com/our-pubs/the-assembly-house
**Opening hours:** 12-11 (midnight Fri & Sat);
12-10.30 Sun

# A hilltop tour of Highgate

**WALK 18**

Deservedly one of London's best-loved urban villages, Highgate commands a hilltop site offering views across London. Historically, Highgate adjoined the Bishop of London's hunting estate. The Gatehouse pub in the centre of the village today marks the site of the tollhouse where the road from London entered his land. In later centuries Highgate was associated with highwayman Dick Turpin, and of course is also renowned for its atmospheric Victorian cemetery, in which Karl Marx is buried. The walk across the Heath from Hampstead is a highly recommended way to start this pub walk around Highgate; but a fine alternative is the Parkland Walk (and its Northern Heights Walk extension, part of the Capital Ring), which, using old rail lines, converges on Highgate Underground station from Finsbury Park, and from Alexandra Palace via Queen's Wood and Highgate Wood.

- **Start:** ⊖ Hampstead then walk via Hampstead Heath or ⊖ Archway and bus via ⇌ Highgate Hill

- **Finish:** ⊖ Highgate

- **Distance:** 1 mile (1.6 km)

- **Access:** Northern Line, to ⊖ Hampstead. Also from ⇌⊖ Finsbury Park via Parkland walk, or ⇌ Alexandra Palace via Capital Ring Walk

- **Key attractions:** Highgate village and cemetery; Hampstead Heath; Parkland Walk (www.parkland-walk.org.uk); Highgate & Queen's Woods; Waterlow Park; Kenwood House

- **THE PUBS:** Flask; Prince of Wales; Duke's Head; Gatehouse; Bull; Wrestlers

- **Timing tip:** If you're visiting on a weekday, which has some advantages, be aware that the Wrestlers does not open until 4.30pm. A leisurely lunchtime in the village and leaving this pub until last should do the trick!

**Highgate Cemetery**

**The front entrance of the Prince of Wales**

As mentioned above there are fine walks converging on the village from several directions, but whether you arrive on foot, or by bus, bike or car, make your way to the pretty green between Highgate West Hill and The Grove, immediately south west of the village centre. This is the way you'll approach the village if you've walked over the Heath. There are some fine buildings on both sides, something Highgate is famed for, and jealously guarded by its active Civic Society. Its website (www.highgatesociety.

**The Flask**

com) also gives details of a circular walk around Hampstead and Highgate taking in Kenwood House, Highgate Cemetery and Waterlow Park.

At a focal point of the green, by the fork in the roads, the 🍺 **Flask** is a bit of a Highgate institution. It's easy to see that the pub is an amalgamation of two buildings, both of which have undergone great alteration. The older, three-storey part is 18th century, and retains the former servery with its glazed sashes. The left-hand part is a later conversion of a former outbuilding. New owners Fuller's have let the vegetation run amok outside so it's more difficult to appreciate the exterior: let's hope they adopt a similar 'hands off' policy inside lest what remains of the pub's rambling character is not lost as a result of any further 'improvements' and tarting up. The garden/patio outside is agreeable enough if not too busy, but the place gets packed at times. Food is the focus, but

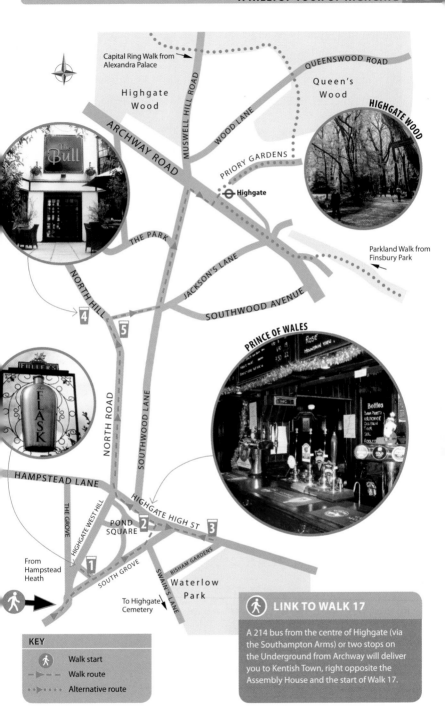

Capital Ring Walk from
Alexandra Palace →

Highgate
Wood

QUEENSWOOD ROAD

Queen's
Wood

HIGHGATE WOOD

MUSWELL HILL ROAD

ARCHWAY ROAD

WOOD LANE

PRIORY GARDENS

The Bull

Highgate

THE PARK

JACKSON'S LANE

Parkland Walk from
Finsbury Park

NORTH HILL

SOUTHWOOD AVENUE

**4**

**5**

PRINCE OF WALES

FULLERS

FLASK

NORTH ROAD

SOUTHWOOD LANE

HAMPSTEAD LANE

HIGHGATE HIGH ST

THE GROVE

HIGHGATE WEST HILL

POND
SQUARE

**2**

**3**

BISHAM GARDENS

From
Hampstead
Heath

**1**

SOUTH GROVE

SWAIN'S LANE

Waterlow
Park

To Highgate
Cemetery

### 🚶 LINK TO WALK 17

A 214 bus from the centre of Highgate (via
the Southampton Arms) or two stops on
the Underground from Archway will deliver
you to Kentish Town, right opposite the
Assembly House and the start of Walk 17.

**KEY**

🚶 Walk start

➡ Walk route

•▶•▶• Alternative route

**The rear entrance of the Prince of Wales leads on to Pond Square**

a wide range of Fuller's beers is available, including Chiswick Bitter, ESB and a seasonal; and there's a non-Fuller's guest.

Now, from the Flask's front door bear left and follow South Grove past the bus stance, and you will see the rear of the **2 Prince of Wales** almost immediately. Either enter here, or walk around onto the High Street, maybe browsing some of the shops before entering via the front door. The Prince is a handsome brick building, certainly the most unspoilt pub in the village, with several distinct but interconnected drinking areas around a central servery. It's exactly the sort of villagey pub you'd expect in Highgate, with bookish locals hopefully plotting the overthrow of capitalism in one of the quiet corners. Adnams Bitter is the regular fixture here, along with three guests; on my last visit they had two from

**Handpumps at the Duke's Head**

North London micro Redemption. The Thai kitchen provides the food, whilst there's an all-day Sunday roast.

Now leaving the pub by the front door, head to your right down the High Street to visit Highgate's newest (and arguably best) ale attraction. The **3 Duke's Head** is across the street and some 100 yards further down. Don't let the rather austere exterior nor the gloomy decor dissuade you at all, for this former coaching inn turned specialist beer house offers the finest range of cask beers in town. Local brewer Hammerton has a fairly permanent presence but on the remaining seven ale handpulls expect to find an excellent range of changing beers sourced from some of the country's best micros, including Weird Beard, Siren, Blue Sky and Magic Rock. There are two real ciders as well, and as many craft

**Cafe in Highgate Woods**

**Façade of the High Point apartment block**

'keg' beers. The long narrow space has limited seating and unfortunately there's no garden, only the side alley, if it gets very busy. Another reason to do a midweek tour if you can.

It's a hard place to leave, but when the time comes to move on, retrace your steps up the hill to the junction at the top, where opposite Highgate School sits a very significant Highgate landmark, the **4 Gatehouse**. The name refers to a former tollgate and archway over the road, for this was the former boundary between Middlesex and London. The earliest mention of the Gatehouse in licensing records is as early as 1670, and amongst the former glitterati who have drunk here were Byron, Dickens and George Cruickshank. The mock-Tudor style of the pub we see today goes back to the early 20th century. The upstairs was previously used as a courtroom, but now it's a very successful fringe theatre. To top it all there is a resident lady ghost! The pub has very recently been acquired by the Urban Pubs & Bars chain and tastefully stripped of its former Wetherspoon raiment. Expect at least three, and up to five, changing cask ales sourced from across the country, along with rather more upmarket food than heretofore.

Leaving the Gatehouse, cross the road to your left and walk along North Road, to the north of the pub, with the school opposite. It's a few minutes' walk along the road to reach the last two pubs on this tour, and they stand almost opposite each other. Pass the Wrestlers

on the right hand side, opposite the listed 1930s High Point apartment block, to reach the **5 Bull** a little beyond. This formal-looking house offers a warmer welcome for drinkers than the painfully smart décor and (to the left on entry) the upmarket dining area might suggest. It's the original home of the London Brewing Company, and although the new brewhouse has been relocated to the pub's sister establishment, the Bohemia at North Finchley, a fine range of at least four well-kept London Brewing ales are available. There may be the occasional guest, and real cider. In addition there are several keg taps serving a good list of both regular and guest beers, together with some Belgian bottles.

**The Bull**

And finally, now for something slightly more traditional. Beyond the Bull, North Road becomes North Hill. Architecture lovers may enjoy a detour along this street and back, since it's regarded as one of the best examples of architectural diversity in London. With or without this detour, and having checked your watch and the opening times, you can safely set off for the last pub, the

The Wrestlers

**6 Wrestlers**, almost opposite the Bull. It has stood on this site since 1547, although the current building dates to 1921. The star of the show is the atmospheric interior with its dark panelling and impressive fireplace, which evidently survived the 1920s rebuild. You can learn for yourself about the curious ancient ceremony of 'swearing on the horns', which apparently goes back to 1623, for the horns in question, and the procedure, are there above the fireplace. The beer menu has improved significantly since the first edition of this guide: London Pride and St Austell Tribute are the regulars, and they're joined by two changing guests with a local flavour. Supporting the cask ales are several 'craft' beers such as the hoppy and refreshing Brooklyn Lager and Chicago's Goose Island IPA. If you're finishing off here and looking

to eat, there's a very extensive menu including Sunday roasts, again available on the pub website.

By now you will be replete and probably ready for a train home! Simply turn down the alley, Park Walk, immediately to the side of the pub, and on reaching the road at the bottom, turn sharp left and follow down the short distance to the Archway Road, where Highgate Underground station (on the Northern Line) is just to your right. If you prefer a bus, the 143 outside the pub will take you down to Archway.

**The Wrestlers**

## PUB INFORMATION

**1 FLASK**
77 Highgate West Hill, Highgate, N6 6BU
020 8348 7346 • www.theflaskhighgate.com
**Opening hours:** 12-11; 12-10.30 Sun

**2 PRINCE OF WALES**
53 Highgate High Street, Highgate, N6 5JX
020 8340 0445
**Opening hours:** 12-11 (midnight Fri & Sat)

**3 DUKE'S HEAD**
16 Highgate High Street, Highgate, N6 5JG
020 8341 1310 • www.thedukesheadhighgate.co.uk
**Opening hours:** 12-midnight (1am Thu-Sat);
12-11.30 Sun

**4 GATEHOUSE**
1 North Road, Highgate, N6 4BD
020 8340 8054 • thegatehousen6.com
**Opening hours:** 11-11 (midnight Fri & Sat);
11-10.30 Sun

**5 BULL**
13 North Hill, Highgate, N6 4AB
020 8341 0510
thebullhighgate.co.uk
**Opening hours:** 12-11 (midnight Fri); 9.30am-
midnight Sat; 9.30am-11 Sun

**6 WRESTLERS**
98 North Road, Highgate, N6 4AA
020 8340 4297 • thewrestlershighgate.com
**Opening hours:** 4.30-midnight (1am Fri); 12-1am
Sat; 12-11 Sun

# A North London 'inside story'

One of CAMRA's campaigning priorities is pub heritage, which is always under threat. In London the enthusiastic members of the CAMRA London Pubs Group, led tirelessly by Jane Jephcote, have worked hard to research, promote and celebrate this heritage. Jane is the co-author of *London Heritage Pubs: An Inside Story* (CAMRA, 2008), the most authoritative and detailed publication on the subject; and she has kindly allowed me to make use of her research in this walk. This particular route, taking in an area of Stoke Newington and Dalston, has the added advantage that all of the pubs offer a very decent pint. The route given here starts in Stoke Newington and works south towards the Regent's Canal; but, of course, if you wish to finish in the Jolly Butchers for a protracted sampling of its lengthy beer menu, there's nothing to prevent you tackling the route in the other direction.

▶ **Start:** ⇌ Stoke Newington

▶ **Finish:** ⟶ Dalston Junction/Dalston Kingsland

▶ **Distance:** 3 miles (4.8 km); 4.5 miles (7.2 km) including Stag's Head

▶ **Access:** From ⇌ London Liverpool Street, or by London Overground services to Dalston Junction/Kingsland then northbound buses on A10

▶ **Key attractions:** Exterior and interior pub architecture; Abney Park Cemetery; Clissold Park; Metropolitan Benefit Society Almshouses; Balls Pond Road

▶ **THE PUBS:** Jolly Butchers; Rochester Castle; Rose & Crown; Lord Clyde; Scolt Head; Duke of Wellington. Try also: Stag's Head

▶ **Timing tip:** This is one for a weekend or a summer afternoon/evening, owing to the late (4pm) weekday opening of both the Jolly Butchers and the Duke of Wellington.

**Metropolitan Benefit Society Almshouses**

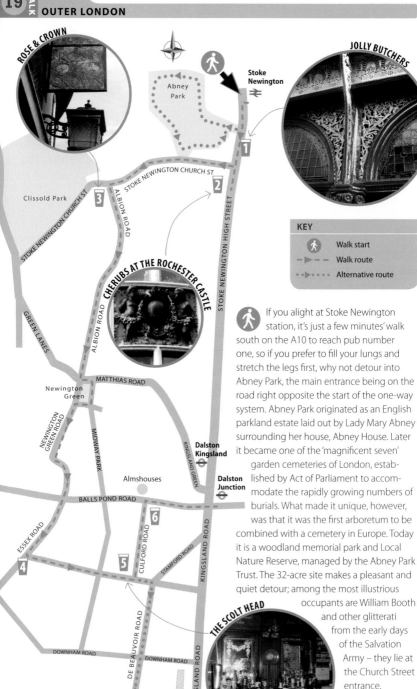

ROSE & CROWN

JOLLY BUTCHERS

Abney Park

Stoke Newington

STOKE NEWINGTON CHURCH ST

Clissold Park

STOKE NEWINGTON HIGH STREET

ALBION ROAD

STOKE NEWINGTON CHURCH ST

GREEN LANES

CHERUBS AT THE ROCHESTER CASTLE

**KEY**

🚶 Walk start

Walk route

Alternative route

MATTHIAS ROAD

Newington Green

NEWINGTON GREEN ROAD

MIDWAY PARK

Dalston Kingsland

KINGSLAND GREEN

Dalston Junction

Almshouses

BALLS POND ROAD

ESSEX ROAD

CULFORD ROAD

STAMFORD ROAD

KINGSLAND ROAD

4

5

6

7

3

2

1

DOWNHAM ROAD

DE BEAUVOIR ROAD

DOWNHAM ROAD

KINGSLAND ROAD

THE SCOLT HEAD

Regent's Canal

ORSMAN ROAD

If you alight at Stoke Newington station, it's just a few minutes' walk south on the A10 to reach pub number one, so if you prefer to fill your lungs and stretch the legs first, why not detour into Abney Park, the main entrance being on the road right opposite the start of the one-way system. Abney Park originated as an English parkland estate laid out by Lady Mary Abney surrounding her house, Abney House. Later it became one of the 'magnificent seven' garden cemeteries of London, established by Act of Parliament to accommodate the rapidly growing numbers of burials. What made it unique, however, was that it was the first arboretum to be combined with a cemetery in Europe. Today it is a woodland memorial park and Local Nature Reserve, managed by the Abney Park Trust. The 32-acre site makes a pleasant and quiet detour; among the most illustrious occupants are William Booth and other glitterati from the early days of the Salvation Army – they lie at the Church Street entrance.

It's only a short stride further down

**The Jolly Butchers**

the road to the **1 Jolly Butchers**. You won't miss the place with its garish red paint job, but most of the heritage interest is on the exterior. The mid-19th-century corner pub has retained its fine half-moon windows, pierced spandrels and cast iron pillars, as well as some impressive iron brackets. The Jolly Butchers, modestly billing itself as 'North London's premier real ale, cider and craft beer house' has reverted to what was once its old name after a pretty grim interregnum. The interior has been stripped out and replaced with… well, not a fat lot, in keeping with the modern style. It also gets very busy with the hip Stoke Newington set, whose cheery chatter reverberates off all the hard surfaces. But, to be fair, there's a great beer list with some of Britain's best breweries showcased regularly here on the six handpumps; a further three pumps offer ciders and parries. There's also an extensive and appealing array of craft-keg 'world beers' on the even more numerous keg founts. Check the 'featured breweries' section of the website for a flavour of what to expect. In short, a temple of great beer, but far from the most comfortable or intimate place to enjoy them.

Walk a bit further down onto Stoke Newington High Street, beyond the junction with Church Street opposite,

and look out for the imposing frontage of the next pub, across the street at No. 143. Whereas the Jolly Butchers is basically a spruced-up, humble, street-corner boozer, the **2 Rochester Castle** is something far grander, architecturally at least, and it's worth lingering for a couple of minutes on the other side of the street to admire the

**The grand façade of the Rochester Castle**

elevation. Despite significant meddling, this late-Victorian pub still presents a striking appearance. The garlanded cupids frolicking around a cartouche between the first- and second-floor bays are particularly attractive, but down at ground-floor level, having crossed the street in one piece, there are some quality columns and tilework to admire. Inside, Wetherspoon have retained the glazed tilework and pilasters, although some of the figurative bordered panels depicting the Seasons had been hidden behind fruit machines when I was there. The bar counter has been shifted to one side and all the one-time partitions (note three sets of former doors) have of course gone. Expect the usual JDW fare of regulars and guests on the handpumps.

Return north to the junction with Church Street and head down here, maybe pausing briefly to admire the attractive exterior (including a pretty wrought iron panel above the door) at the Three Crowns opposite. You could take a bus (73, 393 or 476) for a couple of stops from here, but it's not a bad walk,

**The curving frontage of the Rose & Crown**

and there's a chance to peek into Abney Park again and look at William Booth's grave by the entrance. Either way, when you arrive at the striking Stoke Newington Town Hall – a very impressive Art Deco pile at the junction with Albion Road – look across the street to another impressive building, the **3** **Rose & Crown**. Running elegantly around the corner, this Truman's pub, dating to the mid 1930s, has retained a great deal of original fittings and is one of the highlights of this walk in terms of pub heritage. The five external doorways around the sweep of the façade show the former internal divisions, whilst the clear glazed 'shop window' style on the corner itself actually dates back to the days of the off-sales department, and would have been used to display goods to take away. Note the metal pub signs and lamps outside.

Moving inside, the pub has kept much of its 1930s layout since the screens that once would have divided the various rooms survive in their upper parts. The wood-panelled interior, with its gilded lettering above head height, is typical of the classic Truman's interwar style; whilst the bar counter with its doors to access the beer engines is also original. Some pretty lampshades and the ceiling Vitrolite panels are particularly remarkable survivors, and a key reason for it's recent listing at Grade II by the local council. There are now four handpumps serving a couple of Caledonian beers (including their popular Deuchars IPA), St Austell Tribute and Adnams Southwold Bitter. Food is served throughout most of the day, with roasts on Sunday.

Leaving the pub, Clissold Park is just across the street to the left – if you are looking for a halfway point rest from the rigours of the schedule.

The next pub stop is quite a walk to the south, so I would recommend jumping on a bus: pop back across the road to the bus stop opposite the Town Hall and catch a southbound 73 or 476. It's about eight stops. Alight at Northchurch Road, just a few yards beyond the **4** **Lord Clyde**. (If you decide to walk it, check your map and A to Z, and

**The Lord Clyde**

ensure you take the right route when you get to Newington Green.)

From a pub heritage viewpoint the Clyde is another of the best destinations on this walk, having now reverted to its former name and traditions after a period as Kenrick's bar. Note the unfinished brick courses above the single-storey left-hand end of the pub: according to the licensee, this could be where plans to resume the completion of the remodelled pub after the Second World War were aborted, owing presumably to lack of resources. Inside, the fittings are pure interwar, with a separate public bar to the left, the remains of an off-sales counter between this and the main room (the doorway survives too); the main room would once have been further subdivided, evidenced by the different extent of the old spittoon either side of the curved corner. Also surviving are the good bar counter and bar-back, the latter a rather attractive affair carrying the name of Charrington's, the once-widespread purveyor of bland beer.

On the beer and food front, the place is a metaphor for the transformation of many formerly dismal North London boozers into attractive destinations for the new breed of discerning customer. Expect the ales here to be well kept: Harveys Sussex is a regular here supported by two rotating guests with a strong emphasis on North London micros such as Hackney and Redemption. The food has attracted favourable reviews.

Walk along Englefield Road (on the right, immediately outside the Clyde) and cross the Southgate Road and into the district of De Beauvoir Town. Named after a 19th-century local landowner, there are some handsome Victorian villas in the part you're walking through, which is now a Conservation Area. In little more than five minutes you'll reach the penultimate destination on this tour, the **5** **Scolt Head**, a striking three-storey building occupying a prominent plot. It was formerly the Sussex Arms but the new owners apparently have a predilection for the Norfolk coast, where Scolt Head Island is found. At least they didn't choose 'Fox & Newt' or something similar! Original fittings here are more sparse than at the previous two pubs but the pretty bar-back survives, and the room around to the left may once have been a billiard room. The spacious interior does, however, have a homely, pubby atmosphere, with an attractive open fire (note the painting of the eponymous island above the mantel) and a variety of seating opportunities. It's a bit of a foodie joint but there are three permanent ales, at present Greene King IPA, Truman's Runner and Crouch Vale's excellent Brewer's Gold. There's also a guest beer tap with Brixton Brewery featuring regularly.

**The Scolt Head**

**A little etched glasswork survives inside the Duke of Wellington**

At this point, if you wish to take in the Stag's Head, you need to continue on your former eastward journey along Englefield Road to the next junction, and turn right down De Beauvoir Road. Follow it down, admiring the pretty villas, and crossing the Regent's Canal into a more working-class area, take the first left into Orsman Road. The **7** **Stag's Head** offers a couple of ales from national brewers like Greene King and Charles Wells but has a lot of surviving internal features from its Truman's days, notably a well-preserved off-sales counter between the public and saloon bars. To finish at Dalston, return the way you came, back to the Scolt Head.

From the Scolt Head, a very short walk up the Culford Road to the north will lead you to the last stop, the **6** **Duke of Wellington**, on the Balls Pond Road right opposite the impressive Victorian Metropolitan Benefit Society's Almshouses. As to the pub, it's another one to revert to its old name following a refit and slight repositioning to attract the new clientele of the area. It has retained the surviving bits of its Victorian past, notably some cut and etched glass. The screen that runs across the servery is a pleasing feature, whether original or not; and the bar counter is solidly attractive. In keeping with the high standards of beer quality and choice on this round, the Duke offers a very tempting range of ales, five on tap (Sambrook's Wandle always on, alongside four interesting guests from the SIBA list) and some interesting bottled beers (Kernel, Bristol Beer Factory, etc.) in complement. You'll be able to finish the tour with food (including Sunday roasts) if you wish.

It's a few minutes' stroll to the right down the Balls Pond Road to Dalston Junction/Kingsland for trains and buses.

## PUB INFORMATION

**1** **JOLLY BUTCHERS**
204 Stoke Newington High Street, N16 7HU
020 7241 2185 • jollybutchers.co.uk
**Opening hours:** 4-midnight (1am Fri); 12-1am Sat;
12-11 Sun

**2** **ROCHESTER CASTLE**
143-145 Stoke Newington High Street, N16 0NY
020 7249 6016
**Opening hours:** 9am-midnight (1am Fri & Sat)

**3** **ROSE & CROWN**
199 Stoke Newington Church Street, N16 9ES
020 7923 3337 • roseandcrownn16.co.uk
**Opening hours:** 12-11 (midnight Fri & Sat); 12-10 Sun

**4** **LORD CLYDE**
340-342 Essex Road, N1 3PB
020 7288 9850 • thelordclyde.com
**Opening hours:** 12-midnight (11 Mon); 12-11 Sun

**5** **SCOLT HEAD**
107a Culford Road, N1 4HT
020 7254 3965 • www.thescolthead.co.uk
**Opening hours:** 12-midnight

**6** **DUKE OF WELLINGTON**
119 Balls Pond Road, N1 4BL
020 7275 7640 • thedukeofwellington.london
**Opening hours:** 4-midnight (1am Thu & Fri);
12-1am Sat; 12-11.30 Sun

Try also:

**7** **STAG'S HEAD**
55 Orsman Road, N1 5RA
020 7739 5186 • stagsheadhoxton.com
**Opening hours:** 12-11 (1am Fri & Sat); 12-midnight Sun

# To Homerton & Hackney across Victoria Park

**WALK 20**

One of the new hipster hangouts, the area east and north of Victoria Park was not much of a destination for the beer drinker until very recently. Now, however, this short walk, mostly within the borough of Hackney, reveals some excellent pubs with the now customary wide range of well-kept and interesting tipples to sample: more strong evidence of the shifting centre of gravity of the city. Culture vultures are well catered for, with the National Trust's 16th century Sutton House, right on the route, being a highlight. Another notable stop on the route is the Chesham Arms just a stone's throw from Sutton House, which re-opened in 2015 after a successful three year campaign by CAMRA and others to stop developers turning the pub into flats. Starting at Hackney Wick enables you to enjoy a stroll across Victoria Park at the start with an option of taking in a canalside walk by extending the distance just a little. The People's Park Tavern opens at midday.

- **Start:** ⇌ Hackney Wick via Stratford ⇌ ⇌ ⇌ ⇌

- **Finish:** ⇌ Hackney Central

- **Key attractions:** Victoria Park and Wellstreet Common; Sutton House (www.nationaltrust.org.uk/sutton-house-and-breakers-yard); St John-at-Hackney church and churchyard; Hackney art galleries

- **Distance:** 2.6 miles (4.2km)

- **PUBS:** Peoples Park Tavern; Kenton Arms; Adam & Eve; Chesnam Arms; Cock. Try also: Jackdaw & Star

- **Timing tips:** Sutton House is closed on Mondays and Tuesdays, and closes at 4.30pm on other days. However, don't start the walk too early if you want to get into the pubs! Several do not open their doors on weekdays until 4pm.

**Inside the Adam & Eve, Homerton**

At Hackney Wick station look for Wallis Road which runs west opposite the southbound exit from the station. The pedestrian bridge at the end of the street carries you across the de facto motorway of the A12 East Cross route and straight into Victoria Park at the Cadogan Gate. (If you prefer to take in the pleasant canalside walk along the Hertford Union and enter Victoria Park from the south, consult your A-Z and head to Rothbury Road from the station

where you can pick up the towpath. Enter the park at the lock about 220 yards after passing under the A12 and join the main route by the tennis courts.)

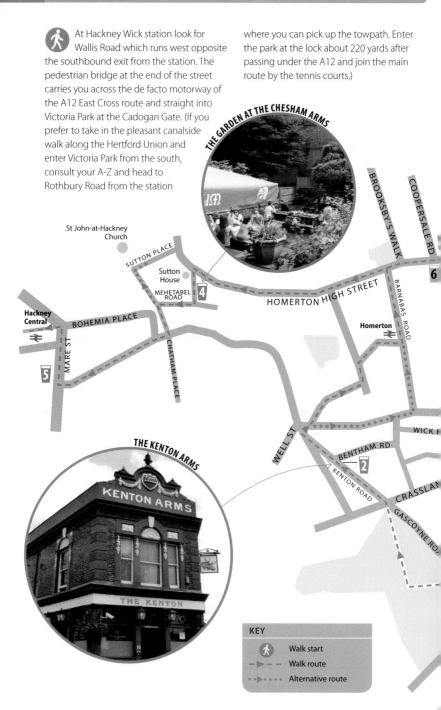

THE GARDEN AT THE CHESHAM ARMS

St John-at-Hackney Church

SUTTON PLACE

Sutton House

MEHETABEL ROAD

**4**

HOMERTON HIGH STREET

BROOKSBY'S WALK

COOPERSALE RD

BARNABAS ROAD

**6**

Hackney Central

BOHEMIA PLACE

MARE ST

CHATHAM PLACE

**5**

Homerton

THE KENTON ARMS

KENTON ARMS

THE KENTON

WELL ST

BENTHAM RD

KENTON ROAD

**2**

WICK R

CRASSLAN

GASCOYNE RO

**KEY**

👤 Walk start

▶ Walk route

▶ Alternative route

134

Go straight ahead at the Cadogan Gate into the park; Victoria Park is London's oldest public park, dating to 1845, and the 'People's Park' has been a vital recreational lung for the working-class areas surrounding it since its inception. This continuing popularity has seen it win the National Green Flag Peoples Choice vote as Britain's favourite park for 2014 and 2015. Read more about Victoria Park in the Regent's Canal II route on page 105. After some 250 yards, at a junction of paths, head slightly right, keeping the newly refurbished tennis courts on your right. If you're coming from the canal you'll be turning left after a similar distance to join the same path. Now it's but a few minutes' stroll until the garden of the **🍺 People's Park Tavern** comes into view on your right, just before you reach the gate onto Victoria Park Road.

**The cheerful, bright interior of the People's Park Tavern**

A striking building in a great location, this large pub has had two other names since its Firkin days in the eighties and nineties before settling on the current name in 2013. It's a cheerful and busy pub with all the cask ales brewed at the on-site microbrewery operated by the Laine brewing company. Expect a decent choice even if the seven handpumps are not all in use when you call. Check the pub's website under 'brewery'

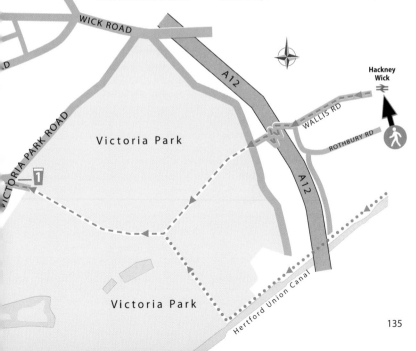

**Great choice of local ales at the Adam & Eve**

to get an idea of what could be in store. In addition, there are interesting keg offerings, a couple of real ciders, and an upstairs taproom which specialises in bottled beers from around the world. There's quite a range, and again the website is informative if you're planning ahead. Traditional pub food is served daily, and if the weather is favourable you might wish to make use of the large and attractive garden overlooking the park, which you saw on the way in.

The onward route heads across the road outside the pub via the crossing and onto Well Street Common. You could follow the edge of the common along Gascoyne Road but it's far nicer to head across the common. Take the right hand fork of the paths, then take a 90 degree right turn and walk towards the junction where Gascoyne Road meets the Cassland Road. Here head straight across into Kenton Road, and now it's but a short walk down the street to the far end where the **2 Kenton Arms** occupies a corner site. Another refurbished and reinvented old pub, the Kenton has a relaxed atmosphere in its comfortably shabby interior. The servery projects into the horseshoe-shaped public room, although there's also small rear room

and an attractive rear yard beyond. There are two cask ales, currently from Hackney and Truman's breweries, although this might have changed when you call in. There are keg and bottled beers in support; and food is available at most times: see the pub's website for the menu. The Kenton picked up the *Time Out* award for London's most loved pub in 2015, so the regulars at least must like it!

Leaving the Kenton, head downhill past the little triangular green to the road junction by the traffic lights. Take the residential road, Flanders Way, off to the right at about 45 degrees, keeping the tower block on your left. This street leads to a footpath skirting the fence of Berger Primary School, beyond which you bear left onto another path past the social club which leads out to Berger Road with Homerton station ahead. The name commemorates the Berger paint factory which was hereabouts until production moved to Chadwell Heath in stages from the 1930s. Walk up to the Barnabas Road junction just beyond the station. If it's dark and/or you prefer not to negotiate the footpaths, the alternative in consultation with your map is to bear sharp right on Wick Road at the lights and first left into Barnabas Road.

Bear left under the rail bridge and walk up to the Homerton High Street. The Homerton University Hospital a little to the north of here has its origins in a fever and smallpox hospital established in the district in the 1840s, and which saw the exodus of the middle classes and confirmed the status of Homerton as a poor and firmly working-class district. Cross the road and bear right for a short distance until you reach the **3** **Adam & Eve**. This huge old pub which was a rough east end boozer for many years and a favourite haunt of the Teddy boys 50 years ago, was given a sympathetic refurbishment in 2014 which has transformed the building and as well as the clientele. The food and drink has also, needless to say, gone upmarket from the lager years and that's why we're here. There's a lot to enjoy in the building for lovers of pub architecture, starting outside with the partially blue tiled façade and the large relief image of Adam and Eve themselves with the date 1915. Internally the terrazzo floor pattern gives some clues as to the former subdivisions of the pub, including a likely and long-gone off-sales corridor, while the old billiard room at the rear is now a dining area. Some stained glass screenwork survives, along with a fine ceiling. And so to the beer menu: an excellent selection of well-kept and changing cask ales on five handpumps, included two from the reliable Wokingham outfit Siren Craft brew on my recent visit. I can testify to the food, which is of high quality. Finally if you head out the rear to the attractive garden, look out for the pub's main curio, the L-shaped pool table!

Across the road from the Adam & Eve is the **6** **Jackdaw & Star**, worth a call if you have the time and the stamina, with two further must-see pubs still to visit. An attractive corner building has been revamped. The place has Five Points Pale Ale on as a regular at the moment with one or two supporting guests, on the cask ale front. The cheery interior is complemented by a rear garden.

It's a 500 yard walk westwards down the Homerton High Street towards our next stop. You can bus it: the 488 from Glyn Road (the stop is a little to the east of the Adam & Eve/ Jackdaw & Star) goes via Homerton Hospital; alight at City Academy. Just beyond the stop is Isabella Road on the left: but before walking down here, just beyond it's worth admiring the exterior of Sutton House, or better still, calling in, perhaps at a weekend when it should be possible to plan to visit the pubs and still arrive here in time to get in! Built in 1535 and the oldest residence in Hackney Borough it's a Tudor building at its core despite the Georgian exterior. It has had a colourful history, being occupied by squatters in the 1980s before being acquired by the National Trust and restored.

At the bottom of Isabella Road, and surrounded by handsome brick terraced houses of a similar age is the **4** **Chesham Arms**. Having been bought by a developer and closed in 2012 it looked like curtains for this locals' boozer. However, a spirited campaign by local people who formed a 'Save the Chesham' group, and sympathetic policies from Hackney Council, including the designation of the Chesham as an 'Asset of Community Value' thwarted the developers' plans. The new owner has granted a 15-year lease to a new publican, and the Chesham

**The Jackdaw & Star**

**Classic interwar Truman's brewery architecture at the Cock Tavern**

is trading once more. It hit the ground running, picking up the local CAMRA branch Pub of the Year award early in 2016, barely six months after re-opening. It's easy to see why when you visit: a welcoming unfussy interior with two distinct areas around the servery, and a leafy garden down steps from a decked seating area; polished floorboards and large windows give the place a bright but pubby atmosphere. There are four changing beers and a real cider. Food is sensibly confined to snacks, pie and mash, for first and foremost it's an unpretentious locals' drinking house, just as it always was.

Bear to your left out of the pub and walk down to the end of Mehetabel Road to join a footpath at right angles. If you briefly detour to your right here you'll quickly reach St John-at-Hackney churchyard and church, and the handsome street of Sutton Place, whose fine listed terraced houses were built by Thomas Sutton, founder of Charterhouse School, around 1790. It's well worth the short detour to admire this little conservation area.

The last section of the route heads south on the footpath however, under the railway and to the right at Morning Lane, from where it's a very short walk down to the bustling centre of Hackney and Mare Street. Almost right opposite, in the restrained brick architecture of the inter war years, and still carrying some reminders of its past as a

Truman's house, stands the **5 Cock Tavern**. This single-room pub (boasting Hackney's smallest beer garden) is yet another which has been recently revamped and re-opened (in this case, in 2012), with an on-site brewery. The latter, Howling Hops, quickly outgrew its first home and moved on (with another smaller outfit installed in its place) but the range and variety of cask ales and ciders (up to eight of each) is undiminished, and the pub regularly showcases relatively rare beer styles, notably mild and porter. There are food and beer pairing nights (with good cheeses making regular appearances) and meet the brewer events. Check the Cock's Twitter page @TheCockTavernE8 if you want to catch one of these.

It's a very short step to the north to reach Hackney Central station with connections to many parts, and of course buses pass outside the pub.

## PUB INFORMATION

**1 PEOPLE'S PARK TAVERN**
360 Victoria Park Road, Homerton, E9 7BT
020 8533 0040 • peoplesparktavern.pub
**Opening hours:** 12-11 (1am Fri; 2am Sat); 11-11 Sun

**2 KENTON ARMS**
38 Kenton Road, Homerton, E9 7AB
020 8533 5041 • www.kentonpub.co.uk
**Opening hours:** 4-11 (midnight Thu & Fri); 12-midnight Sat; 12-11 Sun

**3 ADAM & EVE**
155 Homerton High Street Homerton, E9 6AS
020 8985 1494 • www.adamandevepub.com
**Opening hours:** 4-11 (midnight Thu); 12-1am Fri & Sat; 12-11 Sun

**4 CHESHAM ARMS**
15 Mehetabel Road, Homerton, E9 6DU
020 8986 6717 • www.cheshamarms.com
**Opening hours:** 5-11; 12-11 Fri & Sat; 12-10.30 Sun

**5 COCK TAVERN**
315 Mare Street, Hackney, E8 1EJ
thecocktavern.com
**Opening hours:** 12-11; 12-10.30 Sun

Try also:

**6 JACKDAW & STAR**
224 Homerton High Street, Homerton, E9 6AS
020 7125 7055 • jackdawandstar.co.uk
**Opening hours:** 4-11 (2am Fri); 11-2am Sat; 11-11 Sun

# East beyond the Lea Valley

**WALK 21**

It wasn't long ago that London's eastern postcodes were a significant desert for the cask ale aficionado, and there was little reason to go out of one's way to cross the Lea Valley. Now that has changed, and this bus-assisted tour of E5, E10 and E11 will reward you with some excellent beer and food in a variety of very good pubs. The districts of Clapton, Leyton and Leytonstone were developed as working-class railway suburbs in the late 19th century. Even here, however, some of the pubs were exuberant and impressive in their architecture. Remnants of that are easy to see in the King William IV, Leyton, now the flagship home of Brodie's brewery, and the Red Lion at Leytonstone. The extensive open spaces along the Lea Valley around Hackney Marshes and the river towpath offer an excellent opportunity to stretch your legs before starting the pubs. It's also a route that you can attempt by cycle, if you're confident in traffic.

> **Start:** Lea Bridge Road, by Princess of Wales

> **Finish:** ⬛ Leytonstone

> **Access:** ⬛ Hackney Central then buses 48, 55, to Lea Bridge Road; ⬛ Hackney Downs then bus 56 to Lea Bridge Road. ⬛ Lea Bridge and via Lea Bridge Road. Or ⬛ to Homerton or Hackney Wick, then walk via Lea Navigation towpath. ⬛ Clapton is a short walk from the Lea towpath (see map)

> **Distance:** 7 miles (11.2 km) total (about 2 miles (3.2km) walking)

> **Key attractions:** Hackney & Walthamstow Marshes; Bakers' Almshouses, Leyton;

> **THE PUBS:** Anchor & Hope; Drum; King William IV; Leyton Technical; North Star; Red Lion. Try also: Leyton Orient Supporters' Club

> **Timing tips:** Don't start this route too early as the Anchor & Hope is closed until 1pm (noon on Sunday), and the North Star only opens at 4pm, Monday to Thursday. If you can take in a visit to the award-winning Leyton Orient Supporters' Club bar (open on match days), this will be a feather in your cap.

**Barges on the Lea Navigation**

RIVER LEE NAVIGATION
Capital Ring
Lea Valley
Walk

The walk starts at Lea Bridge Road, which is well served by buses, close to the Princess of Wales; and by the newly reopened Lea Bridge station on the Greater Anglia line. If you've arrived via Clapton station, Southwold Road (to your right) will take you to the Lea towpath, south of the footbridge. When I first visited the Anchor & Hope nearly 30 years ago, the riverside here was dominated by the sheds of Latham's wood yard, to and from which barges made their way up and down the oily, polluted river. Now the industry has gone, replaced by the usual array of modern apartments no doubt occupying a 'stunning water-side location' as per usual, and the river is certainly far cleaner. Head upstream (north) on the wide towpath, noting for the return journey the footbridge after a short way, but keeping to the western bank. Just beyond the rail bridge, and with the expanse of Walthamstow Marshes on the opposite side, you'll spot the first pub of the day.

**The Anchor & Hope**

Overlooked by interwar flats, the diminutive 🍺 **Anchor & Hope** looks slightly out of place among all the modern developments close by. Nonetheless, the pub (one wonders whether the name with the two words in their more unusual order suggests a command rather

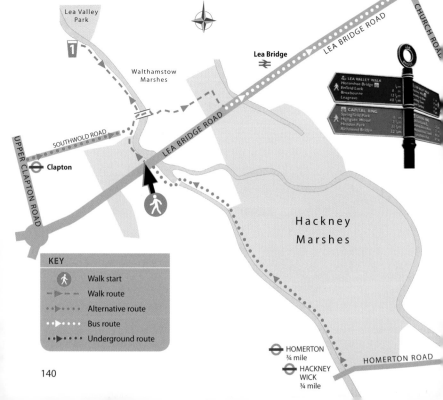

than two nouns?) has long been a beacon of excellence in a beer desert, and in that regard nothing has changed. We owe much to the legendary former landlord, Les Heath, who kept this basic beer house for 50 years. There's an interesting video interview of him at the pub's celebratory party on YouTube. He died in 2003, but not before he was awarded the MBE. The current guv'nor has respected his legacy and expanded the beer range to four handpumps. It's been a Fuller's house for a long while now and, to their credit, refurbishments have been

carried out with a light touch, keeping the simple character of the small interior intact. In addition to staples London Pride and ESB, the beers can include guests from other brewers. All in all, a classic London boozer and not to be missed.

Return down the towpath, and cross the river via the footbridge you passed earlier. Bear round to the right but keeping the Lea Valley Ice Centre on your right, take the path parallel with the Lea Bridge Road for a few minutes, crossing a small wooden bridge, and ahead into the car park which allows you to rejoin Lea Bridge Road at the Ice Centre bus stop.

KING WILLIAM IV

KING WILLIAM THE FOURTH

Bakers' Imshouses

HIGH ROAD LEYTON

EA BRIDGE ROAD

Abbots Park

HIGH ROAD LEYTON

Leyton County Cricket Ground

Leyton Midland Road

Leytonstone

BROWNING RD

CHURCH LN

Leytonstone High Road

CHURCH ROAD

FRANCIS ROAD

A12

OLIVER ROAD

BRISBANE RD

HIGH ROAD LEYTON

BUCKINGHAM ROAD

CATHALL ROAD

HIGH ROAD LEYTONSTONE

N BIRBECK RD

MELON RD

LEYTON TECHNICAL

RUCKHOLT ROAD

A12

Leyton

HIGH RD LEYTON

FRITH ROAD

WAY

Any of the buses (48, 55 or 56) will take you to the High Road Leyton/Bakers Arms stop, just a few yards beyond the striking Bakers Almshouses, and a few yards short of the Drum. The almshouses are well worth a brief look as they are really the architectural highlight of the walk. Built from 1857 in the Italianate style by the Master Bakers' Benevolent Institution, the 50-odd dwellings were intended for 'any respectable member of the baking trade fallen into poverty, eligible according to the rules, or to the widow of such'. They survived an attempt to demolish them by the former Greater London Council and were instead listed, and subsequently purchased and refurbished as flats by Waltham Forest Council. Fifty yards further on, the **2** **Drum** is, by JD Wetherspoon standards, an intimate and cosy corner pub, which has made frequent appearances in past editions of the *Good Beer Guide*. It was one of the very first acquisitions by the well-known chain, but, despite its size, it has a good range of guest beers, including frequent appearances of LocAles from the Hackney and Three Sods breweries. A pleasant little conservatory-style room

**One of JD Wetherspoon's first pubs, the Drum**

at the rear catches the light, and there's a small patio garden beyond. Save some capacity though for the next pub, which is a short walk around the corner, and at least as appealing.

**Traditional décor inside the King William IV**

Cross at the traffic lights and bear right down the Leyton High Road, and on the second left corner, a few yards down, lies the **3 King William IV**. In a fine Victorian building adorned in summer with flowers, newish London brewer Brodie's has resurrected the brewing tradition here and made its home venue a must-do destination in north-east London. The décor inside is very traditional: dark red benches run right round the large bar room, while the red carpet and ceiling complement plenty of dark woodwork on the long bar counter as it snakes around and accommodates one of the largest sets of handpumps you'll see anywhere. They're rarely all in use, other than at the Easter beer festival, but nonetheless you'll have a wide choice from Brodie's own extensive portfolio and other guests, all well kept and at keen prices. Food service starts about 1pm and continues all day.

Walk a few yards further down to the bus stop (Leyton Green) and take the 69 or 97 down towards Leyton Midland Road station. A few stops further down, the football ground of Leyton Orient FC is hidden in the side streets just west of the road. Now, if it's a Saturday, a midweek match day, or an 'ale night' (usually a Thursday preceding a home match Saturday), visitors will be made welcome at the excellent **7 Leyton Orient Supporters Club** bar, which has been a past winner of CAMRA's National Club of the Year award (small admission charge, free to CAMRA members). Expect a couple of Mighty Oak beers supported by several changing guests. Check the opening times and phone number online at www.orientsupporters.org and/or ring ahead before alighting from the bus at Buckingham Road. The club entrance is on Oliver Road to the west of the ground.

Whether or not you take in the club bar, continue by bus (or on foot) down to the Leyton Library bus stop just beyond the massive red brick and stone former Leyton Town Hall. This striking late Victorian complex, a listed building, is now home to one of the latest acquisitions

**The North Star**

of the growing Antic Pub Company, the **4 Leyton Technical**. Carefully restored by Antic the place, with its terrazzo floor, chandeliers and high ceilings, is worth a visit for its architecture, and in common with the rest of Antic's estate there's a satisfying choice of eight cask ales, real cider, and plenty of bottled offerings. Food is available throughout.

Leaving the Leyton Technical, it's a long way to the next stop on this trail so public transport is recommended. By far the easiest option is to walk down to Leyton Underground station and take the train one stop up to Leytonstone, whence it's barely 100 yards down Church Street to reach the Leytonstone High Road, opposite the imposing Red Lion pub. At this point, unless the North Star is yet to open, I recommend leaving this pub until last (it's then an easy return to the tube) and instead either walking north up the High Road, or taking the frequent 257 bus two stops alighting at the notorious Green Man roundabout with the eponymous interchange just ahead of you. Walk back a few yards and across the street is narrow Browning Road. Here, little more than a stone's throw from the roundabout and the speeding cars on the A12 below it, is one of London's more unlikely urban Conservation Areas, a quiet and pleasant little oasis of old workers' cottages, and presided over by the charming

**5 North Star**. A traditional two-room pub arranged pretty symmetrically (note some surviving etched glass in both doorways), it's a proper community local, free of tie and resolutely unpretentious. There are now seven handpumps serving a range of changing beers with regular appearances from Oakham and East London.Whatever's on, you can expect the quality to be good. There's a small but pleasant beer garden, with some tables out front which catch the sun.

Time now to walk back the short distance to the last pub stop. Return up Browning Road to the High Road, and, bearing left to retrace the bus route, it's barely 300 yards back along the road to the **6 Red Lion**. With pubs still closing in large numbers, it's a pleasure to report on the successful refurbishment of a derelict building that had stood empty for some time (although it was briefly an Afro theme bar); now it's helping in the regeneration of Leytonstone. The Antic pub company have carefully restored the landmark building and brought it back to its former glory. It opened in 2011and in my humble opinion it's one of the best of Antic's rapidly growing estate, certainly on the beer front. The internal décor, slightly 'designer shabby', works well for the building, and they've made a good job of the garden too; but it's the beer list, supported by a small but appealing menu, that secures its status. Expect a great range of at least half a dozen ever-changing cask beers with a local emphasis (there are 10 handpumps), and some interesting and often higher-gravity offerings on the five keg founts. There's an excellent range of bottles in the fridges too. The ambience is relaxed and it looks the sort of place that attracts older locals as well as the upmarket younger clientele.

**The Red Lion**

The central location means it's barely five minutes' walk to Leytonstone Underground station, the quickest way to return to Stratford (for excellent onward transport connections) and Liverpool Street. Just bear right out of the pub onto the High Road and take the first left.

## PUB INFORMATION

**1 ANCHOR & HOPE**
15 High Hill Ferry, Clapton, E5 9HG
020 8806 1730 • www.anchor-and-hope-clapton.co.uk
**Opening hours:** 1 (12 Fri & Sat)-11; 12-10.30 Sun

**2 DRUM**
557-559 Lea Bridge Road, Leyton, E10 7EQ
020 8539 9845
**Opening hours:** 10-midnight (1am Fri & Sat)

**3 KING WILLIAM IV**
816 High Road Leyton, Leyton, E10 6AE
020 8556 2460
**Opening hours:** 11-midnight (1am Fri & Sat); 12-midnight Sun

**4 LEYTON TECHNICAL**
265B High Road, Leyton, E10 5QN
020 8558 4759 • leytontechnical.com
**Opening hours:** 12-11 (midnight Thu; 1am Fri & Sat); 12-11 Sun

**5 NORTH STAR**
24 Browning Road, Leytonstone, E11 3AR
020 8530 3197
**Opening hours:** 4-11; 12-10.30 Sun

**6 RED LION**
640 High Road Leytonstone, Leytonstone, E11 3AA
020 8988 2929 • theredlionleytonstone.com
**Opening hours:** 12-11 (midnight Thu; 2am Fri & Sat)

Try also:

**7 LEYTON ORIENT SUPPORTERS CLUB**
Matchroom Stadium, Brisbane Road, Leyton, E10 5NF
020 8988 8288 • www.orientsupporters.org
**Opening hours:** match days from 5.30; 12.30-6 Sat; closed Sun

# Riverbus pub hopscotch

**WALK 22**

▶ **Start:** Embankment Pier

▶ **Finish:** Charing Cross

▶ **Access:** Via Charing Cross

▶ **Key attractions:** River views; Tower of London; Greenwich museums, Observatory and Park

▶ **THE PUBS:** *Greenwich Pier:* Old Brewery; Plume of Feathers. *Canary Wharf Pier:* Ledger Building. *Tower Bridge Millennium Pier:* Draft House Tower Bridge. *Blackfriars Pier:* Black Friar; Cockpit. *Embankment Pier:* Ship & Shovell. Try also: *Tower Bridge Millennium Pier:* Liberty Bounds

As a lifelong Londoner I have to confess I had never been on a river trip until I did the punishing research putting this circuit together. I can only hope you enjoy the route as much as I did: once the commuters have melted away, there's enough space on board the fast and frequent Thames Clipper services to relax and enjoy the views, which are first class throughout. The River Roamer ticket (currently almost £15 but discounted by a third if you have a valid Travelcard) allows you to jump on and off the services at will, which is what we need to visit the pubs on this trail. Check the maps and timetables in advance at www. thamesclippers.com; but you can just turn up at the pier and buy your ticket at the booth at no extra cost. Starting at the Embankment Pier by Charing Cross rail bridge, I recommend heading non-stop down to Greenwich and thence making your way back in several stages, but as usual there's nothing to stop you composing your own variations. The clippers run very frequently, so you can pretty much turn up and go; there are pocket timetables on board – be aware that some services omit some stops, notably Blackfriars.

**Riverside warehouses and the Shard**

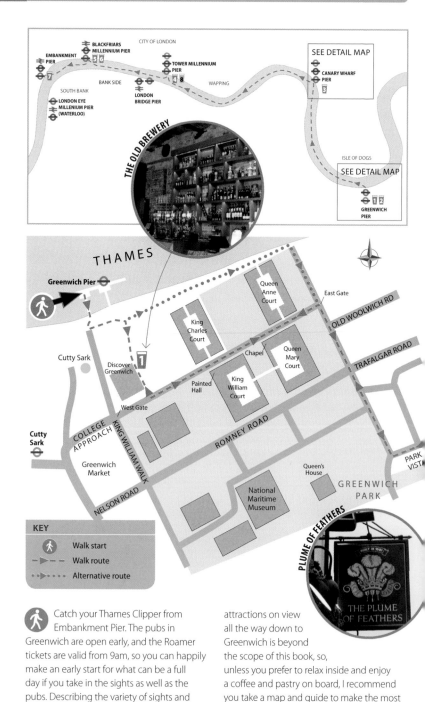

Catch your Thames Clipper from Embankment Pier. The pubs in Greenwich are open early, and the Roamer tickets are valid from 9am, so you can happily make an early start for what can be a full day if you take in the sights as well as the pubs. Describing the variety of sights and attractions on view all the way down to Greenwich is beyond the scope of this book, so, unless you prefer to relax inside and enjoy a coffee and pastry on board, I recommend you take a map and guide to make the most of them. Having said that, it's quite striking how different the view of a familiar city is from the water.

The first stop for the boat (not for us) is the London Eye, and thereafter it's downstream all the way to Greenwich. Obvious highlights are the bridges, the Tower of London, the riverside warehouses, and some fine churches, a few of which are still able to show a face to the river despite the proliferation of brash modern blocks. Look out

**Old Brewery**

in particular for St Paul's Church, Shadwell, close by the Prospect of Whitby at Wapping; the tower is very graceful. The clippers don't hang about, particularly beyond Tower Bridge where they're allowed to get moving. The views of the Docklands towers are very striking, with the original 'Canary Wharf' block – 1 Canada Square, to give it its proper title (the one with the slopy roof!) – now joined by many others of differing heights. Unless you fancy going down to the O2 and back for the ride (and the view of the new cable

car crossing), then alight with most of the other trippers at Greenwich.

There's enough to see in Greenwich that, even if you arrive before opening time, you should be fully entertained. The *Cutty Sark* is of course one of the stars, right in front of you as you exit from the pier. She was the fastest sailing ship of her day, and after being launched at Dumbarton in 1869 she initially sailed the tea route to China, once doing the trip from Shanghai in just 107 days. Later on, she brought back wool from Australia but has been in dry dock in Greenwich since 1954. Bear downstream on the route signed 'cycle path' in front of the Old Naval College buildings, which was originally the Greenwich Royal Naval Hospital. The hospital was built by Christopher Wren between 1696 and 1712 and closed in 1869. Between 1873 and 1998 it functioned as the Royal Naval College. A charitable trust, the Greenwich Foundation for the Royal Naval College, assumed responsibility for

**Greenwich Park and the National Maritime Museum**

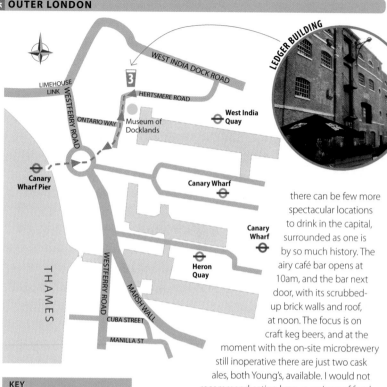

LEDGER BUILDING

the site when the Royal Navy moved out in December 1998. Go to www.ornc.org/visit to see what's on offer here.

One important attraction for us is just yards away, across the lawn in the near side of the cluster of the old College buildings: the **1 Old Brewery** is the microbrewery, bar and café venture which was opened a few years ago by Greenwich-based Meantime Brewing Company, but has now been acquired by Young's. The name celebrates a surprisingly long association with brewing on this site, set out in the timeline running around the wall of the café building that houses the microbrewery. A brewery opened on the site in 1717 to supply the hospital, and operated until 1868. This recent venture gives the buildings an agreeable, but very modern, makeover, and

there can be few more spectacular locations to drink in the capital, surrounded as one is by so much history. The airy café bar opens at 10am, and the bar next door, with its scrubbed-up brick walls and roof, at noon. The focus is on craft keg beers, and at the moment with the on-site microbrewery still inoperative there are just two cask ales, both Young's, available. I would not recommend eating here as reviews of food quality, service and value have taken a (sadly predictable) nosedive since Young's took over. I include it here because of its location and because quite frankly there are few appealing alternatives: Greenwich is still a disappointing place for real ale when almost everywhere else in the capital is better than ever.

That said, my second choice here is a far more traditional affair a few minutes' walk away and is recommended. Either exit the Old Brewery on the town side, onto the main vista running west–east through the Old Naval College site, and walk left to the East Gate onto Park Row; or return to the riverside path and follow it down to the Trafalgar Gate by the big old riverside pub of the same name, turning 'inland' up Park Row. Head away from the river, up Park Row and cross the main road towards the park entrance ahead, following the road left by the park gates into Park Vista, where you'll catch sight of the **2 Plume of Feathers**. This attractive street was at one time the main east–west

**View of Canary Wharf and Dockland from the riverbus**

**'The Walkie-Talkie' and 'The Gherkin' now form part of London's ever-changing skyline**

route through Greenwich, dividing the park from the Tudor palace that stood by the river. Just before you reach the pub, look out for the meridian line, set as series of studs in the road leading to a metal groove in the footpath and a wall plaque on the right. So, once you are safely inside the Plume, the easternmost entry in this guide, you will have drunk in both hemispheres in one day! This comfortable pub dates from 1691 and, not surprisingly given its location, contains many naval artefacts. The carpeted bar assumes a horseshoe shape around the servery, where a choice of four beers (London Pride, Harveys Sussex, Sharp's Doom Bar and one or two guests) can be expected. There's a dining area to the rear with a lunch and evening menu.

Unless you're heading up to the Observatory, the Park or Greenwich's other attractions (all worthwhile, but we've a long day ahead), return back to the pier for a westbound clipper.

Next stop for us is Canary Wharf. As one would expect, the majority of the watering holes in and around the towers of international banking are pretty soulless modern joints designed primarily to unload large sums of cash from the overpaid occupants whilst they talk loudly to each other on their mobiles. Right, now

we have the stereotypes dealt with, let's try a couple of the better places! Ascend the steps from the piazza in front of the pier, and cross the large traffic circus with the original tower, 1 Canada Square, directly in your sights. Once across the two roads, head slightly left through the arch advertising 'Columbus Place' to emerge in a pedestrian courtyard. Over to the left is a piece of artwork in light and dark blue glass, the 'Columbus Screen'. To the right of this is a well-hidden staircase down to the street below. Now follow the sign for the Docklands Museum for about 100 yards and you'll come across the **3 Ledger Building**.

It's refreshing to find a few surviving old buildings here in the midst of the largely mediocre modern stuff, and this one with its classical portico has been restored with the care that characterises the work done by the J D Wetherspoon chain. Its neighbour is the

**The Draft House**

very different but equally attractive Museum of London Docklands. The name of the Ledger Building stems, as one might expect, from the building's original use: to house the ledgers of the West India Docks. The light and spacious bar room, according to reviewers, attracts a slightly lower quotient of suits than neighbouring establishments, so you should have a fighting chance of getting a seat if you want one. There's a good range of up to five interesting guest ales as well as the four 'regulars' further along the bar, and of course the usual JDW fare on the menu.

Return to the pier and head further back upstream to our next port of call, the Tower Bridge Millennium Pier. Here you'll be sharing the stage with a very different clientele: the hordes of tourists who make this the most popular of the Royal Palaces. Unless you've planned a visit yourself, work your way along the riverside back towards Tower Bridge, and, climbing up onto the roadway, cross the bridge to the south shore. The area around Butlers Wharf and Shad Thames on the South Bank here, close to City Hall (the elliptical building you can't miss on the riverside), has been transformed into a bit of a destination, with numerous upmarket bars and eateries where once there were riverside wharves and warehouses. In that sense it's a symbol of the changes you will have seen from the riverbus.

My recommendation for some interesting beers on this strip is the **4 Draft House** Tower Bridge on the left, 200 yards beyond the bridge, past the Bridge House (see below). One of a small but growing chain of alehouses aiming at the new aficionados of beer culture, the place has a layout and atmosphere fairly typical of the new breed of bars, but retains a vestige of 'pubbyness' within too. Drinkers can order third-of-a-pint 'samples', complemented by a range of beer-friendly food. Sambrook's Wandle Ale is the regular fixture at the moment, joined by three changing guests; but there's a good range of both bottled and draught craft keg beers, the latter including popular North London micro Camden Town. The enthusiastic and knowledgeable staff seem to know what they're doing, making the visit a positive experience.

If you're game for another beer, my advice would probably be to stay here, but if it's another nearby pub or bar you're after, you could try the Pommeller's Rest a few doors down. The former Tower Bridge Hotel has had a rather bland (by Wetherspoon standards) conversion, but there's a good selection of beers. The Bridge House, which you passed earlier, is Adnams' only London tied house; it focuses on table service and is food-led, and frankly I find the place rather lacking in atmosphere. It's still worth a call if you have the time, if only for the location and the chance of a decent pint of Adnams.

**The striking exterior of the Black Friar**

**Tower Bridge is one of the Thames' most iconic crossings**

If you'd like a second pub before you return to the boat, turn left out of the Black Friar under the rail bridge and left again up Black Friars Lane, turning right into Playhouse Yard, which becomes Ireland Yard ahead. At the end of this passageway you'll find the **6** **Cockpit**. The dark exterior looks the part, notably the fine entrance on the apex of the two streets. It was adapted from one of the Blackfriars Monastery's gateways. The interior is comfortable, although quite confined, and perpendicular drinking is common here. The story goes that at one time there was cockfighting here until it was outlawed early in Victoria's reign, but the current interior in a curious quasi-medieval style complete with mini minstrel's gallery dates back to an 1890s remodelling. This increasingly popular little pub offers four beers from national brewers. Adnams Bitter and St Austell Tribute were joined by Hog's back TEA on my most recent visit.

If you're pushed for time, then consider the **8** **Liberty Bounds** a couple of minutes' walk from the boat (just keep directly away from the river on the path, weave through the tourists and it's pretty well directly ahead at the road crossing). Another J D Wetherspoon house, in a handsome Edwardian block, there's a decent if smaller than usual (for JDW) range of beers, which, although pricier than normal JDW offerings, are still very good value for the area.

Return to the pier. If you fancy stretching your legs, another option is to head down Queen Elizabeth Street opposite and then make your way down to City Hall and walk along the Thames Path to pick up your boat at the London Bridge City Pier in a few minutes.

Check that your departure is scheduled to stop at Blackfriars, or be prepared to miss out on one of the definite highlights of the tour. Disembarking from the riverbus at Blackfriars Millennium Pier, climb up to the Victoria Embankment and walk back up to Blackfriars Bridge. Crossing the roads here is one of the day's more taxing undertakings, but heading up away from the river you'll spot the distinctive prominent shape of the **5** **Black Friar** on the prominent apex, surrounded by modern buildings jammed against the railway line. For a full description, see its entry on Walk 2, the Central London Pub Heritage tour.

**The Cockpit**

Return to the pier and catch the clipper down to Embankment, where we started. The last stop is reassuringly close. Cross the road by the pier and walk through the concourse to the Underground station, and continue straight up Villiers Street. The street is named after George Villiers, first Duke of Buckingham, who was a fashionable courtier and friend of James I. He had a substantial mansion nearby, the only remnant of which is the York Water Gate in the Embankment Gardens alongside the street. This marked the old line of the Thames before the Embankment reduced its width. Look for the tunnel running under the railway station on the left (and note, for later, the new access to the station immediately on your left as you walk down it).

At the far end of this arch lies the curious **7 Ship & Shovell**. Curious, since it's the only pub in the land which is divided into two parts, on opposite sides of the passage. The spelling of the name refers to Admiral Sir Cloudesley Shovell, whose fleet was grounded on the Scilly Isles in 1707 with the total loss of several of his ships and over two thousand of his crew. His portrait hangs in the main bar. The smaller bar (on the left) is probably the more atmospheric, with some cosy corners and plenty of dark wood

**The Ship & Shovell**

panelling. Of more importance is the beer range, which comes from Hall & Woodhouse and includes favourites such as Tanglefoot and their take on the old King & Barnes Sussex Best Bitter.

You have just passed the nearest British Rail and Underground station – if it's buses you're after, walk up to the top of Villiers Street to the Strand.

---

## PUB INFORMATION

 **OLD BREWERY**
The Old Royal Naval College, Greenwich, SE10 9LW
020 3327 1280 • www.oldbrewerygreenwich.com
**Opening hours:** 11-11; 12-10.30 Sun

 **PLUME OF FEATHERS**
19 Park Vista, Greenwich, SE10 9LZ
020 8858 1661 • www.plumeoffeathers-greenwich.co.uk
**Opening hours:** 11-11 (midnight Fri & Sat);
12-11 Sun

 **LEDGER BUILDING**
4 Hertsmere Road, Canary Wharf, E14 4AL
020 7536 7770
**Opening hours:** 8am-midnight (1am Fri & Sat)

 **DRAFT HOUSE TOWER BRIDGE**
206 Tower Bridge Road, Tower Bridge, SE1 2UP
020 7378 9995 • www.drafthouse.co.uk
**Opening hours:** 12-11 (midnight Fri); 12-10 Sun

 **BLACK FRIAR**
174 Queen Victoria Street, EC4V 4EG
020 7236 5474 • www.nicholsonspubs.co.uk/
theblackfriarblackfriarslondon
**Opening hours:** 10-11 (11.30 Fri & Sat); 12-10 Sun

 **COCKPIT**
7 St Andrews Hill, EC4V 5BY
020 7248 7315
**Opening hours:** 11-11; 12-10.30 Sun

 **SHIP & SHOVELL**
2-3 Craven Passage, WC2N 5PH
020 7839 1311 • shipandshovell.co.uk
**Opening hours:** 11-11; closed Sun

Try also:

 **LIBERTY BOUNDS**
15 Trinity Square, EC3N 4AA
020 7481 0513
**Opening hours:** 8am-11 (midnight Fri & Sat); 8-11 Sun

# A beer circuit of Wandsworth Common

If I had to pick my Desert Island London pub walk, this excellent saunter around Wandsworth Common would have to be a serious contender. Apart from the pleasant if rather fragmented Common itself, there's plenty of appeal in the built environment, from the amazing Royal Victoria Patriotic Building to the bohemian atmosphere of the Northcote Road. Add to this some great pubs and bars scattered liberally at frequent intervals along the way, and it would be a difficult route not to like. Moreover, the last pub is just a step from the station, so there should be no worries about finding your way home. There are eight pubs on this circuit so, depending upon time and capacity, you might wish to be selective.

> **Start/finish:** ⇄ ⊖
> Clapham Junction

> **Distance:** 3 miles (4.8 km)

> **Access:** ⇄ Waterloo, Victoria and East Croydon; or London Overground

> **Key attractions:**
> Wandsworth Common; Wandsworth Nature Study Centre; Royal Victoria Patriotic Building (www. rvpb.com)

> **THE PUBS:** Beehive; Powder Keg Diplomacy; Roundhouse; Le Gothique; County Arms; Eagle Ale House; Draft House Northcote; Falcon

> **Timing tips:** Although an enjoyable route at any time of the week, be aware of the limited weekday opening times at the Powder Keg Diplomacy, and note that Le Gothique is closed on Sundays and often has private functions on Saturdays: always phone ahead to check. However, at the weekend, both the Powder Keg and the Draft House open up at 10am for brunch – what better way to kick off a summer pub walk?

**Victorian grandeur at the Falcon**

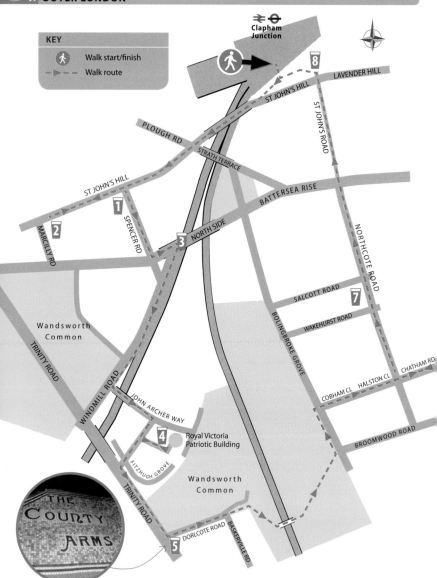

**KEY**

🚶 Walk start/finish

– – ▸ – – Walk route

🚆 ⊖ Clapham Junction

LAVENDER HILL

ST JOHN'S HILL

ST JOHN'S ROAD

PLOUGH RD

STRATH TERRACE

ST JOHN'S HILL

BATTERSEA RISE

MARCILLY RD

SPENCER RD

NORTH SIDE

NORTHCOTE ROAD

SALCOTT ROAD

WAKEHURST ROAD

BOLINGBROKE GROVE

Wandsworth Common

TRINITY ROAD

WINDMILL ROAD

JOHN ARCHER WAY

COBHAM CL   HALSTON CL   CHATHAM RD

BROOMWOOD ROAD

Royal Victoria Patriotic Building

FITZHUGH GROVE

Wandsworth Common

TRINITY ROAD

THE COUNTY ARMS

DORLCOTE ROAD   BASKERVILLE RD

🚶 Start at Clapham Junction – which isn't billed as Britain's busiest railway station for nothing – and head for the new exit at the southern end of the long footbridge which disgorges you onto St John's Hill by the rail bridge. It's not the most inspiring of urban environments, but it will improve! Cross the rail bridge and continue ahead at the traffic lights, beyond which it's a good five-minute walk into a more bohemian area with some trendy shops and eateries before, just beyond Spencer Road on your left, you'll come across a newish bar, which reflects the surroundings.

The oddly named **1 Powder Keg Diplomacy** is a skilful conversion of a former curry house into an appealing modern-style

**The Powder Keg Diplomacy**

and clean, but still retains a public bar atmosphere, which in my book is a definite plus. A seasonal from the Fuller's portfolio sometimes accompanies London Pride, Seafarers and well-kept ESB on the four handpumps. It's primarily a drinker's pub, although bar food is available.

Retrace your steps to Spencer Road, just beyond the Powder Keg Diplomacy, and turn right. At the end of the street you'll catch your first glimpse of Wandsworth Common, although this is a small outlier cut off by the railway line nearby which sliced through the Common in 1837.

Bear left, and on the next corner is the **3 Roundhouse**. The noteworthy mosaic at the entrance suggests that the original name was the Freemasons, and indeed it seems to have switched back and forth between the names over time; but the elegant curving corner façade in fine yellow brickwork, and classy Victorian sash windows justify the current choice. Inside it's a smart gastropub in line with the location: high and airy, with large windows, and there is an array of seating around the bay frontage and good bench seating along the left hand wall. You can sit outside too, although it's rather noisy given its location. The place has built a solid reputation for its beers, with a LocAle emphasis: Sambrook's supply Wandle as the house cask regular, supported by two other rotating guests, all kept in very good condition; and in addition there are several keg taps with one or two interesting offerings, and a bottle list of around 20.

bar and eatery. The bar area is beset with the usual sofas and tables, whilst at the rear there's a classy conservatory for the diners. The website recommends the cocktails, but this is a bar that has definitely set out to make an effort with its beers as well. On handpump, there are three rotating beers with Windsor & Eton and Oakham among the favoured breweries. Complementing these are half a dozen keg taps, which offer some interesting choices from home and abroad; and in addition around 50 bottled beers, with a strong UK emphasis. There are monthly 'meet the brewer' events, and occasional collaborative brews between the staff and Peter Haydon's Head in a Hat brewery at the Florence, Herne Hill. All in all, a welcome addition to the already very good portfolio of drinking holes on this excellent and well-tested circuit.

By way of almost complete contrast, and just a couple of minutes further along the road on foot, the tiny **2 Beehive** remains a traditional, no-nonsense one-bar pub attracting a mainly local clientele. It's smart

**The Beehive**

**The Roundhouse is a smart gastropub with a solid reputation for its beers**

Now leave the pub and cross the main road outside, taking the road opposite (Spencer Park) which runs alongside the railway on one side and the Common on the other. You'll pass the memorial to the Clapham Junction rail disaster of December 1988 which killed 35 people when three rush-hour trains collided in the cutting below. A little further beyond that are the forlorn remains of a smock windmill, all that is left of a project by the then London and South Western Railway to pump water from this railway cutting. (If Le Gothique is closed and you don't want to detour through the grounds, simply continue straight ahead past the windmill and turn left into Trinity Road.)

Just beyond the mill, turn left over the railway into a modern housing development (John Archer Way, which is named after the founding member of the Fourth International and a veteran of the Trotskyist movement who died in December 2000; right here in ultra-Tory Wandsworth). That aside, you're now facing one of South London's architectural treasures and, for its size, a pretty well-hidden one.

The Royal Victoria Patriotic Building, constructed between 1857 and 1859 (another enclosure from the Common, it has to be said), was originally built as an orphanage and later became a school and hospital, along with a wartime home to MI5 and MI6; Rudolf Hess was apparently detained in the cellar dungeon. Having fallen into dereliction after the war, plans were made to demolish it; but after pressure from the Victorian Society and the Wandsworth Society, the building was listed, saving it from destruction. In 1980 it was acquired for £1, subject to the performance of a schedule of repair and restoration works. The magnificent hall with painted ceiling, totally destroyed by arson, was carefully reconstructed, and is accurate to the last detail, even including several errors in the original artwork. It deservedly won a Civic Trust Award, as well as the prized Europa Nostra Order of Merit.

**Le Gothique is housed in the splendid Royal Victoria Patriotic Building**

Now the building houses a Dance and Drama school, flats and studios, workshops, and **5 Le Gothique**, a restaurant and bar extraordinaire, and one of London's first gastropubs. Signs should help you find the bar, sequestered around the rear of this remarkable building: easiest is to bear right around the front elevation, and then left – noting the exit (ahead) you'll need to take later to continue the route – and keep left. Closed on Sundays and usually closed for private parties on Saturdays (ring ahead to check), the attractive bar offers a changing range of ales but in a typical week features beers from Shepherd Neame, Downton and Sambrook's. The twice-yearly beer festivals (held on the last weekends of March and October) are massive events with 150 beers and 30 ciders overflowing into the cloistered garden and restaurant. If you are do-ing the trail during the week, this would make a good lunch stop: the garden eatery in the Victorian cloisters is highly rated.

OK, follow that! Exit the grounds by retracing the route halfway, to the corner of the front wall of the building, and then left, and follow Fitzhugh Way as it twists left and right before disgorging you onto the busy dual carriageway of Trinity Road; ask at the bar if you are unsure. Turn left to keep the (fenced in) Common on your left, but already our next pub can be seen not too far off on the other side of the road.

The **5 County Arms** is an imposing Victori-an building and is difficult to miss. Young's gave this grand old pub a makeover about 10 years ago, bringing it in line with the well-heeled lo-cal clientele, although a few vestiges of the old building remain – a nice entrance mosaic, screenwork (with some good etched glass), splendid fireplaces and decent woodwork. This is joined today by modern seats, chunky tables and an upmarket eating area to-wards the rear. Beyond this there's a large and secluded garden area, which makes a pleasant summer retreat.

There are four handpumps, one of which offers a guest, which may come from beyond the Wells & Young's portfolio.

Right outside there's a handy controlled crossing; using this, walk down Dorlcote Road with the Common on your left and then take the track running at about 45 degrees to your right at a junction of paths, and this will quickly lead to the footbridge over another railway line. Now head half left on a clear path that runs across the Common to meet the B229 road, Bolingbroke Grove. Cross this carefully and, about 100 yards further up the road to the north, look for Cobham Close on the right, just before the modern block of flats. Keep straight ahead when this becomes a footpath, and cross the Northcote Road directly into Chatham Road.

Halfway up here, on the right, you'll find the **6 Eagle Ale House**. In a distinctive and characterful building, this independent establishment offers a relaxing ambience with comfortable seating arranged informally around the L-shaped bar counter. Bookshelves add to the appeal. There are basic bar snacks, but this is a quality beer house first and foremost, which has carried off the coveted local Pub of the Year award for 2012 and again in 2014. Expect between four and eight beers to be available in this LocAle-accredited house, depending upon the time of week: Surrey Hills and Pilgrim are among the favoured brewers in an interesting and changing selection. There is a heated marquee in the rear courtyard garden for special occasions, including beer festivals.

## THE COMMONS OF SOUTH LONDON

It's appropriate to dedicate this walk around Wandsworth Com-mon to those of our forebears who fought to stop greedy land-owners and gentry from enclosing common lands across South London, in particular in the 18th and 19th centuries, enabling us to enjoy the admittedly fragmented and truncated remains of them today. In Wandsworth's case, the main culprit was Earl Spencer (the same family that later gave us Lady Di), who along with others had already done great damage by the time he gave in to popular pressure and agreed to transfer much of what remained to what later became the Wandsworth Common Preservation Society. Read much more about all this and other South London Commons at www.alphabetthreat.co.uk/pasttense/pdf/fences.pdf

**The Draft House Northcote**

Return to the Northcote Road and turn right. The longish walk down this road into Clapham Junction is punctuated by interesting shops, many of which have a bohemian flavour. Another attraction appears a few minutes down on the left: at the junction with Salcott Road stands one of the Draft House chain, which numbers five outlets across London. The **7** **Draft House Northcote**, in keeping with the others in the chain has a very modern internal style, although housed in an attractive old end-terrace Victorian building. Run by avowed beer enthusiasts, the place offers a wide and interesting selection, adding to the already extensive range sampled on this walk: Sambrook's Wandle is the regular, and the two rotating guests have a local emphasis. On keg, look out for Camden Town beers and Budvar Dark, while in the fridge there's a good variety of around 50 bottled beers. Food is available all day from noon, and just in case you're tackling the route in reverse, they're open from 10am at weekends.

For the final stop on this marathon of a pub walk, continue down Northcote Road (or if you prefer, take bus 319 or G1 from the Salcott Road stop, alighting at Clapham Junction: two stops), crossing straight ahead at the traffic lights into St John's Road and, at the far end, on the opposite corner of the crossroads stands the imposing **8** **Falcon**. Aptly described by CAMRA's Heritage Pubs group as 'mightily impressive', inside this late Victorian pub possibly the longest continuous bar counter in the country curves around a spacious servery. A real impression of height prevails in the bar-back and the windows; and some fine screen work survives, as does a stained-glass window depicting the eponymous bird of prey. All this in itself makes the Falcon well worth a visit. Beer range is less exciting than of late but you should still be able to find something to your palate from a decent range in this Nicholson's house; and towards the rear there's a spacious area set aside primarily for diners, which makes a good place to relax and enjoy some food with your ales, before the short walk to your right on leaving the pub to catch your train at the station.

## PUB INFORMATION

**1** **POWDER KEG DIPLOMACY**
147 St Johns Hill, Battersea, SW11 1TQ
020 7450 6457 • www.powderkegdiplomacy.co.uk
**Opening hours:** 4-11; 10-midnight Sat; 10-11 Sun

**2** **BEEHIVE**
197 St John's Hill, Battersea, SW11 1TH
020 7450 1756 • www.beehivewandsworth.co.uk
**Opening hours:** 12-midnight (1am Fri & Sat)

**3** **ROUNDHOUSE**
2 North Side, Wandsworth Common, SW18 2SS
020 7326 8580 • www.theroundhousewandsworth.com
**Opening hours:** 112-11 (midnight Sat); 12-10.30 Sun

**4** **LE GOTHIQUE**
Royal Victoria Patriotic Building, John Archer Way, off Windmill Road, Wandsworth Common, SW18 3SX 020 8870 6567 • www.legothique.co.uk
**Opening hours:** 12-3, 6-11 Mon-Fri; closed Sat & Sun

**5** **COUNTY ARMS**
345 Trinity Road, Wandsworth Common, SW18 3SH
020 8874 8532 • www.countyarms.co.uk
**Opening hours:** 11-midnight; 11-11 Sun

**6** **EAGLE ALE HOUSE**
104 Chatham Road, Battersea, SW11 6HG
020 7228 2328 • www.eaglealehouse.co.uk
**Opening hours:** 4 (3 Fri)-11; 12-11 Sat; 12-10.30 Sun

**7** **DRAFT HOUSE NORTHCOTE**
94 Northcote Road, Battersea, SW11 6QW
020 7924 1814 • www.drafthouse.co.uk
**Opening hours:** 12-11; 10-11 Sat & Sun

**8** **FALCON**
2 St Johns Hill, Battersea, SW11 1RU
020 7228 2076 • www.nicholsonspubs.co.uk/ thefalconclaphamjunctionlondon
**Opening hours:** 11-11.30 (midnight Fri & Sat) 11-11 Sun

# South down the Northern Line

The southern extension to the City & South London Railway as far as Morden was opened in 1926, with several new stations designed by now-iconic architect Charles Holden. All the stations on this pub tour are now listed buildings, having suffered relatively little damage from subsequent development (unlike Morden station itself). The pubs won't let you down either: no fewer than three were in the portfolio of pubco Antic, which has gained a reputation for imaginative refurbishments, although it has now hived off two of these. Thrown in for good measure is a favourite from Young's, the current local CAMRA Pub of the Year, and the Hop Back brewery's only London tied house. The route could also be accomplished by bicycle, but I recommend you take the train. Or, if you are averse to the Underground, take the bus: the 155 down the A24 as far as Tooting Broadway, then the 219 or 57.

> **Start:** ⊖ Clapham South

> **Finish:** ⊖ South Wimbledon (Merton)

> **Distance:** 4.7 miles (7.5 km)

> **Access:** Northern Line from Central London; or via ⇌ Clapham Junction or ⇌ Victoria to ⇌ Balham, then walk

> **Key attractions:** Clapham and Tooting Bec Commons; Wandle Trail; Merton Abbey Mills market; Underground architecture; Tooting curry houses

> **THE PUBS:** Nightingale; Balham Bowls Club; Wheatsheaf; King's Head; Antelope; Sultan; Trafalgar. Try also: Hagen & Hyde

> **Timing tips:** Don't be caught out by the limited hours at several of these pubs. Avoid Mondays, and don't start before late afternoons during the other weekdays, if you want to visit the whole set. That said, weekend evenings can see the pubs crowded and noisy with slow service. Aim for a summer midweek evening if you can.

**The solidly attractive Nightingale**

Clapham South station lies at the southern extremity of Clapham Common, surely the most well known (but not the prettiest) of South London's numerous Commons. Nightingale Lane is the road running off to the left (west) from the station, and our first pub is about half a mile down this road. Alternatively, catch the G1 or 690 bus from around the corner for two stops to Ramsden Road and continue walking for a short way to get to the **1 Nightingale**. A pretty mid-Victorian listed building, it has some handsome brickwork and windows giving it a cottage-style appearance. More importantly, it has so far escaped Young's obsession with turning its pubs into gastro eateries (and turning its back on the humble drinker), although you can certainly eat here. The front bar in particular is much as my generation of former Young's fans remember many of their old South London pubs: a simple but solidly attractive bar counter with a well-worn boarded floor, all in good old-fashioned brown. The very well-kept beers include not only Wells & Young's staples and a seasonal, but also Sambrook's Wandle and often another guest. In addition, Meantime beers are available on

INSIDE THE NIGHTINGALE

Clapham Common

Clapham South

Alternative bus route

Balham

SCREEN GLASS AT THE KI

**KEY**

Walk start

Walk route

Wandle Park

South Wimbledon

Colliers Wood

keg, and you can sample a range, since there are third-pint glasses available. All in all, a pub that has got the balance right and which remains a firm community favourite.

Now, to get to the next pub, you can walk: it's only a few minutes. Follow Western Lane at the side of the pub and swing round left to join Endlesham Road. Turn right, and head south until the junction with Norgrove Street, and turn up here to join Ramsden Road, when a short distance to the right you'll find the distinctive **2 Balham Bowls Club**. (If you want to be a Northern Line purist – and why not? – return to Clapham South, head one stop south to Balham and, upon exit, cross the High Road diagonally and take the second turn left along the road.) The building greets you with a frontage that suggests a more rural location and a previous era, an impression reinforced once you're inside. It still feels like the clubhouse it once was, and much of the old décor remains, in a deliberately retro refurb by Antic in 2006. The rambling interior has several rooms, many with lovely parquet flooring complemented by panelled walls. Seating is eclectic like the rest of the furniture – sofas, old chairs and tables; there's also quite a bit of vertical drinking at the bar. One of the rooms is mainly used as a restaurant, and there's a pleasant walled patio garden, though the old bowling green itself isn't part of the property anymore. On the four handpumps you'll find regular Purity UBU, one from Adnams and a couple of rotating guests. It's a likeable place, but be warned: it can get very, very busy, especially on Friday and Saturday nights.

Walk to the end of the road and turn right onto lively Balham High Road, with the Underground station visible to your right. Balham has come a long way upmarket since Peter Sellers' now very dated and rather corny portrayal of the place as the 'Gateway to the South' in 1958. Even the station has had a facelift! En route to Balham station on the High Road, is **8** **Hagen & Hyde** another Antic acquisition well worth a stop if you have the stamina. Up to ten beers are served in a vintage shop atmosphere with plenty of dark woodwork.

Take the tube down one more stop to Tooting Bec, and emerge onto the crossroads. Let's deal with the funny name first: this part of the home of Citizen Smith is properly

**Balham Bowls Club**

Upper Tooting, but at the time of Domesday was held by the Abbey of Bec-Hellouin in Normandy – whence it acquired its unusual suffix. Now, right across the junction is the **3** **Wheatsheaf**. This Victorian corner pub was extensively refurbished in late 2010 following lease to Antic, with a welcome reinstatement of real ale after many years absence, and soon became the popular pub its location deserves. After a threat of redevelopment in 2013, a vigorous local campaign resulted in its registration by Wandsworth Council as an Asset Of Community Value bolstered by additional protections. It's now part of the Urban Pubs & Bars chain having undergone another major refurbishment in 2015. On the five handpumps expect a changing range of mostly local beers from the likes of Hackney, Wimbledon

**The Wheatsheaf**

**The King's Head is architecturally one of South London's most remarkable pubs**

and the new Truman micro. Food is available both at lunchtimes and in the evenings from five (all day weekends). Once again, I'd issue my warning about Friday and Saturday evenings.

Take to your feet for the next pub on this trip, for it's only a few minutes' walk south down the main road. Upper Tooting Road is lively but rather tatty, with nondescript shops in abundance – an unlikely place to run into our next pub, which has been described as one of the most important historic pub interiors south of the river, a view with which it's almost impossible to disagree. The **4 King's Head**, designed in 1896 by the prolific pub architect W. M. Brutton and regarded as possibly his best work, is a remarkable building on the outside too, best viewed from the other side of the street. Although there has been a degree of opening out inside, there is enough remaining to recall the sheer quality and extravagance of the late Victorian interior. Several splendid screens with fine glass have survived, along with some quality bar fittings. The snug on the left has some good floor tilework, whilst to the right-hand side various doors show how there were formerly several separate areas. Being in the portfolio of Greene King's Spirit group the pub offers GK's IPA but you can expect to find some more local offerings on the other taps, most likely from Sambrook's (who brew the house beer, King's Head Pale Ale) or Twickenham. There are also up to four craft keg beers and some bottled world beers as well as a choice of traditional ciders, but this stop is firmly one to savour for the building, and not to be missed.

Now, if you're planning to take in a Tooting curry house on this tour – and anyone in the know will tell you that there's no better place in London for one just now – the main drag down to Tooting Broadway has some of the finest. Whether you'll feel able to resume the pub tour afterwards is your call, so an alternative option is to finish that first and return to the Broadway, in which case, if you're doing things by the book, the only way is back, to Tooting Bec, for the tube to Tooting Broadway.

From the crossroads at the Broadway turn right out of the station and head along the Mitcham Road (signed to Croydon on the ornate metal fingerboard on the traffic island) for a few minutes. The **5 Antelope** is a conversion of a substantial late Victorian building with some character, now in the Antic portfolio. The spacious interior is dominated by the central servery, with the usual mixture of sofas, chairs and tables making the place feel cosier and more intimate than one might expect for its size. This place takes its food seriously and the dining area at the rear is a good choice if you plan to eat somewhere on this tour. There's also an outdoor drinking area at the rear of the pub. The beer range is wider here, and there are usually four rotating and often interesting guests alongside the Adnams and Purity regulars.

It's a short walk back to Tooting Broadway for the tube to Colliers Wood. Once known as Merton Singlegate after the tollhouse on the turnpike road here, it's now more notorious as the home of the grim tower block that was voted London's ugliest in a 2006 poll. It's being refurbished but it's still grim to this day and only demolition will change that I fear…; but if you can turn a blind eye to it as you cross the road by the station, there are more pleasant sights, and much history, in this locality. One such is Wandle Park on your right. Under the influence of early open spaces campaigners like Octavia Hill, co-founder of not just the National Trust but also the Wandle Open Spaces Committee, Wimbledon Corporation bought the 10-acre estate of Wandle Bank House when it came onto the market in 1907. The house, once home to James Perry, a friend of Admiral Lord Nelson (who lived briefly across the road in Merton), has now gone, but the public park remains. Across the road, on the very site now occupied by the hideous boxy supermarket, once stood William Morris's Merton Abbey Mills workshops and, earlier, Nelson's Merton Place. The much-tormented River Wandle still flows alongside the street, opposite the bus garage.

Walk past all this, and look for Norman Road on your right, a few turnings along. Head down this street of humble Victorian terraces, until on a corner site to your right you see the 6 **Sultan**. A pretty intact post-war pub, which retains its two-room layout, with the addition of a conservatory, the Sul-

**The Sultan, Hop Back brewery's only London pub**

tan (named after a champion stallion) is far better known as the only London pub in the small estate of the Wiltshire-based Hop Back brewery. Its flagship beer Summer Lightning is credited by many as being the first of the new breed of light hoppy beers that we now take for granted, and the pub has won hatfuls of commendations for its well-kept beers ever since it opened under Hop Back's colours in 1993. It now has a microbrewery in the garden which should be in operation by the time you read this; but it is expected that Hop Back's GFB and Summer Lightning will remain on the bar alongside home brewed offerings and maybe a guest from Downton as now. It's not a food pub, so if you're peckish try a packet of crisps!!

**The river Wandle flows past Merton Abbey Mills**

**The Antelope**

Leaving the pub, head back the way you came. When you get back to the main road, Merton High Street, bear right. Note the very striking exterior of the Nelson Arms across the road as you pass. The pub, the nearest to the site of the Admiral's erstwhile home, sports full exterior tiling from its Charrington days and a series of murals by Garters of Poole. Continue beyond the traffic lights as far as Nelson Road, where on the corner sits Nelson Wines beer shop, one of the best bottle shops for miles around. Now, to finish the tour on a high, carefully cross the road here and head down to the end of Pincott Road opposite. On the corner here, tucked away in an unlikely spot, you'll find the  **Trafalgar**. After a long career as an award-winning freehouse under the stewardship of Dave Norman, this little Victorian pub has now been taken on by another independent outfit headed by the man behind the successful Hope in nearby Carshalton, Rodger Molyneux. A careful refurbishment has improved this corner local (and removed all but one of the TV sets!) whilst retaining its unique character. And, as I frequently moan about poor pub signs, let me commend the new management for commissioning a very good one here. Regular beers are Downton Quadhop and Surrey Hills Shere Drop, while four more handpumps dispense a changing variety of interesting beers. In support are a variety of bottled beers, including a good selection from Belgium, and key-keg beers. There is live music including jam sessions on some evenings. It is the current (2015-6) local CAMRA Pub of the Year.

To reach South Wimbledon Underground station, the nearest, head back up Pincott road and bear left onto the Merton High Street; and it's a further couple of minutes' walk.

## PUB INFORMATION

 **NIGHTINGALE**
97 Nightingale Lane, Balham, SW12 8NX
020 8673 1637 • www.thenightingalebalham.co.uk
**Opening hours:** 12 (11 Sat)-midnight; 11-11 Sun

 **BALHAM BOWLS CLUB**
7-9 Ramsden Road, Balham, SW12 8QX
020 8673 4700 • www.balhambowlsclub.com
**Opening hours:** 4-11 (midnight Fri); 12-midnight Sat; 12-11 Sun

 **WHEATSHEAF**
2 Upper Tooting Road, Tooting, SW17 7PG
020 8672 2805 • www.thewheatsheafsw17.com
**Opening hours:** 12-midnight (1am Fri & Sat); 12-11 Sun

 **KING'S HEAD**
84 Upper Tooting Road, Tooting, SW17 7PB
020 8767 6708 • www.kingsheadpub-tooting.co.uk
**Opening hours:** 12-11 (midnight Fri & Sat)

 **ANTELOPE**
76 Mitcham Road, Tooting, SW17 9NG
020 8672 3888 • www.theantelopepub.com
**Opening hours:** 4-11 (midnight Thu; 1am Fri); 12-1am Sat; 12-11 Sun

 **SULTAN**
78 Norman Road, Wimbledon, SW19 1BT
020 8544 9323 • www.hopback.co.uk/our-pubs/the-sultan.html
**Opening hours:** 12-11 (midnight Fri & Sat)

 **TRAFALGAR**
23 High Path, Merton, SW19 2JY
020 8542 5342 • www.trafalgarfreehouse.co.uk
**Opening hours:** 12-11

**Try also:**

**8** **HAGEN & HYDE**
157 Balham High Road, Balham, SW12 9AU
020 8772 0016 • hagenandhyde.com
**Opening hours:** 12-11.30 (2am Fri & Sat); 12-10.30 Sun

# Croydon – London's Edge City

With a population well in excess of Southampton or Brighton, Croydon functions in all but name as London's 'edge city', hence my licence with the title of this walk. Croydon retains a strong identity of its own, and despite the sixties demolitions, the 'concrete jungle' image and its recent troubles many of its inhabitants are fiercely loyal to the place; if you've never ventured this way, this walk is a great opportunity to find out why. Its once numerous traditional pubs have suffered tremendous loss and damage, but true to form, it has bounced back, and today the centre of this vibrant town is a great place for a pub walk. Perhaps it's in keeping with the rest of the place that the majority of the destinations on this tour are modern conversions rather than traditional old pubs, but all in all this is a top-notch pub walk which can hold its own with central London.

▶ **Start:** East Croydon

▶ **Finish:** The Skylark, South End (with buses back to centre)

▶ **Distance:** 2 miles

▶ **Access:** East Croydon, fast and frequent trains from Central London

▶ **Key attractions:** Whitgift Hospital, Croydon Old Palace (www.friendsofoldpalace.org), Surrey Street market; London's only on-street trams

▶ **THE PUBS:** Oval Tavern; George; Dog & Bull; Green Dragon; Spread Eagle; Royal Standard; Skylark. Try also: Surrey Cricketers

▶ **Timing tips:** The Oval Tavern opens at noon. This route works well at any time of the day or year, with all the pubs open throughout the day. A daytime visit will (except on Sunday) allow you to enjoy the open-air market on Surrey Street. One word of warning: this route is less of the walk and more of the pub: you don't get much chance to walk off the beer between one pub and the next, so pace yourself!

The Green Dragon

The modernised East Croydon station makes a good starting point for this walk, but the first pub is further east still. Coming out of the station with the tram stop right in front of you, bear left, but pause to look at the striking geometric concrete tower overlooking the transport interchange. This is 'No. 1 Croydon', but known more fondly to Croydonians as the threepenny bit tower (after the old twelve-sided coin). Built in 1968 by Siefert and Partners, it's regarded as perhaps their most intact remaining work, and was (unsuccessfully) forwarded for listing by the Twentieth Century Society in 2013. It still qualifies as the most identifiable symbol of the brave new Croydon of the sixties and is certainly far better than some of the recent additions to Croydon's striking skyline.

Head left again down Billington Hill which has been a building site for some time, passing the much-altered Porter & Sorter pub and following the road round to join the A232. Here, bear left yet again, with new flats going up all round you, and cross the road here, taking the second road on your right, Oval Road. Follow this Victorian suburban street for five minutes forking left at the one way signs to reach the **1** **Oval Tavern**

**Croydon is home to London's only tram network**

almost immediately. This imposing three storey Victorian pub has been revitalised by popular landlady Esther Sutton who moved here in early 2014 after a long and successful spell at the Green Dragon. The large bar room is a relaxing place in which to enjoy a beer from a range on the six handpumps where changing offerings from South London micros including Cronx, Sambrook's and Belleville support Robinson's Trooper and St Austell Tribute. Meantime's Yakima Red on keykeg and bottled beers are also available. A full menu of home cooked food, including a good choice for vegetarians, is available throughout the day until 9pm. There's a large garden and patio at the rear of the pub. As befits a champion of Croydon's music scene Esther hosts regular live bands including Sunday lunchtime jazz sessions.

Retrace your steps to East Croydon station, where the stylish thing to do is to take the tram, just one stop westbound, to George Street. If you prefer to walk, just follow the tracks at a safe distance! Close to George Street tram stop is the **2** **George**. This excellent Wetherspoon town centre shop conversion is one of the chain's busiest pubs, and deservedly so if the beer range and quality is any guide. Among the regular beers is Thornbridge Jaipur, but there are usually around ten rotating guests as well as the regulars. Expect Dark Star Hophead and Oakham JHB, along with a great range of changing guests, with local micros much in evidence. Don't miss the second array of handpumps at the rear of the pub.

Continue, on foot, to follow the tram lines, reaching the crossroads at the epicentre of the town, adjacent to the Whitgift almshouses. And what a remarkable building this is, surrounded by modern temples of capitalism and consumerism! Croydon's own Archbishop of Canterbury, John Whitgift (c.1530–1604) obtained permission from Queen Elizabeth I to build a hospital and school in Croydon and, in 1596, he laid the foundation stone for the Hospital Of The Holy Trinity, now known as the Almshouses. This handsome building has survived against all the odds, notably in 1923,

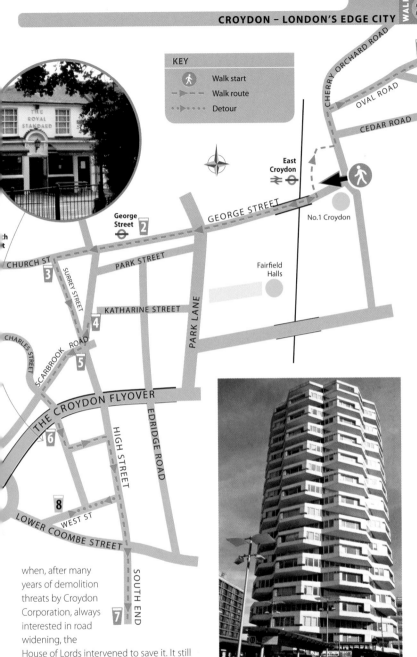

**KEY**

🚶 Walk start
- - - Walk route
•••••• Detour

CHERRY ORCHARD ROAD

OVAL ROAD

CEDAR ROAD

East Croydon ⇌ ⊖

George Street ⊖ **2**

GEORGE STREET

No.1 Croydon

Fairfield Halls

CHURCH ST **3**

PARK STREET

SURREY STREET

KATHARINE STREET

PARK LANE

CHARLES STREET

SCARBROOK ROAD **5**

**4**

THE CROYDON FLYOVER

EDRIDGE ROAD

HIGH STREET

**6**

**8**

WEST ST

LOWER COOMBE STREET

SOUTH END

**7**

when, after many years of demolition threats by Croydon Corporation, always interested in road widening, the House of Lords intervened to save it. It still provides sheltered accomodation.

Head down Crown Hill, still following the tram lines, and turn left into Surrey Street in 100 yards. This area was once known for its markets and fairs, with the first reference

**Seifert's striking geometric 'No. 1 Croydon'**

**Surrey Street market and the Dog & Bull**

to a market being as early as 1276; and this street, once called 'Butcher's Row' still sports a surviving remnant of the butchers' shambles supported by iron and timber columns supporting galleried upper floors above the shops. Across the street, sporting a handsome brick frontage, is the **3 Dog & Bull**. This Young's house (with beers from the Wells/Young's stable) is almost certainly the oldest pub in town today; it has a Georgian frontage, of very attractive dark brickwork, complemented by a pleasing pendant lantern and a hanging pub sign. The recent blue paint job hasn't done it any favours though. It's easy to see where an adjacent shop has been absorbed into the pub; this took place about 30 years ago. It's always been a market pub, and when the market was bigger and livelier than today the pub was an urban classic, bustling with traders and customers, resolutely working-class in character with plain and simple fittings, but clean and well-kept. Today it's lost a lot of that character; it's still likelier to be busier during the day than in the evenings, although the conversion of the old Dog & Bull Yard into an attractive garden has drawn in a new crowd, and there has been a certain smartening-up inside. I think this has gone quite far enough and I hope Young's refrain from further 'improvements' and respect the location and history of this old pub. The

interior retains its island bar, with a separate rear room and the area off to the left in the former shop already referred to. Incidentally, this is the pub which in 1994 HRH Prince Charles, Prince of Wales, visited and was photographed pulling a pint of bitter in the same way that his grandmother had done in an earlier well-known picture which also used to hang in many pubs in Young's estate.

Returning to the street, walk further along, passing an area where modern building on both sides (most recently a pretty grim wall of apartments, thrown up in what's meant to be a Conservation Area!) has spoilt the character of the street; but down to the right on Matthew's Yard good conservation has taken place. Whilst the Victorian gasworks and flour mill have been lost, the old 1880 granary of the former Page & Overton brewery, with its original Victorian hoists, pulleys and loading bays has been restored and part of it is now a nightclub. The impressive and striking castellated building on nearby Overton's Yard is part of Croydon's first waterworks which supplied a million gallons of water a day from 1851. It took advantage, like the brewery, of strong springs which rose immediately west of Surrey Street and fed the headwaters of the River Wandle, whose valley you walked downhill to enter at the start of the walk. The river itself has been buried in Central Croydon today, sadly…

**The Spread Eagle and Croydon clock tower**

Take the steps opposite and climb back out of the valley to re-enter the High Street in the centre of what is very much the 'yoof strip' of town at night, and turn right. Just a short step opposite, and on the corner of Katherine Street by Croydon's impressive Victorian town hall, is the **4** **Spread Eagle**. This is a very good bank conversion by Fuller's inside a fine building. The ambience is relaxed, the fittings do justice to the gravitas of the building, and the décor is smart but traditional. There's even a small terrace outside under the adjacent clock tower. A wide range of Fuller's beers are available, and they offer a discount on production of a current CAMRA membership card. There's a full food menu if you're feeling peckish.

On leaving the Spread Eagle, it's only a short stroll south along the High Street, past the old Ship Inn, and you'll spot the next port of call, across the street where the top end of Surrey Street rejoins the High Street.

**Croydon Water Tower**

The **5** **Green Dragon** is another bank conversion, this one currently in the estate of the Stonegate pub company. This successful and vibrant urban pub offers a welcome to a remarkably diverse clientele, and has been a past winner of the local CAMRA Pub of the Year award. With six handpumps and two gravity dispenses there's a good range of beers to choose from, with Dark Star, Hog's Back and Westerham among the regularly represented breweries. There's often live music upstairs at the weekends.

Leave the Dragon and drop back down the surprisingly steep hill (on Scarbrook Road alongside the pub's side wall) onto the old floodplain of the River Wandle. Once the site of the Scarbrook Pond, the foot of the road now plays host to a couple of ugly car parks and a couple of modern blocks of apartments. You'll also catch a good view of Croydon's well-known flyover, built in the late 1960's

as part of its Brave New World of skyscrapers and urban freeways. In connecting the town centre across the Wandle Valley to Duppas Hill and the west, wholesale demolition of narrow terraced streets took place, and a large number of old pubs were lost. Our next call is one of the survivors, but only just! Turn left and walk under the flyover; and on the corner, opposite the grim multi-storey car park and with its garden pretty well under the flyover itself, lies the **6** **Royal Standard**. Despite the compromised location (but to be fair the street beyond the pub remains an area relatively untouched by the march of modern Croydon), the pub is a classic street corner local, a real gem, the likes of which are becoming rarer all the time. With no fewer than four old doorways pointing to its former compartmentalised interior, it's now all interconnected although with some interesting nooks and corners. The area around to the rear, with its own serving hatch, is the result of a 1980s extension to the public space which improved the pub immensely. A good range of Fuller's beers, usually four, is available. It doesn't get so busy as once it did, but the Standard is still a great Croydon boozer.

Continue along the street, now called Wandle Road, noting the Bull's Head with its rather garish blue and red décor at the next corner. The paint job resulted from the landlord losing a bet that Croydon's football team, Crystal Palace, would not get promoted at the end of the 2012-13 season! Architecture buffs might detour left back to the High Street here (100 yards each way) to inspect the handsome listed Wrencote House straight ahead, reputedly designed by a pupil of Sir Christopher Wren and built around 1720, before following Wandle Road to the 'T' junction with West Street in a further 200 yards. Now, turn left to follow the main route to the last pub. Worth a try if you

**The handsome art deco Skylark**

have time, and just down to the right at the next junction is the  **Surrey Cricketers** which has a few heritage features of interest and a couple of cask beers. Its rather tatty exterior, which nonetheless has some fine brown glazed tilework and retains opaque leaded glass windows throughout, gives way to a comfortable opened out triangular space inside, with wood panelling and carpets. Another features of note is the remarkably high number of former doorways suggesting a heavily compartmentalised interior and a different layout of the servery. The 'public bar' door on the West Street frontage has some stained glass set in the intricate leadwork.

On handpump expect Harveys Sussex Bitter, Sharp's Doom Bar and sometime a third, maybe from Sharp's.

With or without the detour to the Cricketers, the last featured stop is beyond the traffic lights where the High Street becomes South End. Pass the cycle shop on the opposite side of the road. On 'our' side of the street a little further is the  **Skylark**. Croydon is fortunate in having a couple of well above-average Wetherspoon outlets as far as beer range and quality is concerned; and this handsome art deco building is no exception. Although the interior follows the well-established JDW pattern, the spacious drinking area is arranged on two levels and the ambience is very relaxed. Beer range is nearly always good, and often includes locally-sourced microbrewery offerings; quality is good, and the pub is another *Good Beer Guide* regular.

By now, you may either be ready for a walking workout – in which case you may appreciate the opportunity to walk back into town along the main road, which will take about ten minutes; or you'll be dead on your feet, and in that event I would recommend the bus – any bus heading north will take you back into the centre.

## PUB INFORMATION

 **OVAL TAVERN**
131 Oval Road, Croydon, CR0 6BR
020 8686 6023
**Opening hours:** 12-11 (midnight Fri & Sat)

**GEORGE**
17-21 George Street, Croydon, CR0 1LA
020 8649 9077
**Opening hours:** 8am-midnight (1am Fri & Sat)

 **DOG & BULL**
24 Surrey Street, Croydon, CR0 1RG
020 8667 9718 • www.rampubcompany.co.uk/visit-pubs/dog-and-bull
**Opening hours:** 12-11 (11.30 Fri); 11-11 Sat;
12-10.30 Sun

**GREEN DRAGON**
58 High Street, Croydon, CR0 1NA
020 8667 0684 • www.thegreendragoncroydon.co.uk
**Opening hours:** 10-midnight (1am Fri & Sat);
12-10.30 Sun

 **SPREAD EAGLE**
39-41 Katharine Street, Croydon, CR0 1NX
020 8781 1134 • www.spreadeaglecroydon.co.uk
**Opening hours:** 11-11 (midnight Fri & Sat);
12-10.30 Sun

**ROYAL STANDARD**
1 Sheldon Street, Croydon, CR0 1SS
020 8688 9749 • www.royalstandard-croydon.co.uk
**Opening hours:** 12-midnight; 12-11 Sun

 **SKYLARK**
34-36 South End, Croydon, CR0 1DP
020 8649 9909
**Opening hours:** 8am-midnight (1am Fri & Sat)

**Try also:**

 **SURREY CRICKETERS**
23 West Street, Croydon, CR0 1DJ
020 8288 1781
**Opening hours:** 12-midnight (1am Fri & Sat)

# Carshalton & the Wandle Trail

**WALK 26**

Despite being overwhelmed by suburban development nearly a century ago, locals still talk about 'the village', and the centre of Carshalton stills retains a distinctive identity. Several parks and open spaces, some quite small, straddle Carshalton's river, the Wandle; and there are a number of attractive buildings, especially those assembled around Carshalton Ponds. The Wandle Trail offers a pleasant stroll along an almost continuous ribbon of open spaces from Morden, three miles north; and for the more energetic, I would strongly recommend this well-signed walk to build up a thirst – it's full of interest all the way. Start at Morden Hall Park, just minutes from the Underground station.

**Start/finish:**
⇌ Carshalton (NB not Carshalton Beeches); or ⬦ Morden and walk via Wandle Trail

**Distance:** 2 miles (3.2 km)

**Access:** Trains from ⇌ Victoria (30 mins) or via Thameslink services from ⇌ Blackfriars (30 mins)

**Key attractions:** Wilderness Island Local Nature Reserve; River Wandle Trail; Grove Park; Honeywood Museum; Carshalton House Water Tower

**THE PUBS:** Railway Tavern; Lord Palmerston; Sun; Windsor Castle; Racehorse; Hope. Try also: Greyhound

**Timing tips:** Best enjoyed in daylight hours to get the most from the riverside and the open spaces. If you tackle this route on a summer Sunday, you'll have an opportunity to visit the Carshalton House Water Tower, which opens to the public on Sunday afternoons.

The Lord Palmerston

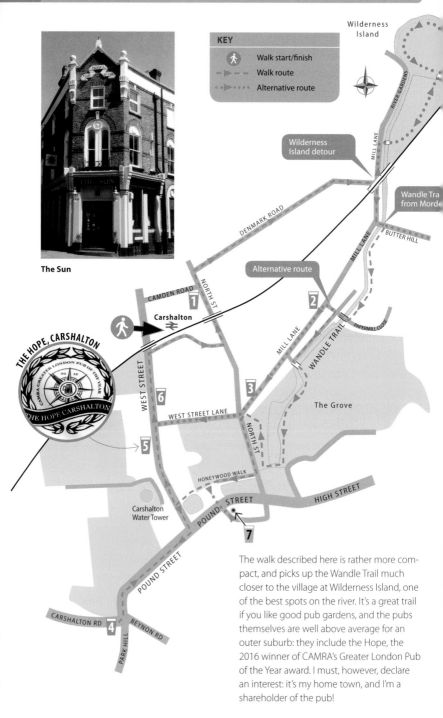

The Sun

**KEY**

🚶 Walk start/finish

Walk route

Alternative route

Wilderness Island

Wilderness Island detour

Alternative route

Wandle Trail from Morden

The Grove

Carshalton Water Tower

THE HOPE, CARSHALTON

THE HOPE CARSHALTON

The walk described here is rather more compact, and picks up the Wandle Trail much closer to the village at Wilderness Island, one of the best spots on the river. It's a great trail if you like good pub gardens, and the pubs themselves are well above average for an outer suburb: they include the Hope, the 2016 winner of CAMRA's Greater London Pub of the Year award. I must, however, declare an interest: it's my home town, and I'm a shareholder of the pub!

**Horseshoe bar inside the Railway Tavern**

Head left out of the station and walk down to North Street at the foot of the hill. Turn left again, under the bridge, and you've already arrived at the first stop of the day. The **Railway Tavern** is a plain but attractive brick built corner local. Like a number of Carshalton pubs it was a former Charrington's house until about 1980 when it was acquired by Fuller's. It now has a single drinking area around the horseshoe bar. Currently there are four ales, three from Fuller's including London Pride, Gales Seafarers and their seasonal ales; and a guest. Food in this wet-led pub is confined to traditional filled rolls. A previous guv'nor developed the attractive garden at the side of the pub, which is a very pleasant retreat for an early pint. If you've opted for the walk from Morden, you'll miss this pub at the start but in consultation with your map you can include it later in the round.

From here, cross North Street and head down Denmark Road, almost opposite. Five minutes of mundane suburbia will bring you down to the River Wandle at the far end of the street. Cross to the riverside and turn downstream, away from the striking Three Arch Bridge, for just a few yards, and over the river bridge to the entrance to Wilderness Island. There are no pubs here, but a detour to take in this small but well-wooded local

nature reserve is recommended: it's an area with quite a history. At the far end of the site, over another bridge, is the confluence of the two branches of the river, from Croydon and Carshalton. It was a very important mill site, and the terminus of a branch of the old Surrey Iron Railway, the world's first public railway. For those with an interest in this small river with a big history, I might humbly recommend my book *A River Wandle Companion* (www.wandlebook.co.uk).

Back at the entrance to the reserve, walk back upstream now, under the bridge, and reach the road junction of Mill Lane and Butter Hill. Here, the corner building is the much-disguised remains of an old snuff mill; but maybe of more interest is the fish pass running up the former wheel pit, installed by the Wandle Trust to assist trout in getting to the upper reaches of the river, and visible from the bridge. Cross the bridge and turn sharp right along the riverside, along a restored stretch, which until 20 years ago was factory land with no public access. Now it's a link in the Wandle Trail which hugs the riverside almost continuously from the source to its confluence with the Thames at Wandsworth. Pass the wooden footbridge and meet a road shortly beyond. Unlikely as it may now seem, here once stood one of the most celebrated paper mills in England. Only the name of the road is left to offer a link to the past.

Turn right here to rejoin Mill Lane right by the **Lord Palmerston**. The only survivor of several working men's pubs that once stood on this street, the 'Palm' has recently had a significant makeover and acquired its striking new exterior livery. The interior although modernised in a contemporary style, retains its traditional, two-room layout: public bar and saloon. The public (left-hand) bar has an open fire while you may be able to spot the old pewter sinks which have survived here. In the saloon there's another TV but the wood panelled walls (now painted) have been retained. The enthusiastic new management have started out with Harveys Sussex Bitter and Sharp's Doom Bar, but there may be other offerings by the time you visit.

**The redesigned interior of the Sun**

Return to the Wandle Trail, which now runs on the right-hand bank of the river (walking upstream). In just 100 yards turn left and cross the river again, and follow the path into The Grove, an attractive riverside park, which allows you to follow the river right up to Carshalton Ponds, the present-day source of the Wandle, in the village centre. Following the riverbank, pass the cascade and the large house, also known as The Grove, on your left. The park was formerly the grounds of this once private mansion, bought by the local council for the town in 1924. At the graceful and slender Leoni Bridge pause to admire the view across the pond to the substantial parish church, before crossing the bridge and following the main path, away from the river a little, round and down to exit onto North Street. If it's after sunset, the gates into the park will be closed and you'll need to continue along Mill Lane.

A few yards further on, unmissable and very distinctive on a prominent corner site, stands the **3** **Sun**. As one might expect from the size and decoration of the building, this was in the past a far more important and imposing hostelry than the others we have visited so far. Built in 1870, just after the coming of the railway, it was a hotel aimed at the new trade and traffic the railway would

bring. The name is said to derive from the fact that the windows in the hotel rooms could expect sunlight nearly all day on account of the orientation of the building. After a period of ups and downs the Sun has been given a completely new lease of life under its new owners. I have to admit that the total redesign of the interior with some very good-quality fittings has more than compensated for the otherwise regrettable loss of the separate public bar. The smart but tasteful refurbishment is complemented by a total transformation outside too: the owners have removed the awful paint from the lovely old tiles, and commissioned replacement for those lost, which together with a tasteful repainting has resulted in the pub looking more attractive than it has done in living memory. Moreover the back yard has been converted into a charming pub garden which is a very popular hangout in almost all weathers. Although the pub majors on good-quality food, it has also installed a set of six handpumps offering a changing and interesting range of beers, often from small independent breweries like Brighton Bier Co and Arbor.

It's possible at this point to shorten the route by heading up West Street Lane across the road from the Sun, to rejoin the trail at the Racehorse (see map); but the official route heads back up North Street, between the walls, and into Honeywood Walk, on your right, alongside the western of the town's twin ponds. There's a great view of the parish church, the Greyhound (see below) and, to the right, Honeywood, an Edwardian mansion that now functions as a museum and tea room. If you wish to take in the **7** **Greyhound,** this is the time to do so: it's a building with a lot of history and has been a Young's house for well over a century but many locals complain about alterations which have seen the pretty 'Swan Bar' at the front often closed and rarely manned, while a large TV screen frequently comes down in the main bar. Currently (mid 2016) the pub is closed for yet another revamp which will see yet more emphasis on food. Beers are from Wells & Young's, with guests. If you do visit, look for the lovely old greyhound floor mosaic at the Swan Bar entrance.

Return, if need be, to the route at the corner of the pond, by the little gatehouse to The Lodge and at the entrance to Festival Walk, a pleasant footpath that leads past a venerable old London

**The river Wandle runs through The Grove**

plane tree, the capital's largest specimen, and the entrance to the grounds of the Ecology Centre, with views of the unusual water tower ahead. The unique Grade II-listed building contained a water-powered pump, which supplied water to Carshalton House (still standing behind the high wall, and now a school) and the fountains in its garden. However, the building was and is much more than this as it contains a suite of rooms, the highlights being an orangery and a remarkable early 18th-century bathroom with a plunge bath lined with Delft blue tiles. It's open to the public only on summer Sundays (check the website: www.carshaltonwatertower.co.uk).

Follow the wall south alongside West Street to the junction 50 yards away and follow the road round to the right up to the traffic lights in 300 yards (you might prefer to cross to the other side, where the footway is wider). At the lights, occupying a prominent position, is another well-known drinking landmark, the **4 Windsor Castle**. This *Good Beer Guide* regular is a spacious one-room pub with a pleasant garden, which you may need help in finding. Once a de facto free house and an erstwhile winner of CAMRA's London Pub of the Year award, the Windsor is now in the hands of Shepherd

Neame, offering a rare local opportunity to sample a range of three of its beers. However, the tradition of offering guest beers here continues, and a further three handpumps dispense two rotating guests and Long Man Best Bitter from the eponymous Sussex micro. Food, from simple bar snacks and light bites to a restaurant menu, is available at most times, with a Sunday carvery (check the website for menus). The Windsor traditionally hosts a May Bank holiday beer festival.

Retrace your steps down to the Water Tower, but this time continue along West Street, passing some attractive old weatherboarded houses on the right. The buildings on either side of the entrance to Old Swan Yard on the left are both interesting. That on the near corner is the former Swan itself (now a private house), from where the daily coach to London once departed; the larger one on the opposite corner is the former National Schools building. A short step beyond and a rather poor new pub sign announces the **5 Racehorse**. This substantial looking 19th century pub has had a tasteful recent refurbishment throughout, which happily has not removed the public bar (although I regret the loss of the benches). It's also the second pub on this trail to have a rather fine floor mosaic in the entrance

**There's always a plenty of choice at the Hope**

lobby. Go to the left if you want to eat. The pub, in the Enterprise Inns estate, has had more than one change of management of late and majors on food but has upped its game on the beer front recently and now offers four ales, Timothy Taylor Landlord and Sharp's Doom Bar as regulars with two rotating guests, often Otter Bitter which the regulars like, and a St Austell beer.

The final port of call is visible by its sign another 100 yards down the road when you leave the Racehorse. For London beer scene aficionados it may need no introduction, for the **6** **Hope** has just notched up its third CAMRA Greater London Pub of the Year award in five years, a remarkable rags-to-riches story for a pub that came close to calling time forever just a few years ago. A group of local people got together and negotiated a long free-of-tie lease from Punch Taverns, and in 2015 bought the freehold outright. Starting with a couple of cask ales, the beer range has expanded steadily under the careful and knowledgeable stewardship of the young cellar manager and his team so that it is now among the most ambitious outside of Central London, and quality is second to none. On handpump, expect two regular beers (Downton New Forest Ale and Windsor & Eton's Knight of the Garter) plus five rapidly rotating guests from some of Britain's best micros, among them Arbor, Magic Rock, Siren Craft Brew and Redemption. Additionally there are some exciting and rarely seen (even in London) craft keg offerings, often at industrial-grade gravities; and a small but serious list of

bottled beers. All draught beers are available in multiples of one third of a pint, a useful option if you're going up-gravity.

The pub is a real community hub and you can expect a friendly welcome. Local events are advertised here and there are frequently impromptu music sessions and other happenings. Check the website for details of upcoming beer festivals, usually themed, and taking place with remarkable frequency in the spacious garden.

If you miss the last train home (and it's a hard pub to leave), ask at the bar for directions to bus stops: the 157 in particular runs a late service and will take you to the Underground railhead at Morden, or into Croydon for all-night trains.

## PUB INFORMATION

**1** **RAILWAY TAVERN**
47 North Street, Carshalton, SM5 2HG
020 8669 8016 • www.railwaytaverncarshalton.co.uk
**Opening hours:** 12-11; 12-10.30 Sun

**2** **LORD PALMERSTON**
31 Mill Lane, Carshalton, SM5 2JY
020 8647 1222
**Opening hours:** 11.30-11; 11-11 Sun

**3** **SUN**
4 North Street, Carshalton, SM5 2HU
020 8773 4549 • www.thesuncarshalton.com
**Opening hours:** 12-(10 Mon) 11; 12-midnight Fri & Sat; 12-10.30 Sun

**4** **WINDSOR CASTLE**
378 Carshalton Road, Carshalton, SM5 3PT
020 8669 1191 • www.windsorcastlepub.com
**Opening hours:** 12-11 (11.30 Fri & Sat); 12-10 Sun

**5** **RACEHORSE**
17 West Street, Carshalton, SM5 2PT
020 8773 1429
**Opening hours:** 11-11 (midnight Thu-Sat); 11-11 Sun

**6** **HOPE**
48 West Street, Carshalton, SM5 2PR
020 8240 1255 • www.hopecarshalton.co.uk
**Opening hours:** 12-11; 12-10.30 Sun

**Try also:**

**7** **GREYHOUND**
2 High Street, Carshalton, SM5 3PE
020 8647 1511 • www.greyhoundhotel.net
**Opening hours:** 7am-midnight Mon-Thu; 8am-1am Fri & Sat; 8am-11 Sun

# An Ealing Edwardian expedition

**WALK**
**27**

This fine bus-assisted route takes in several award-winning pubs, on account either of their (mainly Edwardian) architecture, or of their well kept beers, or both. No fewer than three of the entries are listed by CAMRA as having interiors of either National, in the case of the Forester, or Regional heritage significance. It's a very urban route so I strongly recommend counterbalancing that by taking in a couple of miles on the Grand Union towpath first to work up a thirst, if you have the time. This can be done either from Brentford, or, for a shorter canalside walk, from Boston Manor Underground station. You could also combine part of this route with Walk 28 which passes through Brentford.

> **Start:** Brentford (Grand Union Canal) or ⊖ Boston Manor or ⇌ Hanwell

> **Finish:** Acton High Street

> **Distance:** 7.2 miles (11.7 km) from Brentford

> **Key attractions:** Grand Union Canal towpath walk, Elthorne and Gunnersbury Parks. Edwardian pub architecture.

> **THE PUBS:** Fox; Grosvenor; Forester; Ealing Park Tavern; Aeronaut; George & Dragon

> **Timing tips:** Tackle this route in the order recommended as the George & Dragon doesn't open until 4pm during the week. Note also that Hanwell station is closed on Sundays!

**Hanwell Locks, near the Fox**

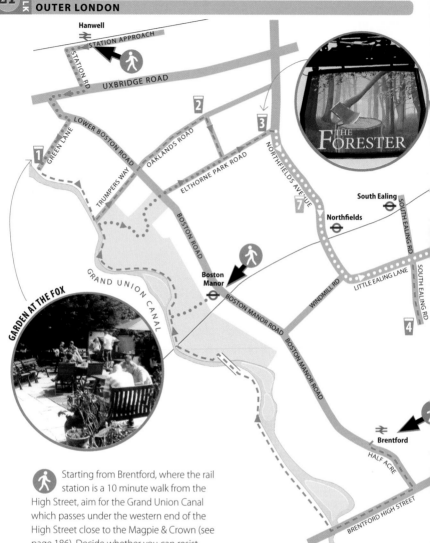

Hanwell
STATION APPROACH
STATION RD
UXBRIDGE ROAD
LOWER BOSTON ROAD
GREEN LANE
TRUMPERS WAY
OAKLANDS ROAD
ELTHORNE PARK ROAD
BOSTON ROAD
GRAND UNION CANAL
NORTHFIELDS AVENUE
South Ealing
Northfields
SOUTH EALING RD
SOUTH EALING RD
WINDMILL RD
LITTLE EALING LANE
Boston Manor
BOSTON MANOR ROAD
BOSTON MANOR ROAD
Brentford
HALF ACRE
BRENTFORD HIGH STREET

THE FORESTER

GARDEN AT THE FOX

1 2 3 4 7

Starting from Brentford, where the rail station is a 10 minute walk from the High Street, aim for the Grand Union Canal which passes under the western end of the High Street close to the Magpie & Crown (see page 186). Decide whether you can resist temptation before setting out northwards towards Hanwell on the towpath, negotiating first the former busy docks, now an area of modern apartments. The Grand Union Canal, originally called the Grand Junction, was completed between Birmingham and London in 1820, just a few years before the first railways arrived. Today the well-maintained towpath, part of the Capital Ring path, is a very pleasant saunter especially in summer when the sight if not the sound of the all-too adjacent M4 motorway is pretty

well hidden and the route takes on a surprisingly rural feel. It's a little over two miles to Hanwell along the canal: before reaching the M4 motorway bridge pass Clitheroe's lock, and beyond this, cross the picturesque black and white painted Gallows Bridge. This graceful cast iron structure, dated 1820, may well be the work of Thomas Telford.

Pass under the noisy M4 motorway (where you'll join the route if you opted for the shorter alternative start from

Ealing Common

UXBRIDGE ROAD

Ealing Common

Acton Central

CHURCHFIELD ROAD

NORTH CIRCULAR

GUNNERSBURY LANE

HIGH STREET

HIGH STREET

POPES LANE

POPES LANE

GUNNERSBURY LANE

BOLLO LANE

Acton House

Gunnersbury Park

LIONEL ROAD

**KEY**

 Walk start

– ▶ – – Walk route

• • ▶ • • • Alternative route

• • ▶ • • • • Bus route

## 🚶 🚊 HANWELL START

Provided it's not Sunday there's a half hourly service from Paddington. Exit from the south side of the station onto Station Approach. It's a short if unexciting walk to the Fox on Green Lane via Station Road, Westminster Road and the Lower Boston Road. Check your A to Z !

## 🚶 ⊖ BOSTON MANOR START

Exit the station and turn left along Boston Road. When you reach the Harvester pub-restaurant take the road on your left, signposted 'canal walk'. Cross Southdown Avenue and continue ahead, entering the park. Immediately bear left and, following the waymark, join the path next to the wooded area and sports pavilion. Continue ahead to more woodland, again following the markers. Reach the canal by the M4 bridge and turn right to follow the towpath.

Boston Manor). Continue north, passing Gunnersbury Lock and about half a mile beyond, pass under a bridge with Patterson's factory opposite. Also on Trumpers Way above the canal is the Weird Beard Brewery (www.weirdbeardbrewco.com) which has several open days a year, and which you may therefore be able to fit into your itinerary with a bit of forward planning.

It's not far now, having passed houses on your right, until you arrive at Hanwell by a marker post sighed 'Green Lane'. Leave the towpath here and emerge onto a picturesque lane of old Victorian cottages. 75 yards up on your right is the **1** **Fox**.

Although dating from 1848 this handsome and interesting building has a distinct Edwardian air about it, due in no small part to the part-leaded and stained windows which are redolent of that period. This popular freehouse, which has won the local CAMRA Pub of the Year gong on many occasions, offers several cask beers including Fuller's London Pride and Timothy Taylor's Landlord. There are two guest beers. Food is of good quality and value, with Sunday lunches especially popular. There's a pretty and generously proportioned beer garden with a quirky 'tea barn' in one corner.

**The ever-popular Fox**

**Surviving screenwork inside the Grosvenor**

Retrace your steps (or if arriving from Hanwell station read the text backwards!) to the canal and then south to the Trumpers Way overbridge, just beyond which a path gains the road by the entrance to Elthorne Waterside Park. Now in consultation with your map you can either take the direct and easy-to-navigate route up the road to the right, crossing straight over the Boston Road into Oaklands Road. This leads directly to the second pub in a few minutes further. Alternatively for a more adventurous and greener walk head into the park, keeping to the main path for a few minutes before veering round to the left by the children's playground into the more formal garden and past the bandstand to reach the Boston Road opposite Elthorne Park Road. Now cross over and walk down as far as Seward Road and bear left to reach the imposing exterior of the **2 Grosvenor** in a couple of minutes.

There's no doubting the Edwardian credentials of this handsome old building, it dates from 1904. Given the size and erstwhile importance of the building, (the owners, Brentford's Royal Brewery, had to surrender three licences on other smaller premises to get permission for the project in the face

of temperance opposition) it may possibly have been the work of celebrated pub architect Nowell Parr, but this is speculation. A recent tasteful makeover has retained the venerable, possibly original bar counter with its black and white mosaic surround. Some glazed screenwork also survives. There's plenty of beer choice (with a local emphasis) on no fewer than seven handpumps, but if you can't find the right cask ale there's a good range of bottle-conditioned beers and a large and varied range of local keg beers too, with enthusiastic and attentive staff on hand to advise.

From the Grosvenor walk down Seward Road to the east as far as the T-junction in 300 yards and turn left into Leighton Road. Another few minutes along here brings you to the perhaps the architectural highlight of the walk, the high Edwardian **3 Forester**. Large and imposing on a corner site, it was completed in 1909 for the Royal Brewery and designed by noted pub architect Thomas Nowell Parr. You can still see some of his trademark Tudor-style arches inside. It remains a fine example of suburban pub architecture for its period, displaying columned porticoes, green-glazed brickwork and prominent gables. Some of the windows still contain some pretty art nouveau panels. It still retains four distinct rooms, and two very unusual features, namely, a publican's office set into the servery, and, uniquely in London, bell-pushes for service in one of the rooms fronting Leighton Road. Grade II-listed, it features on CAMRA's inventory of pub interiors of national significance. The beer's not bad either: since being bought by Fuller's in 2012 it offers a range of Fuller's beers plus a guest or two, often the Fuller's-brewed Gales HSB. There's a well-regarded Thai restaurant on site.

**Ealing Park Tavern**

It's a long haul on foot to our next destination, so, leaving the pub, cross Seaford Road and the main Northfield Road by the allotments, bearing right to reach the Hessel Road bus stop in about 50 yards. It's worth noting before you board the bus that, as we go to print, permission for a new micropub has been granted at the **7 Owl & the Pussycat**, just one stop down the road. Check the pub website for updates.

The frequent E3 bus will take you past Northfields Underground station and on to the South Ealing Road stop where you need to alight for the next pub. (If you wish to shorten things and head straight to Acton, stay on the E3 and alight at Acton Fire Station). Alighting from the bus at South Ealing Road, walk up to the lights and bear right whence it's less than a five minute walk to reach, opposite the gates to the cemetery, the **4 Ealing Park Tavern**. Like the Fox at Hanwell this magnificent and striking building was built in the Victorian period but has a distinctly Edwardian appearance, dominating its corner site completely. It's worth admiring from the other side of the road to appreciate the building. Although not listed, it does feature on CAMRA's London Regional Inventory of Pub Interiors of Special Historic Interest; once again it was built for the Royal Brewery Company at Brentford, whose monograms are still visible in the arch of the porch. Note also the now rather obscure green tiled porch with Art Nouveau-style lettering spelling out 'saloon' as you enter. Inside, the new owners have given the place a rather heavy makeover, removing some historic features, whilst restoring others like the fine wood panelling and bar counter. It focuses on food but an on-site brewery opened in 2015, and its 'Long Arm' cask beers are sold alongside an interesting range of bottle-conditioned and keg beers. A word of warning: the place occasionally shuts completely for private functions, a practice which I find quite inappropriate for a 'public house' but one which seems to be growing. In the case of this establishment, these days are at least advertised on the pub's website so I advise consulting this before you set out, especially at weekends.

Return to the same bus stop and wait for the next E3 to Acton. Readers wishing to end up in Ealing and shorten the day at this point could, as an alternative, take the 65 bus to Ealing Broadway from the stop almost right outside the Ealing Park Tavern, calling en route

**The Forester has a wealth of architectural interest**

**The George & Dragon**

(alight Warwick Road stop) at the Red Lion, a Fuller's house and *Good Beer Guide* regular.

The E3 takes you past Acton Town station and into the centre of town where you should alight at the Fire Station and walk up to the junction by the Red Lion & Pineapple, a striking building at the junction now in the J D Wetherspoon estate and worth a call for those with plenty of stamina. Across the road and a little to the right is the remarkable  **Aeronaut**. This ex-Truman's house has been transformed into a themed pub with a difference; a circus and cabaret performance space to one side of the bar, and a remarkable garden at the rear make this perhaps the most unusual venue listed in this book; but the humble beer drinker

has not been forgotten either; the on-site Laine Brewery which is visible behind the servery turns out some interesting brews of all strengths, and real cider is also available. All in all, quite an experience and certainly something new for Acton!

To finish this marathon, walk east along the High Street (right hand fork at the roundabout) and you'll reach the  **George & Dragon** in about five minutes. In total contrast to the Aeronaut, this externally handsome Grade II-listed brick pub has three separate areas inside, all with plenty of character. An dark and atmospheric front room, with a list of landlords dating back to 1759, leads through to a rear bar with exposed panelling, and beyond to a cavernous but tastefully remodelled room which houses the on-site Dragonfly Brewery. All Dragonfly's cask beers are served, including two changing seasonal ales, and usually two real ciders. There's an outside courtyard leading from the servery. It's a very good finale to a rewarding tour, but you'll probably by now be looking for an exit strategy… fortunately Acton is well placed with plenty of local buses running along the main road and rail stations spaced around the George & Dragon in all main directions. Plan ahead depending on your destination.

## PUB INFORMATION

 **FOX**
Green Lane, Hanwell, W7 2PJ
020 8567 4021 • www.thefoxpub.co.uk
**Opening hours:** 11-11; 12-10.30 Sun

 **GROSVENOR**
127 Oaklands Road, Hanwell, W7 2DT
020 8840 0007 • www.foodandfuel.co.uk/our-pubs/
the-grosvenor-hanwell
**Opening hours:** 12 (9am Fri)-11; 12-10.30 Sun

 **FORESTER**
2 Leighton Road, West Ealing, W13 9EP
020 8567 1654 • www.theforesterealing.com
**Opening hours:** 11-11.30 (midnight Wed & Thu; 1am
Fri & Sat); 11-11 Sun

**4 EALING PARK TAVERN**
222 South Ealing Road, South Ealing, W5 4RL
020 8758 1879 • www.ealingparktavern.com
**Opening hours:** 11-11 (midnight Thu-Sat); 11-10.30 Sun

 **AERONAUT**
264 Acton High Street, Acton, W3 9BH
020 8993 4242 • www.aeronaut.pub
**Opening hours:** 12-midnight (1am Thu; 1.30am
Fri & Sat); 12-midnight Sun

**6 GEORGE & DRAGON**
183 High Street, Acton, W3 9DJ
020 8992 3712
**Opening hours:** 4-11; 12-1am Fri & Sat; 12-10.30
Sun

Try also:

 **OWL & THE PUSSYCAT**
106 Northfield Avenue, West Ealing, W13 9RT
markopaulo.co.uk
**Opening hours:** 12-3, 5-10; 12-10.30
Fri; 11-10.30 Sat

# Isleworth to Kew along the Thames via Syon Park

This is a varied walk of about three miles, full of interest, and strongly recommended for a sunny weekend. It takes us through Old Isleworth on the bank of the Thames, into Syon Park and on to Brentford, where we rejoin the river before crossing Kew Bridge and finishing at the Botanist, close to Kew Green. Throw in several top-notch pubs, offering between them among the widest variety of beers from independent breweries in South West London, and it's easy to see why this is such a popular walk. As an alternative with a canalside walk, divert at Brentford onto the Grand Union Canal and take in at least the Fox at Hanwell (see Walk 27).

**WALK 28**

▶ **Start:** ⇌ Isleworth

▶ **Finish:** Kew Green, for ⇌ Kew Bridge or ⇌ ⟷ Kew Gardens

▶ **Distance:** 3.6 miles (5.8 km)

▶ **Access:** From ⇌ London Waterloo & Clapham Junction

▶ **Key attractions:** Kew Botanic Gardens; Kew Steam Museum; Osterley Park; Syon Park House and gardens

▶ **THE PUBS:** Red Lion; London Apprentice; Magpie & Crown; Brewery Tap; Watermans Arms; Express Tavern; Botanist

▶ **Timing tip:** A good route for the daytime, when you'll get the most from the views of the river and the parkland between Isleworth and Brentford. Most of the pubs are open all day, but watch out for limited hours at the Express, and see the note under the entry for the Watermans Arms, below.

**London Apprentice on the Thames**

**Kew Bridge**

This involves a train trip, so start at Waterloo or Clapham Junction and take the frequent South West Trains service to Isleworth (35 mins from Waterloo). Come out of the main entrance of the station at Isleworth, turn right, and right again under the rail bridge. This is Linkfield Road, and it's only a short walk down here to the first pub. For a shorter version of this trail, omitting the first two pubs and the walk through Syon Park, alight at Brentford station, two stops before Isleworth, and walk down the main road southwards to the main Brentford High Street by the Beehive, a Fuller's house. Then turn right and walk along the High Street for five minutes to reach the Magpie & Crown (below).

The **1 Red Lion** is a large and distinctive building in a fairly nondescript suburban street, but it's also out of the ordinary in terms of its status both as a hub of the local community and as a beacon of beer excellence which has regularly scooped the local CAMRA branch's top pub gong over the past decade. It's no surprise that it's recently been designated as an Asset of Community Value (ACV). The large and homely public bar offers plenty of drinking areas, and there's a separate, comfortable lounge. The new tenant has continued to offer

**RED LION**

**KEY**

🚶 Walk start

- - ▸ - - Walk route

a wide range of beers: expect one or two regulars from Sharp's, and up to half a dozen mainly localled-sorced and changing guests from the likes of Twickenham, Sambrook's and Belleville. There always seems to be something happening here, including live music and a biannual beer festival showcasing champion beers. If you're after a lunchtime bite, avoid Mondays, but otherwise you'll be in luck. It's a good pub to kick off any trail, and a hard one to leave, but there's a task ahead!

Leaving the Red Lion, continue down to the far end of Linkfield Road, where turn right onto the main road, and almost immediately bear left by the river bridge into Mill Platt, an ancient route, now a pedestrian alleyway. Just south of the Platt is the bridge over the Duke of

Northumberland's River – an artificial river, a branch of the River Colne, constructed sometime in the 15th or 16th century to provide power to the manorial water mill at Isleworth just downstream from here. Pass the Ingram Almshouses, a terrace of six built by Sir Thomas Ingram, erstwhile Chancellor of the Duchy of Lancaster, and emerge by the site of the old mill

EXPRESS TAVERN

**Kew Bridge**

**Brentford**
¼ mile

Link to Walk 27

ROYAL
BOTANIC
GARDENS,
KEW

Palm House

SYON
PARK

Syon House

OLD
DEER PARK

THAMES

Kew Gardens

**KEW GREEN**

**KEW ROAD**

**LINK TO WALK 27**

The bridge on the Grand Union Canal is the starting point for Walk 27, and makes an alternative onward route, either before or after visiting the Magpie & Crown.

by the Thames in Old Isleworth village. Saunter left here through the old village street down to the **2** **London Apprentice**.

This large, attractive pub has early 18th-century origins and takes its name from the City livery company (trade association) apprentices, who stopped here for refreshments after their long row upstream. The interior subdivisions have gone, only the multiple doorways remain, but there's enough historic interest for it to merit a Grade II* listing. Look out for the fine 'Isleworth Ales' etched glass (the Isleworth Brewery was bought out by Watneys in 1923). The beer menu has improved significantly in the past few years and you can now choose from up to four guests (Adnams Ghost Ship is a regular guest) in addition to the regulars, Greene King IPA and London Glory. If you didn't eat at the Red Lion, you'll be pleased to learn that food is on offer here throughout the day and evening. The upstairs Riverside Room offers great views over the Thames if it's not being otherwise used; there's also a riverside terrace.

Moving on, continue along the street, passing some handsome old buildings and then the pretty tower of Isleworth church; it's now flanked with incongruous modern buildings, after schoolboys burnt the rest of it down in the 1940s! Just along the riverside past the church, pick up the well-signed Thames Path leading to the right into Syon Park. Originally the site of a medieval abbey, and described by John Betjeman as 'The Grand Architectural Walk', Syon House and its 200-acre park is the London home of the Duke of Northumberland (he of the river), whose family has owned it for 400 years. Walk up the roadway through the park (the house and gardens are open Wednesdays, Thursdays and Sundays in season; for details and admission rates, see www.syonpark.co.uk).

Beyond, keep to the cycle route through the car park and house precincts if you

feel you are about to lose your way, but the Thames Path then emerges on the busy A315 road just west of Brentford High Street. Turn right, pass two or three pubs and the Grand Union Canal bridge before, tucked a little bit back off the street frontage, you'll come upon the next official stop, the **3** **Magpie & Crown**. A *Good Beer Guide* regular, this is a very good pub which has long been a great supporter of microbreweries and interesting beers. Since licensee Tam took over a few years ago she has re-established the place as Brentford's premier ale house, and offers the customer a wider-than-ever choice with, usually, six ales (including one from well-regarded local micro Twickenham), a cider and a perry, at reasonable prices. There's also a decent range of draught and bottled continental (mainly Belgian) beers. All in all, it's another pub that can easily kill off a pub walk and turn it into a long sedentary session! Did you spot the old Watneys badge above the pub sign?

Continue east along the High Street for a short while, and, before the traffic lights

**Watermans Arms**

**The Great Conservatory in Syon Gardens**

and the Beehive opposite, turn right down Catherine Wheel Road. This is an area of mixed land use, industry giving way in places to new river- and canalside apartments. Right by the junction of the canal and the river, and accessed via steps, which is a reminder of the flood risk here, stands the **4** **Brewery Tap**. This Fuller's local, whose name recalls a long-defunct takeover victim, still has a community feel and some vestiges of its former multi-roomed layout. Expect four Fuller's beers plus a rotating guest. Upon exit, a narrow path opposite leads across a creek to the Grand Union Canal. Follow along to the lock and cross the bridge, but don't turn right (upstream) here on the Thames Path; rather, head downstream and follow the path along the wharfage with new developments and a marina as company.

At Ferry Road, after circumnavigating a small inlet, and by a section of old wharf-side rail line, head up between the new apartments with an older brick house ('Peerless Pumps') on the corner, to the attractive **5** **Watermans Arms** on the corner of the main road. With a fine period frontage featuring half-timbering, tiles and leaded windows, this appealing house, smartly traditional inside too, has had a recent change in ownership but Gordon,

the tenant, is still here offering the safe choices of Fuller's London Pride and Wells Bombardier. His guest ale is usually from Twickenham's portfolio. This Greene King house has a welcoming appearance. Inside, despite a recent makeover, it's still quite traditional in layout. The interesting menu features Japanese as well as more traditional dishes. The pub usually closes in the afternoons during the midweek, especially in winter, but if you phone ahead in good time, they may stay open for a group.

Leaving the pub and walking the few steps up to the main road, the continuation to Kew Bridge is a walk of a shade over half a mile to the east (right). You could take the bus – the frequent 65 will drop you at the Express Tavern in no time – but to walk along the river, follow the road to the traffic lights and return to the riverside by the 'Thames Path via Watermans Park' sign. Current redevelopment hereabouts may open up more of the riverfront, so you could take local advice or check. It's a pleasant stroll past an array of houseboats, emerging at Kew Bridge.

Now, assuming you have done your homework with the opening times, the **6** **Express Tavern** is a short walk back to the left, right on the busy road junction. Those readers who haven't visited the

**The bar at the Botanist**

Express for a while will be in for a shock once they step inside this handsome brick pub, but the clue is on the external frontage which advertises 'Cider and Ale House'. Now run by the same people who brought you the award-winning Sussex Arms in Twickenham (see page 193) – the beer range and choice has been transformed: the pub's trademark Draught Bass is still a regular, with Haresfoot Lock Keeper's Launch, and with no fewer than eight changing guests. A range of up to five ciders/perries are also available, advertised on the handpumps in the left hand room. The historically-interesting interior has been given only the lightest of redecorations, respecting the character of this multi-room pub, particularly in the rear room with its 1930s features and not originally part of the public drinking area. A framed award commemorates the founding of the local branches of CAMRA in this pub in 1974; and it has seen very frequent appearances in the *Good Beer Guide* since.

Cross the bridge and walk down on the main road to the south side of Kew Green, the centre of the old village, now riven in two by the nasty and busy South Circular road. Just beyond the green, on the right, lies the **7 Botanist**. This former brewpub was converted from a row of shops just a few years ago, hence the varied character of the separate areas inside. It's now in the hands of M&B who took over in 2014 and removed the in-house brewery; but the place is still worth a visit in view of its good range

of beers (four changing guests in addition to the regular beer, Sharp's Doom Bar). It has a covered, heated garden and the bright and cheery interior is quite tastefully done and makes for an invigorating contrast to the largely traditional pubs earlier on this walk. Needless to say, you can eat here – the menu is good and aimed at the affluent locals.

From here, Kew Bridge station is back across the river and just beyond the Express Tavern; and Kew Gardens on the Underground and Overground is a similar distance in the opposite direction – consult your A to Z, or ask. Alternatively, buses 65 and 391 from the opposite side of Kew Green will take you down to Richmond station and town in about 20 minutes.

## PUB INFORMATION

**1 RED LION**
92-94 Linkfield Road, Isleworth, TW7 6QJ
020 8560 1457 • www.red-lion.info
**Opening hours:** 12-11.30 (11 Tue; midnight Fri & Sat); 12-11 Sun

**2 LONDON APPRENTICE**
62 Church Street, Isleworth, TW7 6BG
020 8560 1915 • www.thelondonapprentice.co.uk
**Opening hours:** 11-11 (midnight Fri & Sat)

**3 MAGPIE & CROWN**
128 High Street, Brentford, TW8 8EW
020 8560 4570 • www.magpieandcrown.co.uk
**Opening hours:** 12-midnight (1am Thu-Sat)

**4 BREWERY TAP**
47 Catherine Wheel Road, Brentford, TW8 4BD
020 8560 5200 • www.brewerytapbrentford.co.uk
**Opening hours:** 12-midnight (2am Fri; 1am Sat); 12-midnight Sun

**5 WATERMANS ARMS**
1 Ferry Lane, Brentford, TW8 0AW
020 8560 5665 • www.watermans-arms.com
**Opening hours:** 12-2.30, 5-11.30 Mon-Thu; 12-11.30 Fri-Sun

**6 EXPRESS TAVERN**
56 Kew Bridge Road, Brentford, TW8 0EW
020 8560 8484
**Opening hours:** 11-11 (midnight Fri & Sat); 12-11 Sun

**7 BOTANIST**
3-5 Kew Green, Kew, TW9 3AA
020 8948 4838 • www.thebotanistkew.co.uk
**Opening hours:** 12-11 (midnight Fri & Sat); 12-10.30 Sun

# Richmond & Twickenham via the Thames Path

**WALK**

**29**

Richmond is one of London's most elegant suburbs and occupies an enviable position on one of the loveliest reaches of the Thames. Once a favoured royal residence, Richmond Palace was rebuilt under Henry VII and renamed after his earldom in Yorkshire. Oliver Cromwell destroyed most of it after 1649. This walk takes in several pubs in the town before leading off upstream into Twickenham, with another handful of very good drinking options. Provided the ferry is operating (see below), the riverside walk is best down on the Surrey side, before crossing into Middlesex and continuing into Twickenham. En route there are also cultural opportunities, notably at Ham House. For those who prefer to leave the bulk of the drinking until the walking is done, consider leaving some or all of the Richmond stops until the end, returning by train or bus to Richmond from Strawberry Hill. The best pubs for beer range are the Roebuck and the Sussex Arms.

▶ **Start:** Richmond

▶ **Finish:** Strawberry Hill

▶ **Distance:** 4.5 miles (7.2 km)

▶ **Access:** From Waterloo/Clapham Junction

▶ **Key attractions:** Richmond; Ham House; Marble Hill House and park; Orleans House Gallery; Eel Pie Island; Thames Path

▶ **THE PUBS:** Waterman's Arms; White Cross; Victoria; Roebuck; White Swan; Sussex Arms; Rifleman; Prince of Wales

▶ **Timing tip:** If planning to use Hammerton's Ferry, it's strongly recommended you establish that the service is definitely operating by phoning ahead (020 8892 9620). There's no service in November and a limited one in winter. Given the attractive riverside views, this is a walk best enjoyed on a long sunny day. At very high water levels, be warned that both riverside paths are liable to flooding.

**The White Cross on the banks of the Thames**

**The White Cross**

**KEY**

🚶 Walk start

– – ▶ – – Walk route

•••••••• Alternative route

Start at Richmond station with its frequent and fast trains from Central London. Upon exit, cross the road at the pelican crossing and head through the covered passageway directly ahead (Capital Ring path sign), meeting a quieter road (Little Green) in 50 yards, where bear left. Cross the railway bridge and pass Richmond Theatre to arrive at the corner of Richmond Green. This open space was originally a common where villagers pastured their sheep, later becoming a medieval jousting ground alongside Richmond Palace. It's now a haven of tranquillity very close to the centre of

town and bordered by attractive, mostly Georgian houses. The terrace on the far side next to the old Palace is called Maids of Honour Row, so named as this was where the unmarried daughters of monarchs once lived. Stay on pretty much the same bearing, on the path, keeping to the left-hand side of the green as you look at it. At the far side, swing left and exit into the town centre via King Street. There are maps on the green if you need help!

Turn down Water Lane by the Old Ship. This narrow and atmospheric street runs down to the river, and the ① **Waterman's Arms** still

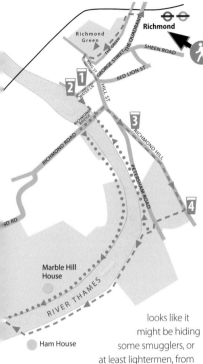

looks like it might be hiding some smugglers, or at least lightermen, from the days of river trade. It started life as a simple beer house, originally named the King's Head. Inside it's still quite intimate and retains some more traditional fixtures and fittings. It offers Young's staple beers and seasonals, and Twickenham's Naked Ladies is a fixture here, too. For a small pub the menu is extensive (available all day), and features Thai and Chinese dishes alongside more traditional fare. Whether these continue with the imminent retirement of the current licensee, time will tell.

Just yards down the lane you'll reach the river, and the elegant Richmond Bridge. Constructed in 1777, this is the oldest Thames bridge still in use and arguably one of the most handsome. To your right is the **2** **White Cross**, a Richmond institution. The name stems from a convent built by Henry VII in 1499, with a white cross being the friars' insignia. There has been a pub here since at least 1780, although the present building dates from 1835. It's a very spacious but popular pub and at certain times you might find it difficult to get a seat. For this

iconic pub it's all about location, with great views over the water from the window seats; in fact the pub is so close to the river that the tide regularly inundates the shore here, and entry to the pub is only via the side steps. The interior is smart but not vulgar, and I'm pleased that they have retained a floorboard covering around the bar. Beers are of course from Young's, with seasonals which can feature other breweries; and there are beer festivals at least twice annually – check the website. It's a pleasant place when it's quiet earlier in the day; if it's overrun by the hordes in high summer, it's perhaps best to leave this one and move on.

Walk to the bridge, and gain the roadway either via the slope or the steps. Turn left up to the road junction (note the 1930s Art Deco Odeon cinema with Egyptian-style decoration on the exterior). Turn right onto Hill Street and, crossing the road, fork to the left onto Hill Rise, keeping the little green on your right. Here sits Richmond's smallest pub, the **3** **Victoria**. There's only a single room, although clearly there were once at least two. On the comfortable seats overlooking the green you can enjoy a choice of three ales: Sharp's Doom Bar, Young's Bitter and a guest. An alternative place to sit is the rear courtyard. Appropriately for such a small pub, food is confined to simple snacks.

**Waterman's Arms**

**The Victoria – Richmond's smallest pub**

For the last official stop in town, and the widest beer choice in Richmond, continue up Hill Rise for the best part of half a mile – the distance will go quickly, though, for as you climb higher onto Richmond Hill, you'll be able to cut into the Terrace Gardens on the right-hand side of the road, with an increasingly wide panorama across the river and the country beyond. It's one of London's iconic views, which has long inspired writers and artists, and along the terrace here you'll find the **4** **Roebuck**. It would be worth coming here for the view alone, but these days the pub is also a destination in its own right for its great choice of well-kept ales. Expect no fewer than seven changing beers from near and far (London Pride, the eighth, is a regular). There's also decent food menu available at most times. Looking out, you should be able to pick out several landmarks, from the roof of Ham House close to the river below you, to the rugby stadium at Twickenham across the river further right.

There's a set of steps, a few yards right of the pub, from the terrace down towards the riverside. Take these, and at Petersham Road, look for the entry to the riverside path a few yards to the right again. Now it's decision time. If you're confident of your ferry connection, bear left along the riverside past Petersham Meadows, and it's a few more minutes of pleasant riverside path before you arrive by Ham House, and the ferry pontoon. Ham House is a very worthwhile detour if you've built it into your itinerary; the National Trust describes it as 'unique in Europe as the most complete survival of 17th-century fashion and power'. Once across the ferry, at a point close to Marble Hill Park, pick up the route at ✳ below.

The alternative route at the riverside is to head back downstream to Richmond Bridge and cross to the Twickenham (north) side, and pick up the Thames Path heading upstream. It's a very nice walk along the banks of the river passing Marble Hill House, a fashionable Georgian villa in the Palladian style, built for Henrietta Howard, mistress of King George II when he was Prince of Wales. The grounds are also open to the public. Pass the ferry pontoon (✳ where readers taking the ferry join us) and continue a little further to where the Thames Path leaves the riverside by Orleans House. Originally built as a country retreat, it features the distinctive Octagon Room, built around 1720, and is now a gallery in the hands of the local authority (see www.richmond.gov.uk/orleans_house_gallery for opening hours and admission details).

The pleasant little lane, called Riverside, winds beyond the gallery; and in this old part of Twickenham is the next pub stop, the **5** **White Swan**. Sited a safe distance from the water's edge (though the basement is reserved for the facilities, and you need to climb up to enter the pub), this is an attractive old building, which has been tastefully brought up to date inside, with stripped floors and a classy paint job on the interior timber. There's plenty of seating inside, including a nice window bench; if you're lucky, you might be able to bag the outside veranda seats with river views. The Swan is now a free house, and the five beers are sourced from all over but with a local emphasis: Twickenham and Sambrook's are favoured micros alongside regular Sharp's Doom Bar. There's a wide menu available all day at weekends, with an afternoon break during the week.

**The Sussex Arms**

Carry on down the lane, passing some pretty houses, until you emerge by the Barmy Arms and the footbridge onto famous Eel Pie Island. This little ait in the Thames has had a remarkable history, perhaps most notably as a venue for all sorts of famous rock and blues artists, who performed at the legendary Eel Pie Hotel on the island, particularly during the 1960s. The hotel was destroyed by fire in 1971, but not before it had been occupied by an anarchist/ hippy commune including illustrator Clifford Harper. The Who frontman Pete Townshend had his studios here, but these days it's most well known as an artists' retreat. You can cross onto the island via the footbridge and walk around.

Head directly away from the river here into King Street in Twickenham town centre. The walk to the next pub has little to recommend it, so jump on a bus (this side of the road, westbound). Take route 110, 490 or H22, for four stops, just past Twickenham Green, to First Cross Road. If you do decide to walk it, fork right at the junction just up to the left, and walk along

**White Swan**

the northern side of Twickenham Green. The bus will deposit you almost outside the **6 Sussex Arms**. It presents a handsome frontage to the street, and inside this pre-war local there are still some period features such as wood panelling and brickwork, but the real draw is the remarkable range of beer and cider taps, which currently stands at 18. This follows a recent makeover as an ale and cider house. Expect rapidly rotating and interesting stuff from all over the place, supporting independent breweries. The informed service and well-kept beer, supported by well-regarded food, has made the Sussex a firm favourite with just about all its visitors, and there can be few if any suburban pubs that offer such a range of ales. The interior ambience is pleasant enough, but there's also a large garden, which features a boules pitch.

Continue along the Staines Road for five minutes or so until you reach Fourth Cross Road, and head down the street of pleasant late-Victorian villas. Right near the bottom of the road is a traditional old street-corner local that offers a nice contrast to the Sussex.

The 7 **Rifleman**
now sports a new pub
sign, dedicating the pub
to local Rifleman Frank
Edwards, the 'Footballer
of Loos'. Ask about the
story inside. The Rifleman
retains a traditional feel
with seating arranged
on the wooden floor
around the horseshoe
bar; and despite the
presence outside of
the Courage cockerels,
these days the beers are
more diverse, with half a
dozen solid regulars from
Twickenham, Butcombe and
Dark Star among others. This well-regarded
pub was voted as the local CAMRA branch
Pub of the Year in 2014.

**The Rifleman**

and rather formal rooms,
with a variety of seating
including leathery sofas.
The beer range and
quality, as testified by a
2011 local CAMRA Pub
of the Year award, is light
years ahead of its former
Watneys days. Expect
seven, with one from the
local Twickenham micro
among the fixtures. There's
food available each day
except Monday, ranging
from snacks to a serious
menu. In good weather,
check out the spacious
garden, but be prepared to
share it with dogs and free-range children.

It's only the shortest of steps to the last
pub: simply head down to the bottom
of the road and you'll see it there on
the corner. The 8 **Prince of Wales** is a
substantial double-fronted Victorian house
with some period detail remaining, among
those a badge from former owners the
unlamented Watneys atop the pub sign.
Inside, the central bar dominates the smart

To get home, or to return to Richmond, it's
a 10-minute walk to Strawberry Hill station:
cross the Hampton Road, bear right and
take Wellesley Road, the first left. If you don't
fancy the walk, step up to the bus stop, on
the same side of Hampton Road as the pub,
and take bus 267 or 281 to Twickenham
station, for trains back to either Richmond, or
Clapham and Central London. The frequent
R70 bus leaves from the same stop and goes
all the way to Richmond.

## PUB INFORMATION

**1 WATERMAN'S ARMS**
2 Water Lane, Richmond, TW9 1TJ
020 8940 2893 • www.rampubcompany.co.uk/visit-
pubs/watermans-arms
**Opening hours:** 12-11; 12-9 Sun

**2 WHITE CROSS**
Riverside, Water Lane, Richmond, TW9 1TH
020 8940 6844 • www.thewhitecrossrichmond.com
**Opening hours:** 10-11; 10-10.30 Sun

**3 VICTORIA**
78 Hill Rise, Richmond, TW10 6UB
020 8940 2531 • www.vicinnrichmond.com
**Opening hours:** 11-11 (midnight Fri & Sat); 12-10.30 Sun

**4 ROEBUCK**
130 Richmond Hill, Richmond, TW10 6RN
020 8948 2329 • www.taylor-walker.co.uk/pub/
roebuck-richmond/s5628
**Opening hours:** 12-11 (midnight Fri & Sat); 12-10.30 Sun

**5 WHITE SWAN**
Riverside, Twickenham, TW1 3DN
020 8744 2951 • whiteswantwickenham.com
**Opening hours:** 11 (10 Sat)-11; 11-10.30 Sun

**6 SUSSEX ARMS**
15 Staines Road, Twickenham, TW2 5BG
020 8894 7468 • www.thesussexarmstwickenham.
co.uk
**Opening hours:** 12-11; 12-10.30 Sun

**7 RIFLEMAN**
7 Fourth Cross Road, Twickenham, TW2 5EL
020 8893 3836 • www.theriflemanpub.co.uk
**Opening hours:** 12 (2 Mon & Tue)-11; 12-10.30 Sun

**8 PRINCE OF WALES**
136 Hampton Road, Twickenham, TW2 5QR 020 8894
5054 • www.princeofwalestwickenham.co.uk
**Opening hours:** 12 (4 Mon)-11 (midnight Thu-Sat);
12-10.30 Sun

# Kingston & Teddington via Bushy Park and the Thames Path

**WALK 30**

Nowhere near as well known as Richmond Park, Bushy Park is also a Royal Park, originally laid out for hunting, but these days the stags have an easier time of it. At just half the size of Richmond that still makes it pretty large: 450 hectares. It's big enough for London to feel a long way off – the perfect place for a longer walk before enjoying the first pint of the day. There are options to lengthen the Bushy Park section by taking in the woodland gardens riverside walks along the Longford River. The pubs selected here offer between them a wide choice of beers, and if the sun is out when you arrive at the Boaters, you may well wish to linger by the riverside with the option of an all-day food menu. Be aware that it's about three miles to the Roebuck from Kingston station. If you get cold feet (or it starts raining), catch a 285 (towards Heathrow) from Wood Street in Kingston to the Roebuck instead!

**Start:** ⇌ Kingston (or ⇌ Fulwell for linear walk omitting Bushy Park).

**Finish:** ⇌ Kingston

**Distance:** 6.6 miles (10.7 km) for the circuit from Kingston

**Access:** From ⇌ Waterloo/Clapham Junction; or by X26 express bus: Croydon–Carshalton–Kingston–Heathrow

**Key attractions:** Bushy Park; Thames Path

**THE PUBS:** White Hart; Roebuck; Masons Arms; Clock House; Boaters Inn

**Timing tip:** It's worth getting an early start on a sunny day to enjoy this route to the full, and the Roebuck opens at 11am (11.30 on Friday and Saturday and noon on Sunday).

Bushy Park in autumn

**The inter-war mock-Tudor style White Hart**

Arriving by train at Kingston (the X26 stops in Wood Street, which is much closer to Kingston Bridge), you don't see the town at its best, so pick your feet up and head along the foot/cycleway sharp right out of the station and follow it for about 250 yards before it leads you to the right under the railway (still on the cycle route), and then sharp left to the riverside, where head left along the Thames and under Kingston Bridge, turning up the slope on the north side to join the road on the bridge. Things improve quickly from here starting with the option of an early 'swift one' before you set off across Bushey Park. This breaks my normal rule of not drinking (too much anyway) before a longish walk, and you can always miss it out, but the **1 White Hart** is strategically placed on the roundabout at Hampton Wick. The smart inter-war mock-Tudor style building is now an hotel but with a front bar and dining area open to all, refurbished in a modern style. This Fuller's house offers well-kept in-house ales, London Pride, ESB and Gales Seafarers complemented by a Fuller's seasonal beer. It's probably too early for food but it's there if you want it, and service is attentive and efficient.

From the White Hart head south-west on the Hampton Court Road turning right in 100 yards by the Old King's Head into Church Grove. Look for the gateway with the London Loop sign in about 100 yards and head onto the gravel path lined with chestnuts, past the skate park.

THE DIFFICULT-TO-MISS ROEBUCK

Fullwell
½ mile

HIGH STREET

Hampton Hill Pond

Waterhouse Pond

Fishes Pond

This brings you into Bushy Park proper in a few moments. The deer park stretches away from you towards the horizon, without any sign of the next pub! There are around 300 red and fallow deer still roaming freely throughout the park, just as they would have done when Henry VIII hunted here.

There are good maps at each of the entrances, so you can plot your own way across the park. To follow the route described here, head across the grass track leaving at about 45 degrees right beyond the cricket square, reaching the left-hand edge of the plantation of deciduous trees ahead (the Oval Plantation). Keep close to the edge of the trees

as the tracks bifurcate, bringing you quickly to the Heron Pond, a pleasant spot to stop for refreshment from your flask if you have one with you.

From here track around the pond to the south (left) and cross the first rustic wooden bridge at the far end, as the car park looms into view. Now bear half left away from the pond and head obliquely towards the road across the park, Chestnut Avenue, crossing this close to the palisaded compound, which is part of the woodland gardens. Keep these on your immediate left as you follow parallel to the road on a good path. Bear left to follow another road and pass the two gatehouses to Bushy House as you take the right fork at the sign to 'Water Gardens and Hampton Hill'. It's another mile or so via this untrafficked road, and then a short

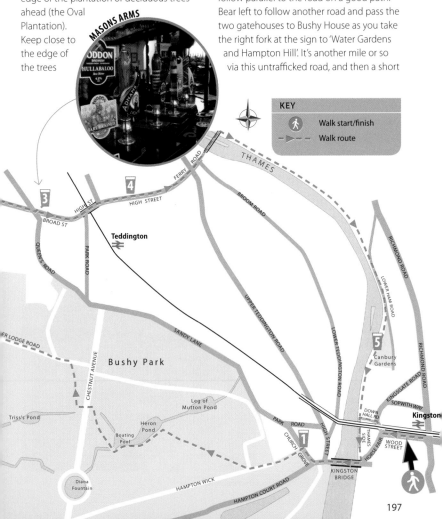

**MASONS ARMS**

**KEY**

🚶 Walk start/finish

– – ▷ – – Walk route

**The listed suspension bridge at Teddington Lock**

path section where it bears left to the water garden, before you reach the Laurel Road gate. Once you get there, it's straight up the road ahead to the junction with Hampton Road and left, where you'll see the second stop of the day on the next corner.

The **2** **Roebuck** stands out a little too much with its gaudy red paint job, but once inside it's a different story. Homely and intimate with numerous nooks and corners in its opened-out layout, every surface is covered with a remarkable collection of ephemera, and each time you visit you'll doubtless see something new. In one corner there's a display of the various awards the pub has picked up for its beer and its flower displays. This local is well patronised, and no wonder, for apart from the inviting atmosphere there's a tempting range of beers: regulars Young's Bitter, St Austell Tribute and Sambrook's Junction are joined by two constantly changing guests; expect them to be in very good condition. To complement this on weekday lunchtimes (until 2pm), there's a tempting array of food from sandwiches to full meals. You

may not fall victim to them, but traffic lights in the bar and garden turn amber, then red, as 'time' looms.

The next leg involves a traverse of about half a mile down the Hampton Road to Teddington, with not much to recommend it, so I would favour catching a bus (either the 285 or R68 will do) three stops down to Teddington Memorial Hospital at the junction with Stanley Road. Cross Stanley Road, and between the two modern blocks at the junction you'll see the **3** **Masons Arms** down the pedestrian alley. The part-tiled exterior goes back to a mid twentieth-

**The Roebuck**

**The Masons Arms**  **Teddington Lock**

century rebuild, and the most interesting thing about it is arguably that there are no fewer than five separate doorways, most now blocked off, of course. For a suburban pub it's very rare to see quite this many. The entrance on the corner has only recently been brought back into use, and it's been done to blend in well. In the capable hands of licensee Rachel (Rae to the regulars), who has 20 years' experience in the place, the Masons has now become a must for discerning beer drinkers in Teddington, winning the local CAMRA branch's Pub of the Year award for 2015 and 2016. A comfortable carpeted drinking area, with stove at one end, wraps around the spacious servery. Choose from four ales: regulars Tillingbourne A.O.N.B and Sambrook's Junction joined by two changing guests. Some interesting old prints on the wall show the changing appearance of the pub over the years, but pride of place (in what was once a Watney's house) must surely go to the ancient and unopened 'Party Seven' can of Red Barrel behind the bar. Oh, the sheer nostalgia…

Continue along Teddington's main street (or take the bus, 285 or R68) two more stops over the railway bridge and into the High Street, where opposite Field Lane you won't miss the **4 Clock House** in a prominent location despite advertising itself as Teddington's 'hidden gem'!? Maybe to a blind man… Like the Masons, this was once

in the estate of the old Isleworth brewery, but a major makeover about five years back has pretty well obliterated anything of the past. The interior is intensely modern: high seats, floorboards, straight lines, around a horseshoe bar with an outside paved area and a rear dining room. The result is not particularly to my taste, but it may be to yours. Expect Fuller's London Pride, Young's Bitter and two from Sharp's with a fifth guest pump offering regional beers from larger brewers. Food on weekday lunchtimes is available until 3pm, if you're planning ahead.

The walk continues by following the length of Teddington High Street (pleasanter than most) to the junction with the A310 Kingston Road, where you cross ahead into Ferry Road for the short walk down to the Thames. You'll pass two more pubs at this point – the Tide End Cottage (Greene King) and the Anglers (Fuller's) – quite satisfactory as additional stops, although not, I would suggest, at the expense of the next official call on the walk. To get there, cross the river

### 🚶 STARTING AT FULWELL STATION

It's only about five minutes down to the Roebuck from Fulwell station: exit onto the A311 Wellington Road, and turn left (south) heading down to the traffic lights. Here, turn left again, and the Roebuck is the unmissable building on the next corner.

The Boaters with its river-view terrace

Handpumps at the Boaters

and the navigation by Teddington Lock here, the former on a pretty suspension bridge, which dates back to 1888 and was listed in 2005. The lock itself, at the highest point of the tidal Thames, was constructed in 1811–12. Once on the Surrey side, it's simply a matter of following the river closely on the path (the cycle path is a few yards 'inland') along a pleasant mile or so, lined with boats, until, approaching Kingston once more, you reach the narrow riverside park of Canbury Gardens and, adjacent, a boathouse, which gives the pub its name: the **5 Boaters**. The building would win no architectural awards, but the location is its trump card, right on the river and with an outside terrace to complement the room-with-a-view within. The other draw of course is the beer menu: Greene King, who own the pub, have sensibly chosen to showcase a changing list of guest beers and keep only one of the five handpumps for their own IPA. Local microbreweries are prominent, and the increasingly popular 'tap takeover' evenings now feature here one evening each month. Bottled and keg offerings from the likes of Sambrook's and Meantime complement the cask ales. With this the last stop on the route it's useful to know that a full food menu is available pretty much throughout, with a brief afternoon interregnum during winter; phone ahead if it's critical.

A short walk further along the riverside will return you to the path you walked on to reach the Thames earlier in the day if you started here, just before the rail bridge, where head inland and keep to the cycle route back to the station in about five minutes. If you're of a mind to linger in Kingston for more refreshment, consult your *Good Beer Guide* along with your street map.

## PUB INFORMATION

**1 WHITE HART**
1 High Street, Hampton Wick, KT1 4DA
020 8977 1786 • www.whitehartoteluk.co.uk
**Opening hours:** 7am-11; 8am-11 Sun

**2 ROEBUCK**
72 Hampton Road, Hampton, TW12 1JN
020 8255 8133 • www.roebuck-hamptonhill.co.uk
**Opening hours:** 11-11 (11.30 Fri & Sat); 12-4, 7-10.30 Sun

**3 MASONS ARMS**
41 Walpole Road, Teddington, TW11 8PJ
020 8977 6521 • the-masons-arms.co.uk
**Opening hours:** 12-11 (11.30 Fri & Sat); 12-10.30 Sun

**4 CLOCK HOUSE**
69 High Street, Teddington, TW11 8HA
020 8977 3909 • www.theclockhousepub.com
**Opening hours:** 11-11.30 (midnight Fri & Sat); 11-11 Sun

**5 BOATERS**
Canbury Gardens, Lower Ham Road, Kingston, KT2 5AU
020 8541 4672 • www.boaterskingston.com
**Opening hours:** 11-11 (midnight Sat)

# PUB INDEX

**Charles Lamb p97**

**Harp p40**

**Jerusalem Tavern p76**

**Powder Keg Diplomacy p154**   **King William IV p143**   **White Cross p191**

# BEER INDEX

# PLACES INDEX

**Royal Courts of Justice, p31**

**Huguenot Houses, Spitalfields p80**

# BOOKS FOR BEER LOVERS

**CAMPAIGN FOR REAL ALE**

CAMRA Books, the publishing arm of the Campaign for Real Ale, is the leading publisher of books on beer and pubs. Key titles include:

## GOOD BEER GUIDE 2017

### Editor: Roger Protz

*CAMRA's Good Beer Guide* is fully revised and updated each year and features pubs across the United Kingdom that serve the best real ale. Now in its 44th edition, this pub guide is completely independent with listings based entirely on nomination and evaluation by CAMRA members. This means you can be sure that every one of the 4,500 pubs deserves their place, plus they all come recommended by people who know a thing or two about good beer.

**£15.99     ISBN 978-1-85249-335-6**

## THE YEAR IN BEER: 2017 DIARY

Discover a beer for every week of the year with *CAMRA's Year in Beer 2017 Diary*. The best beers from around the world are linked to key events and dates through the year, with comprehensive tasting notes. Major anniversaries, religious feasts and important birthdays are highlighted, along with commemorations, carnivals and some more eccentric events.

**£9.99     ISBN 987-1-85249-337-0**

## YORKSHIRE PUB WALKS

### Bob Steel

CAMRA's Yorkshire Pub Walks guides you round the best of England's largest county, while never straying too far from a decent pint. A practical, pocket-sized guide to some of the best pubs and best walking in Yorkshire, this fully illustrated book features 25 walks around some of Yorkshire's most awe-inspiring National Parks and landscapes, and its most vibrant towns and cities. Full-colour Ordnance Survey maps and detailed route information, plus pub listings with opening hours and details of draught beers, make *CAMRA's Yorkshire Pub Walks* the essential guide for anyone wanting a taste of 'God's Own County'.

**£9.99     ISBN 978-1-85249-329-5**

Order these and other CAMRA books online at **www.camra.org.uk/books**, ask at your local bookstore, or contact: CAMRA, 230 Hatfield Road, St Albans, AL1 4LW.
Telephone 01727 867201

## LONDON'S BEST BEER, PUBS & BARS

### Des de Moor

The essential guide to London beer, completely revised for 2015. *London's Best Beer, Pubs & Bars* is packed with detailed maps and easy-to-use listings to help you find the best places to enjoy perfect pints in the capital. Laid out by area, the book will be your companion in exploring the best pubs serving the best British and world beers. Additional features include descriptions of London's rich history of brewing and the city's vibrant modern brewing scene, where brewery numbers have more than doubled in the last three years. The venue listings are fully illustrated with colour photographs and include a variety of real ale pubs, bars and other outlets, with detailed information to make planning any excursion quick and easy.

**£12.99     ISBN 978-1-85249-323-36**

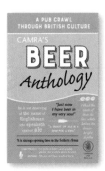

## CAMRA'S BEER ANTHOLOGY

### Edited by Roger Protz

Beer is deeply engrained in the culture and history of the British Isles. From the earliest times, the pleasures of ale and beer have been recorded for posterity. Shakespeare, Dickens and Hardy all wrote on the delights of beer and pubs. They are joined today by a small army of writers with a different aim: they are not commenting on beer in passing, as part of a literary endeavour, but are dedicated full time to researching, promoting and championing beer. From bards to biographers to beer bloggers, explore the world of beer as seen through the eyes of writers as diverse as Bill Bryson, William Blake, Douglas Adams, Melissa Cole, Dylan Thomas, Breandán Kearney, James Joyce, Thomas Hardy, Jeff Evans and George Orwell.

**£9.99     ISBN 978-1-85249-333-2**

## CAMRA'S BEER KNOWLEDGE

### Jeff Evans

A fully revised and updated collection of conversation-starting anecdotes, useful pub facts and figures, and trivia, *CAMRA's Beer Knowledge* is the perfect gift for any beer lover. More than 200 entries cover the serious, the silly and the downright bizarre from the world of beer. Inside this pint-sized compendium you'll find everything from the biggest brewer in the world to the beers with the daftest names. A quick skim before a night out and you'll always have enough beery wisdom to impress your friends. Meticulously researched by award-winning beer writer Jeff Evans, CAMRA's Beer Knowledge is the beer book that everyone should own.

**£9.99     ISBN 978-1-85249-338-7**    Published October 2016

## SO YOU WANT TO BE A BEER EXPERT?

### Jeff Evans

More people than ever are searching for an understanding of what makes a great beer, and this book meets that demand by presenting a hands-on course in beer appreciation, with sections on understanding the beer styles of the world, beer flavours, how beer is made, the ingredients, and more. Uniquely, So You Want to Be a Beer Expert? doesn't just relate the facts, but helps readers reach conclusions for themselves. Key to this are the interactive tastings that show readers, through their own taste-buds, what beer is all about. *CAMRA's So You Want to Be a Beer Expert?* is the ideal book, for anyone who wants to further their knowledge and enjoyment of beer.

**£12.99     ISBN 978-1-85249-322-6**

## BRITAIN'S BEST REAL HERITAGE PUBS

### Geoff Brandwood

This definitive listing is the result of 25 years' research by CAMRA to discover pubs that are either unaltered in 70 years or have features of truly national historic importance. Fully revised from the 2013 edition, the book boasts updated information and a new set of evocative illustrations. Among the 260 pubs, there are unspoilt country locals, Victorian drinking palaces and mighty roadhouses. The book has features describing how the pub developed, what's distinctive about pubs in different parts of the country, how people a century ago could expect to be served drinks at their table, and how they used the pub for take-out sales in the pre-supermarket era. There is a bonus listing of 70 pubs that, while not meeting CAMRA's national criteria for a heritage pub, will still thrill visitors with their historic ambience.

**£9.99     ISBN 978-1-85249-334-9**

## BRITAIN'S BEER REVOLUTION

### Roger Protz and Adrian Tierney-Jones

UK brewing has seen unprecedented growth in the last decade. Breweries of all shapes and sizes are flourishing. Established brewers applying generations of tradition in new ways rub shoulders at the bar with new micro-brewers. Headed by real ale, a 'craft' beer revolution is sweeping the country. In *Britain's Beer Revolution* Roger Protz and Adrian Tierney-Jones look behind the beer labels and shine a spotlight on what makes British beer so good.

**£14.99     ISBN 978-1-85249-321-9**

# A CAMPAIGN OF TWO HALVES

## Campaigning for Pub Goers & Beer Drinkers

CAMRA, the Campaign for Real Ale, is the not-for-profit independent voice of real ale drinkers and pub goers. CAMRA's vision is to have quality real ale and thriving pubs in every community. We campaign tirelessly to achieve this goal, as well as lobbying government to champion drinkers' rights. As a CAMRA member you will have the opportunity to campaign to save pubs under threat of closure, for pubs to be free to serve a range of real ales at fair prices and for a long-term freeze in beer duty that will help Britain's brewing industry survive.

## Enjoying Real Ale & Pubs

CAMRA has over 180,000 members from all ages and backgrounds, brought together by a common belief in the issues that CAMRA deals with and their love of good quality British beer. From just £24 a year* – that's less than a pint a month – you can join CAMRA and enjoy the following benefits:

- Subscription to *What's Brewing*, our monthly colour newspaper, and *Beer*, our quarterly magazine, informing you about beer and pub news and detailing events and beer festivals around the country.

- Free or reduced entry to over 160 national, regional and local beer festivals.

- Money off many of our publications including the *Good Beer Guide*, the *Good Bottled Beer Guide* and *So You Want to Be a Beer Expert?*

- Access to a members-only section of our website, **www.camra.org.uk**, which gives up-to-the-minute news stories and includes a special offer section with regular features.

- Special discounts with numerous partner organisations and money off real ale in your participating local pubs as part of our Pubs Discount Scheme.

Log onto **www.camra.org.uk/join** for CAMRA membership information.

*£24 membership cost stated is only available via Direct Debit, other concessionary rates available. Please note membership rates stated are correct at the time of printing but are subject to change. Full details of all membership rates can be found here: **www.camra.org.uk/membershiprates**